LIBRO DE EJERCICIOS

NIVEL 1 INICIAL

Autor

Thomas Booth ha trabajado durante 10 años como profesor de inglés en Polonia y en Rusia. Actualmente vive en Inglaterra, donde trabaja como editor y autor de materiales para el aprendizaje de la lengua inglesa, principalmente manuales y vocabularios.

Consultor del curso

Tim Bowen ha enseñado inglés y ha formado profesores en más de 30 países en todo el mundo. Es coautor de libros sobre la enseñanza de la pronunciación y sobre la metodología de la enseñanza de idiomas, y autor de numerosos libros para profesores de inglés. Actualmente se dedica a la escritura de materiales, la edición y la traducción. Es miembro del Chartered Institute of Linguists.

Consultora lingüística

La profesora **Susan Barduhn** cuenta con una gran experiencia en la enseñanza del inglés y la formación de profesores. Como autora ha participado en numerosas publicaciones. Además de dirigir cursos de inglés en cuatro continentes, ha sido presidenta de la Asociación Internacional de Profesores de Inglés como Lengua Extranjera y asesora del British Council y del Departamento de Estado de Estados Unidos. Actualmente es profesora de la School for International Training en Vermont, Estados Unidos.

ENGLISH
FOR EVERYONE

LIBRO DE EJERCICIOS

NIVEL 1 INICIAL

SEGUNDA EDICIÓN
Edición sénior Ankita Awasthi Tröger
Edición Beth Blakemore
Edición de arte Amy Child
Edición ejecutiva Carine Tracanelli
Edición ejecutiva de arte Anna Hall
Edición de producción Gillian Reid
Control de producción sénior Poppy David
Diseño de cubierta sénior Surabhi Wadhwa-Gandhi
Dirección de desarrollo de diseño de cubierta Sophia MTT
Dirección editorial Andrew Macintyre
Dirección de arte Karen Self
Dirección de publicaciones Jonathan Metcalf

DK INDIA
Coordinación sénior de cubiertas Priyanka Sharma Saddi
Diseño de maquetación Rakesh Kumar

PRIMERA EDICIÓN
Asistencia editorial Jessica Cawthra, Sarah Edwards
Ilustración Edwood Burn, Denise Joos, Michael Parkin, Jemma Westing
Producción de audio Liz Hammond
Edición ejecutiva Daniel Mills
Edición ejecutiva de arte Anna Hall
Dirección de proyecto Christine Stroyan
Producción, preproducción Luca Frassinetti
Producción Mary Slater
Diseño de cubierta Natalie Godwin
Edición de cubierta Claire Gell
Dirección de desarrollo de diseño de cubierta Sophia MTT
Dirección editorial Andrew Macintyre
Dirección de arte Karen Self
Dirección de publicaciones Jonathan Metcalf

DK INDIA
Edición sénior Vineetha Mokkil, Anita Kakar
Edición sénior de arte Chhaya Sajwan
Edición del proyecto Antara Moitra
Edición Agnibesh Das, Nisha Shaw, Seetha Natesh
Edición de arte Namita, Heena Sharma, Sukriti Sobti, Shipra Jain, Aanchal Singhal
Asistencia editorial Ira Pundeer, Ateendriya Gupta, Sneha Sunder Benjamin, Ankita Yadav
Asistencia editorial de arte Roshni Kapur, Meenal Goel, Priyansha Tuli
Ilustración Ivy Roy, Arun Pottirayil, Bharti Karakoti, Rahul Kumar
Documentación iconográfica Deepak Negi
Edición ejecutiva Pakshalika Jayaprakash
Edición ejecutiva de arte Arunesh Talapatra
Dirección de proyecto Pankaj Sharma
Dirección de preproducción Balwant Singh
Diseño de maquetación sénior Vishal Bhatia, Neeraj Bhatia
Diseño de maquetación Sachin Gupta
Diseño de cubierta Surabhi Wadhwa
Edición ejecutiva de cubiertas Saloni Singh
Diseño de maquetación sénior Harish Aggarwal

DE LA EDICIÓN EN ESPAÑOL
Servicios editoriales Tinta Simpàtica
Traducción Anna Nualart
Coordinación de proyecto Cristina Sánchez Bustamante
Dirección editorial Elsa Vicente

Publicado originalmente en Gran Bretaña en 2016, 2024 por Dorling Kindersley Limited
DK, 20 Vauxhall Bridge Road, Londres, SW1V 2SA
Parte de Penguin Random House

006-339236-Feb/2026

Título original: *English For Everyone. Practice Book. Level 1. Beginner*
Segunda edición: 2026

ISBN: 979-8-2171-3534-9

Impreso y encuadernado en China

www.dkespañol.com

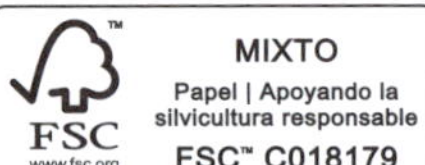

Este libro se ha impreso con papel certificado por el Forest Stewardship Council™ como parte del compromiso de DK por un futuro sostenible. Más información: **www.dk.com/uk/information/sustainability**

Contenidos

Cómo funciona el curso

English for Everyone está pensado para todas aquellas personas que quieren aprender inglés por su cuenta. Como cualquier curso de idiomas, cubre las habilidades básicas: gramática, vocabulario, pronunciación, escucha, conversación, lectura y escritura. A diferencia de otros cursos, todo ello se practica y aprende de forma enormemente visual, con el apoyo de gráficos e imágenes que te ayudarán a entender y a recordar. Los ejercicios de este volumen están pensados para consolidar lo aprendido en el libro de estudio. Sigue las unidades por orden y utiliza al máximo los audios disponibles en la web.

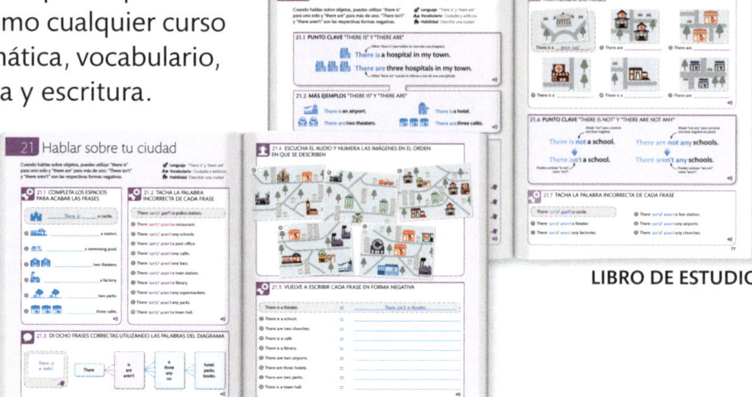

LIBRO DE ESTUDIO

LIBRO DE EJERCICIOS

Número de unidad Este libro está dividido en unidades. En cada una de ellas se practica lo aprendido en la misma unidad del libro de estudio.

Qué vas a practicar La unidad comienza con un resumen de lo que practicarás en ella.

Módulos Cada unidad se compone de distintos módulos que debes seguir por orden. Puedes tomarte un descanso tras completar cualquiera de ellos.

15 Frases negativas con "to be"

Para hacer una frase negativa se utiliza "not" o la forma contraída "n't". Las frases negativas con el verbo "to be" siguen reglas diferentes que las formadas con otros verbos.

Lenguaje Frases negativas con "to be"
Aa Vocabulario "Not"
Habilidad Decir lo que las cosas no son

15.1 VUELVE A ESCRIBIR LAS FRASES PONIENDO LAS PALABRAS EN SU ORDEN CORRECTO

o'clock. 5 not is It — *It is not 5 o'clock.*

1 teacher. Paula not is a
2 are not England. We from
3 my This phone. not is
4 years Kirsty not old. 18 is
5 is not Frank my father.
6 This my not purse. is
7 not They are engineers.
8 is That salon. not a
9 Kim a teacher. is not

15.2 COMPLETA LOS ESPACIOS PARA CONSTRUIR FRASES NEGATIVAS

They *are not* hairdressers.

1 That ______ a castle.
2 They ______ at school.
3 He ______ a grandfather.
4 We ______ engineers.
5 She ______ 70 years old.
6 You ______ French.
7 This ______ my dog.
8 I ______ a doctor.
9 It ______ 11 o'clock.

46

15.3 ESCUCHA EL AUDIO Y NUMERA ... EN QUE SE DESCRIBEN

A B 1

15.4 COMPLETA LOS ESPACIOS PARA ... DISTINTAS

She is not a nurse. She's ...
1 Fredo'...
2 Susie is not my cat.
3
4 They're no...

15.5 LEE EL BLOG Y CONTESTA LAS PREGUNTAS

Mia is 45 years old. True
1 She lives in California. True
2 She's a waitress in a restaurant. True
3 She isn't Mexican. True
4 Franco isn't an engineer. True
5 They have a daughter in college. True

Vocabulario Las páginas de vocabulario ponen a prueba tu memoria sobre las palabras y las expresiones clave que has aprendido en el libro de estudio.

Guía visual Imágenes y gráficos te dan pistas visuales que te ayudan a fijar en la memoria las palabras más importantes.

Audio de apoyo La mayoría de los módulos cuentan con audio grabado por hablantes nativos que te ayudará a mejorar tu expresión y tu comprensión.

AUDIO GRATUITO
www.dkefe.com

Módulos de ejercicios

Cada ejercicio está cuidadosamente graduado para que profundices y contrastes lo que has aprendido en la unidad. Si haces los ejercicios a medida que avanzas, asimilarás y recordarás mejor los conceptos, y tu inglés será más fluido. Cada ejercicio indica con un símbolo qué habilidad vas a practicar con él.

GRAMÁTICA
Aplica las nuevas reglas en distintos contextos.

LECTURA
Analiza ejemplos del idioma en textos reales en inglés.

ESCUCHA
Comprueba tu comprensión del inglés hablado.

VOCABULARIO
Consolida tu comprensión del vocabulario clave.

CONVERSACIÓN
Compara tu dicción con los audios de muestra.

Número de módulo Cada módulo tiene su propio número, para que te sea fácil localizar las respuestas y el audio correspondiente.

Instrucciones En cada ejercicio tienes unas breves instrucciones que te dicen qué debes hacer.

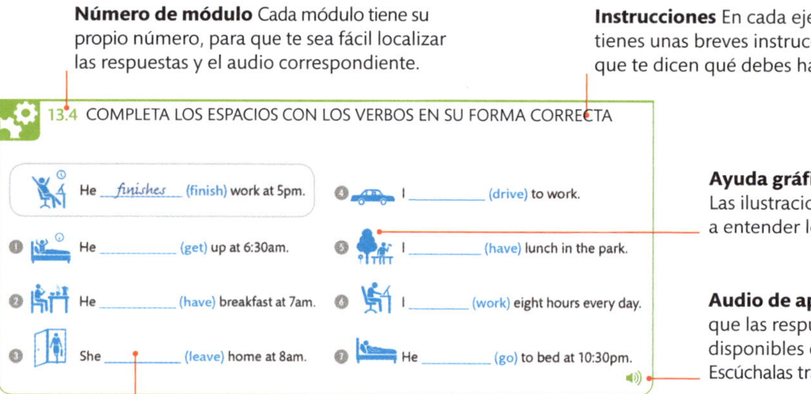

Ayuda gráfica
Las ilustraciones te ayudan a entender los ejercicios.

Audio de apoyo Este símbolo indica que las respuestas a los ejercicios están disponibles en grabaciones de audio. Escúchalas tras completar el ejercicio.

Espacio para escribir Es útil que escribas las respuestas en el libro, pues te servirán para repasar lo aprendido.

Ejercicio de conversación Este símbolo indica que debes decir las respuestas en voz alta y compararlas a continuación con su audio correspondiente.

Respuesta de ejemplo
La primera respuesta ya está escrita, para que entiendas mejor el ejercicio.

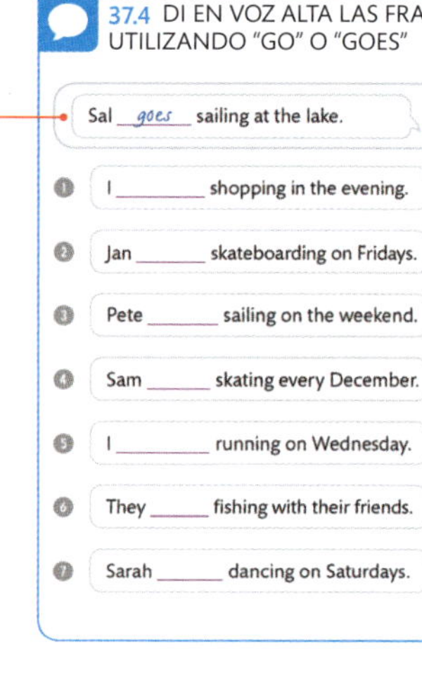

Ejercicios de escucha Este símbolo te avisa de que debes escuchar el audio para poder responder a las preguntas.

Audio

English for Everyone incorpora abundantes materiales en audio. Te recomendamos que los utilices al máximo, pues te ayudarán a mejorar tu comprensión del inglés hablado y a lograr una pronunciación y un acento más naturales. Escucha cada audio tantas veces como quieras. Páusalo y vuelve atrás en los pasajes que te resulten difíciles, hasta que estés seguro de que has entendido bien lo que se dice.

EJERCICIOS DE ESCUCHA
Este símbolo indica que debes escuchar el audio a fin de poder responder las preguntas del ejercicio.

AUDIO DE APOYO
Este símbolo indica que dispones de audios adicionales que puedes escuchar tras completar el módulo.

Respuestas

Al final del libro tienes una sección con las respuestas correctas de todos los ejercicios. Consúltala al terminar cada módulo y compara tus respuestas con los ejemplos para comprobar si has entendido bien los contenidos que has estado practicando.

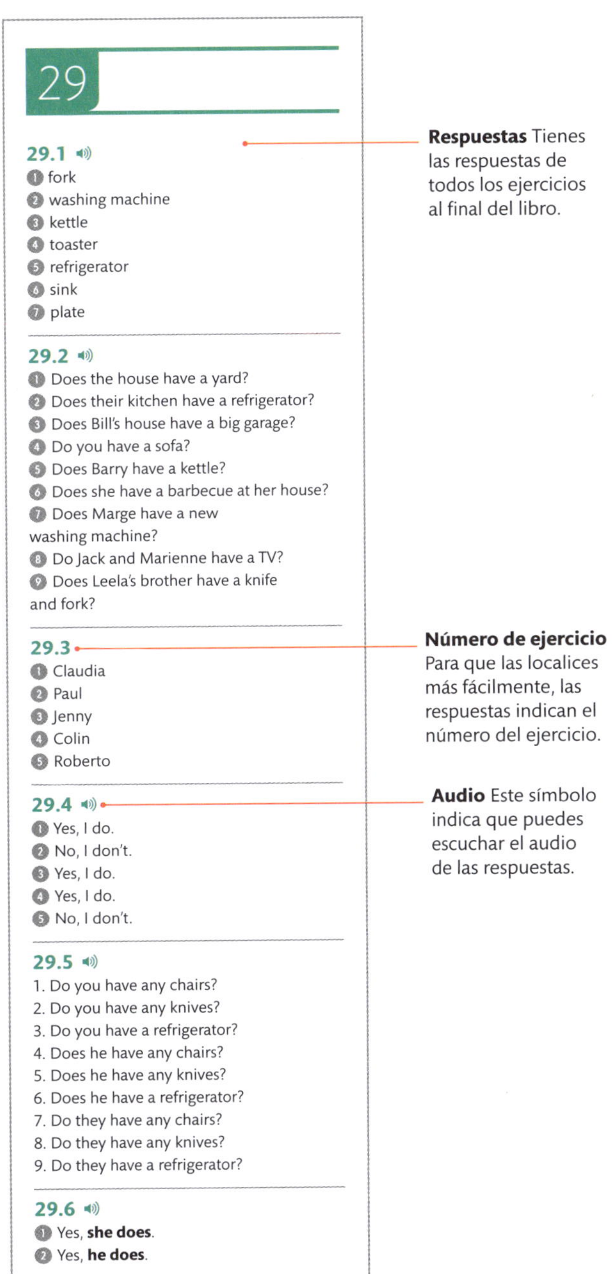

29

29.1
1 fork
2 washing machine
3 kettle
4 toaster
5 refrigerator
6 sink
7 plate

29.2
1 Does the house have a yard?
2 Does their kitchen have a refrigerator?
3 Does Bill's house have a big garage?
4 Do you have a sofa?
5 Does Barry have a kettle?
6 Does she have a barbecue at her house?
7 Does Marge have a new washing machine?
8 Do Jack and Marienne have a TV?
9 Does Leela's brother have a knife and fork?

29.3
1 Claudia
2 Paul
3 Jenny
4 Colin
5 Roberto

29.4
1 Yes, I do.
2 No, I don't.
3 Yes, I do.
4 Yes, I do.
5 No, I don't.

29.5
1. Do you have any chairs?
2. Do you have any knives?
3. Do you have a refrigerator?
4. Does he have any chairs?
5. Does he have any knives?
6. Does he have a refrigerator?
7. Do they have any chairs?
8. Do they have any knives?
9. Do they have a refrigerator?

29.6
1 Yes, **she does**.
2 Yes, **he does**.

Respuestas Tienes las respuestas de todos los ejercicios al final del libro.

Número de ejercicio Para que las localices más fácilmente, las respuestas indican el número del ejercicio.

Audio Este símbolo indica que puedes escuchar el audio de las respuestas.

01 Presentarse

Puedes saludar a otras personas diciéndoles: "Hello!" o "Hi!". Preséntate con la expresión: "I am". A veces tendrás que deletrear tu nombre.

Lenguaje Usar "to be" con nombres
Aa Vocabulario Nombres y letras
Habilidad Decir tu nombre

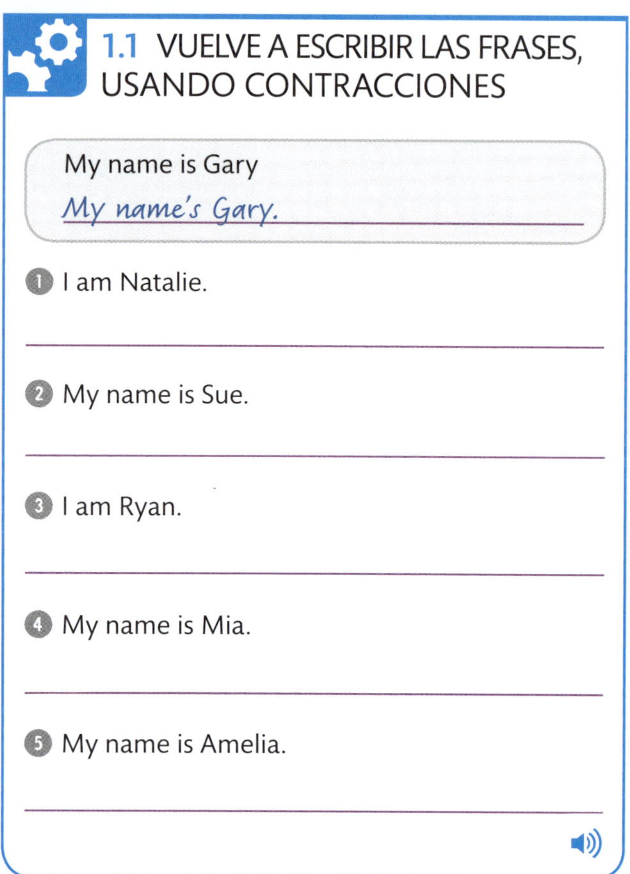

1.1 VUELVE A ESCRIBIR LAS FRASES, USANDO CONTRACCIONES

My name is Gary
My name's Gary.

1. I am Natalie.
2. My name is Sue.
3. I am Ryan.
4. My name is Mia.
5. My name is Amelia.

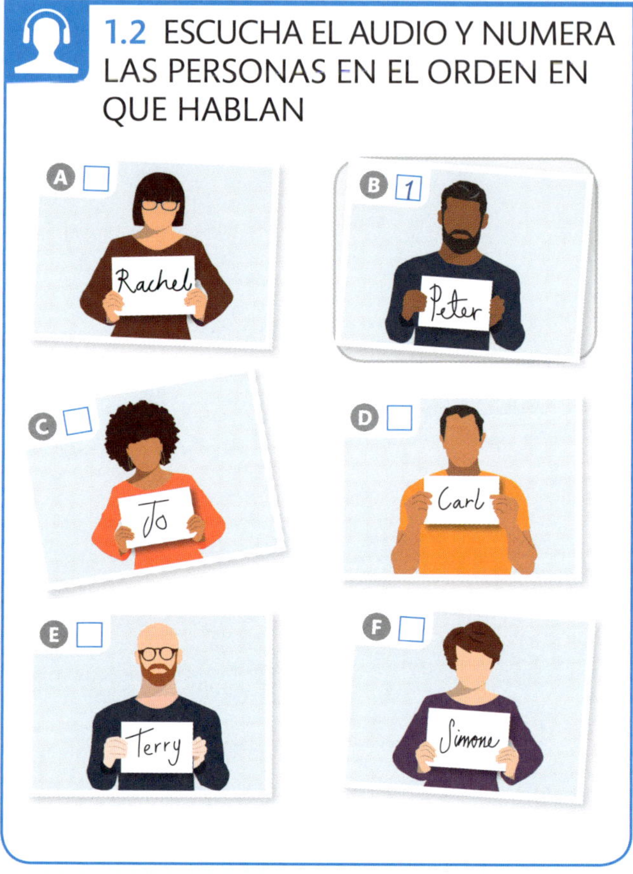

1.2 ESCUCHA EL AUDIO Y NUMERA LAS PERSONAS EN EL ORDEN EN QUE HABLAN

1.3 USA EL DIAGRAMA PARA DECIR 12 SALUDOS EN VOZ ALTA

1.4 ESCUCHA EL AUDIO Y DELETREA LOS NOMBRES QUE ESCUCHES

R-A-C-H-E-L H-A-R-P-E-R

1 ______________________
2 ______________________
3 ______________________
4 ______________________
5 ______________________
6 ______________________
7 ______________________
8 ______________________
9 ______________________
10 ______________________
11 ______________________
12 ______________________
13 ______________________
14 ______________________
15 ______________________

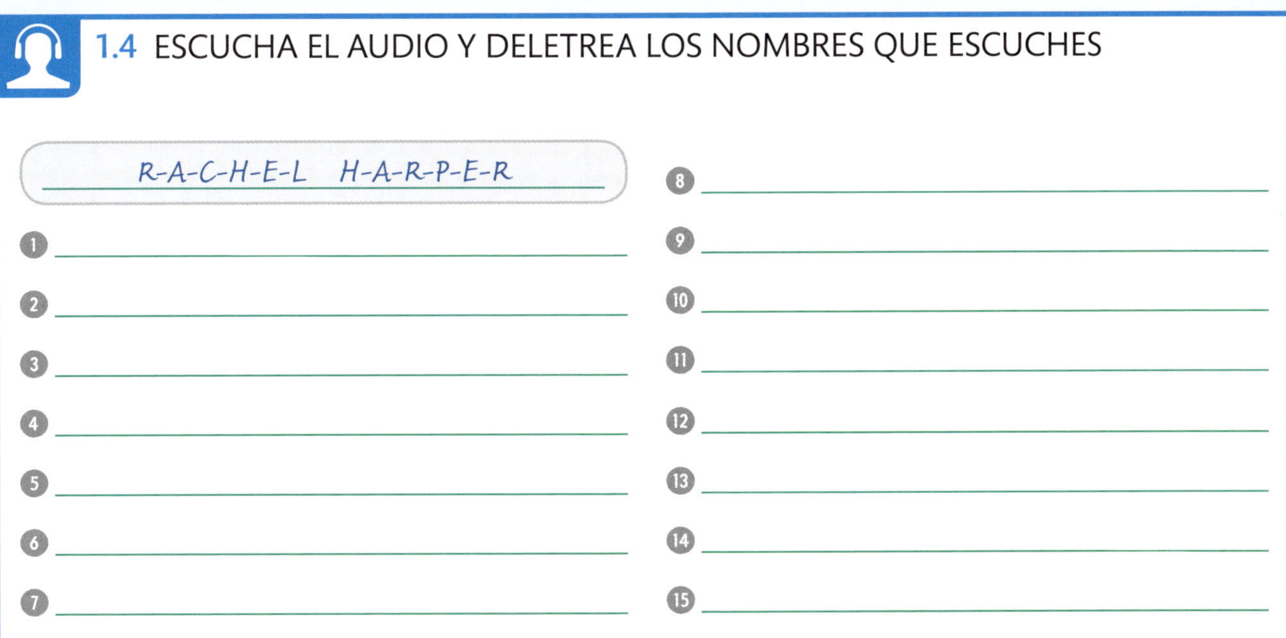

1.5 DELETREA EL NOMBRE DE CADA PERSONA Y LEE LAS FRASES EN VOZ ALTA

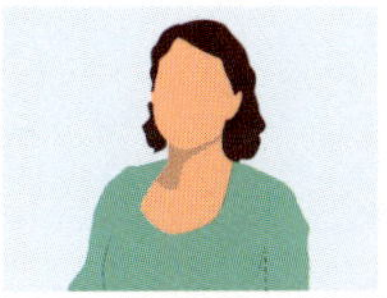

I'm Marina,
M-A-R-I-N-A.

1

My name is Terry,
____

2

My last name is Singh,
____

3

I'm Mario,
____

4

My name is Yasmin Khan,
____

5

I am Jacob,
____

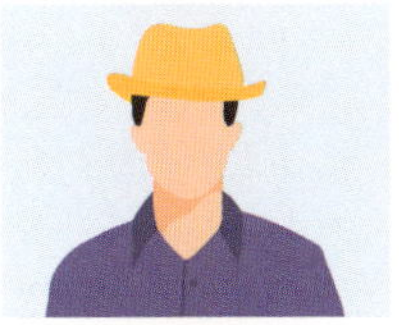

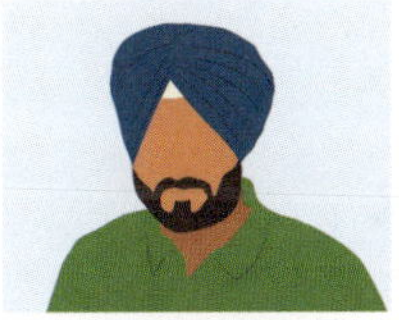

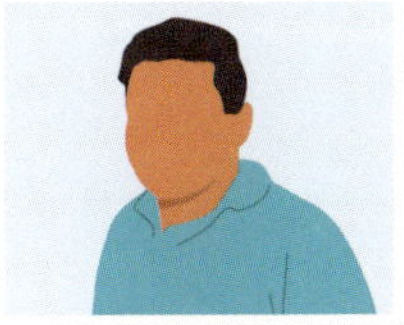

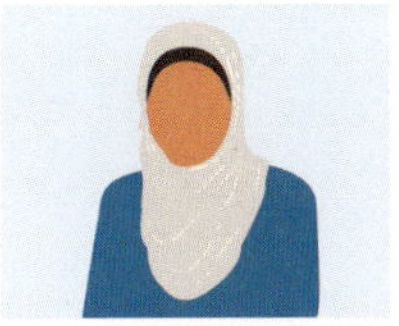

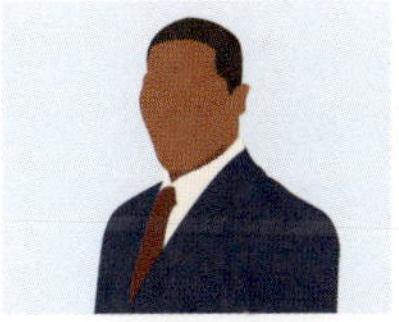

02 Vocabulario

Aa 2.1 **PAÍSES** ESCRIBE LOS NOMBRES DE LOS PAÍSES DEL RECUADRO BAJO SU CORRESPONDIENTE BANDERA

1 ______

2 ______

3 ______

4 ______

10 ______

11 ______

12 ______

13 ______

14 ______

20 ______

21 ______

22 ______

23 ______

24 ______

30 ______

31 ______

32 ______

33 ______

34 ______

Republic of Ireland Greece Singapore France Russia Thailand Argentina
South Africa ~~Turkey~~ Mexico New Zealand Mongolia China Poland India Brazil
Egypt Canada Japan Slovakia Australia Netherlands Philippines Portugal Austria
South Korea Spain United Kingdom Pakistan Czech Republic
Indonesia United Arab Emirates Germany United States of America Switzerland

03 Hablar de ti

Es útil saber cómo decir tu edad y de dónde eres. Para ello, puedes utilizar el verbo "to be".

Lenguaje "To be" con edades y nacionalidades
Vocabulario Números y nacionalidades
Habilidad Hablar de ti

3.1 ESCRIBE ESTOS NÚMEROS EN CIFRAS

Three = *3*

1. Eighty-five = ______
2. Twenty-one = ______
3. Ninety = ______
4. Seventeen = ______
5. Eighty-four = ______
6. Sixty-two = ______
7. Forty-seven = ______
8. Fifty = ______
9. Seventy-one = ______
10. Twelve = ______
11. Thirty-three = ______

3.2 VUELVE A ESCRIBIR LAS FRASES, CAMBIANDO LAS CIFRAS POR PALABRAS

Pamela is 42 years old.
Pamela is forty-two years old.

1. Chloe is 31 years old.
2. Heidi is 52 years old.
3. Zach is 16 years old.
4. Charlie is 10 years old.
5. Marcel is 80 years old.
6. Claire is 21 years old.
7. Dan is 36 years old.
8. Eleanor is 28 years old.
9. Rebecca is 43 years old.

3.3 USA EL DIAGRAMA PARA CREAR NUEVE FRASES CORRECTAS Y DILAS EN VOZ ALTA

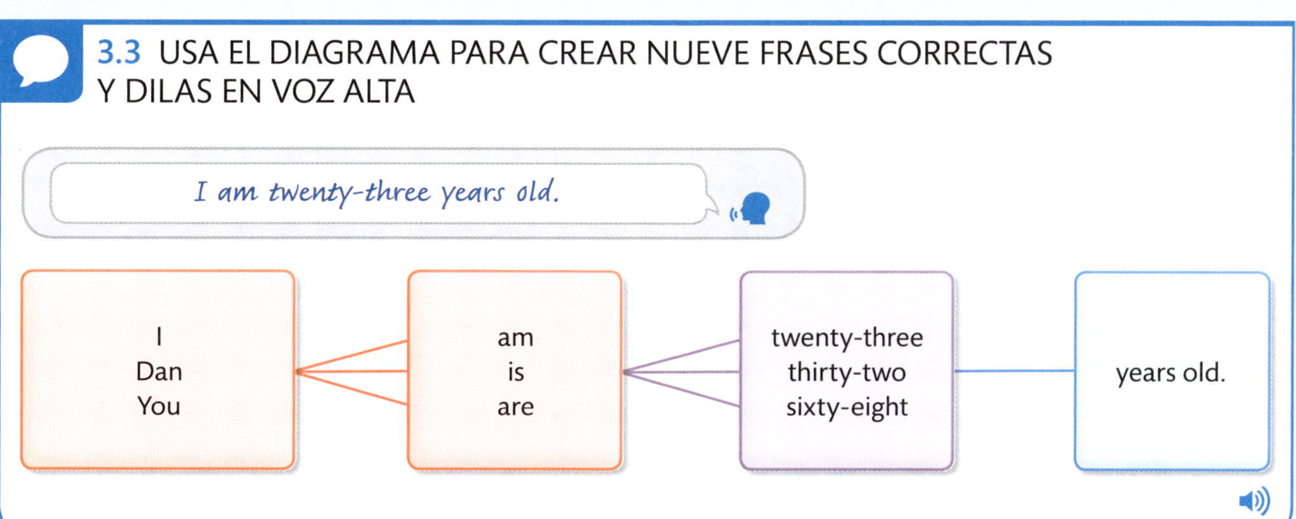

3.4 COMPLETA LOS ESPACIOS CON LAS FORMAS CORRECTAS DE "TO BE"

Alfonso *is* 87 years old. He *is* Spanish.

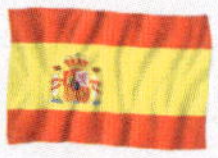

1. Abe ______ 72 years old. She ______ Japanese. 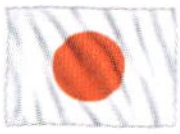
2. Mia and Leo ______ 12. They ______ from Italy. 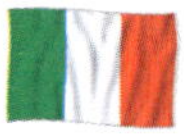
3. Chantal ______ 66 years old. She ______ French. 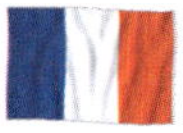
4. Amir and Aamna ______ 90 years old. They ______ from Pakistan. 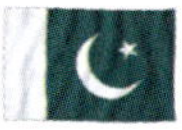
5. I ______ 24 years old. I ______ Irish. 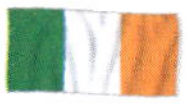
6. Max ______ 47 years old. He ______ German. 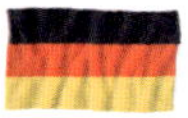
7. We ______ 38 years old. We ______ from New Zealand. 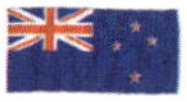
8. My sister ______ 4 years old. She ______ from Canada.

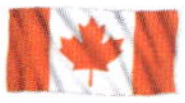

Aa **4.1 LA FAMILIA DE PABLO** ESCRIBE LAS PALABRAS DEL RECUADRO EN SU LUGAR EN EL ÁRBOL GENEALÓGICO DE LA FAMILIA DE PABLO

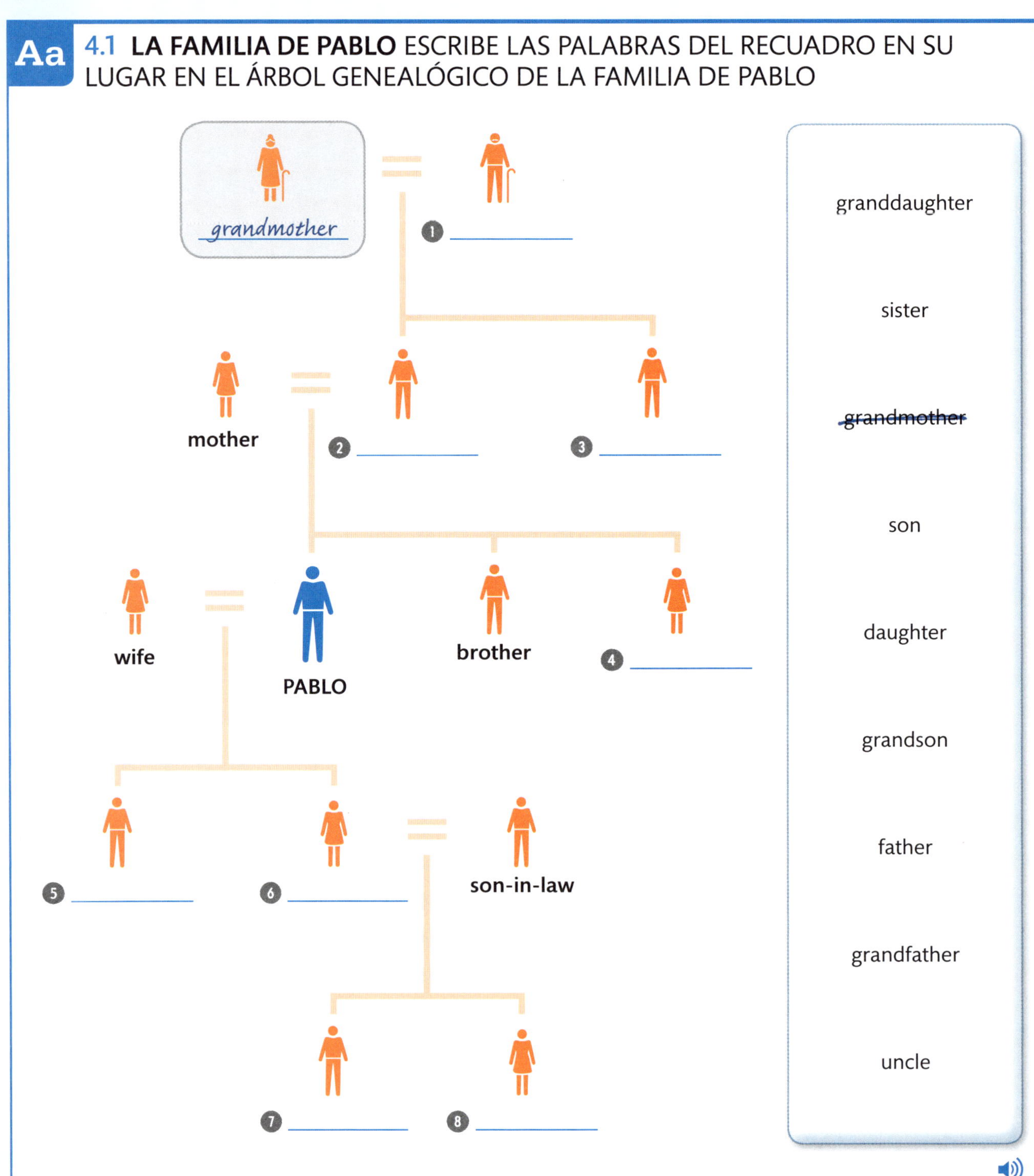

Aa **4.2 MASCOTAS Y ANIMALES DOMÉSTICOS** ESCRIBE LAS PALABRAS DEL RECUADRO DEBAJO DE LAS IMÁGENES CORRECTAS

hamster

1 ________

2 ________

3 ________

4 ________

5 ________

6 ________

7 ________

8 ________

9 ________

10 ________

11 ________

guinea pig
parrot
dog
chicken
snake
~~hamster~~
cat
rabbit
fish
tortoise
pig
horse

05 Tus cosas

Los adjetivos posesivos nos indican a quién le pertenece algo (una mascota, por ejemplo). "This" y "that" son determinantes. Señalan a una persona o un objeto concretos.

Lenguaje Adjetivos posesivos, "this" y "that"
Aa Vocabulario Animales y familia
Habilidad Hablar de a quién pertenecen las cosas

5.1 COMPLETA LOS ESPACIOS CON LOS ADJETIVOS POSESIVOS CORRECTOS

Her (She) fish is called Nemo.

1 ________ (They) dog is called Beth.
2 ________ (He) tortoise is 50 years old.
3 ________ (I) cat is called Sam.
4 ________ (We) lion is from Kenya.
5 ________ (You) rabbit eats grass.
6 Here is ________ (it) bed.
7 ________ (They) snake is called Sid.
8 Buster is ________ (I) monkey.
9 ________ (You) parrot is from Venezuela.
10 ________ (She) cat is called Tabatha.
11 ________ (They) monkey is from Morocco.
12 ________ (She) pig lives on a farm.
13 ________ (He) horse is called Prancer.
14 ________ (We) chicken lives in the garden.

5.2 VUELVE A ESCRIBIR LAS FRASES CORRIGIENDO LOS ERRORES

It is she horse.
It is her horse.

1 Fido is I dog.
2 Cookie is he cat.
3 It is we chicken.
4 Ziggy is you parrot.
5 Hiss is they snake.
6 Max is we monkey.
7 It is she rabbit.
8 Ed is I horse.
9 Rex is you dog.
10 Nemo is she fish.
11 It is we sheep.

5.3 COMPLETA LOS ESPACIOS USANDO "THIS" O "THAT"

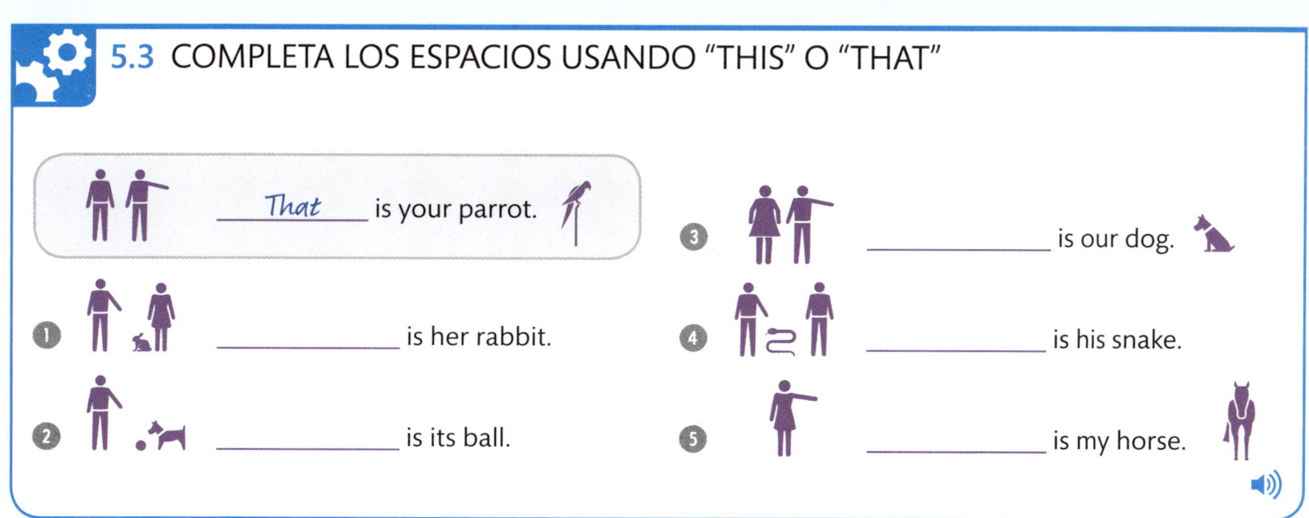

5.4 VUELVE A ESCRIBIR LAS FRASES PONIENDO LAS PALABRAS EN SU ORDEN CORRECTO

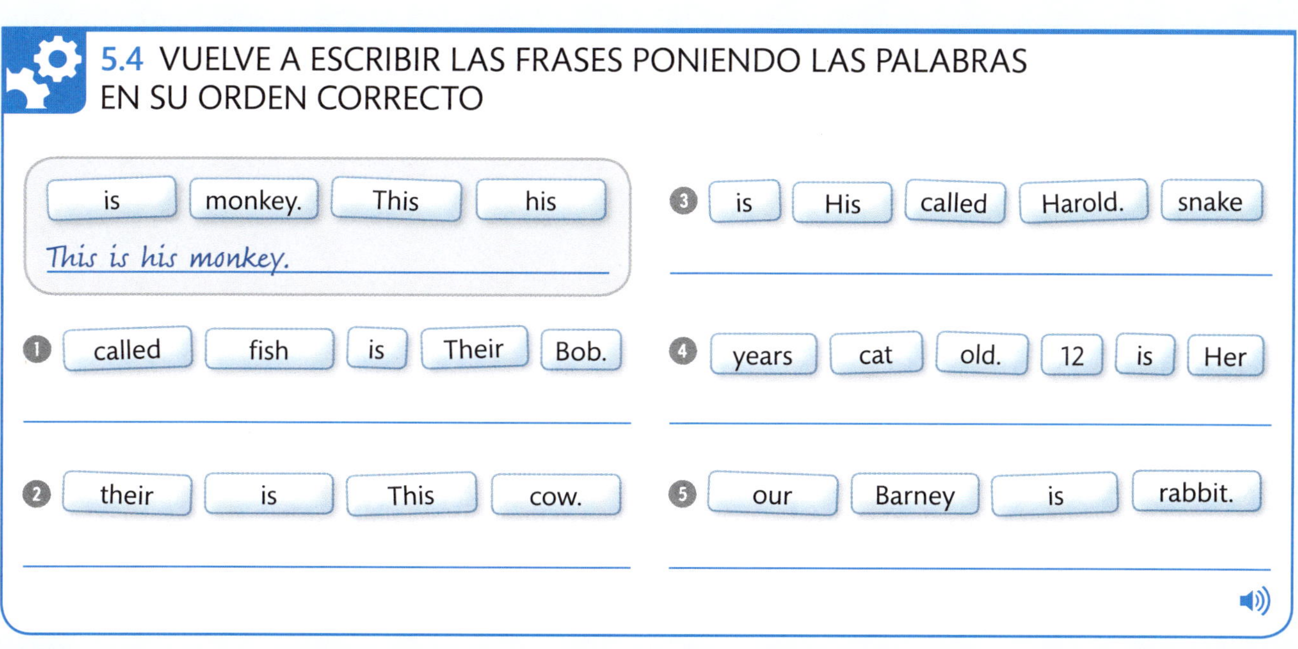

5.5 USA EL DIAGRAMA PARA CREAR 12 FRASES CORRECTAS Y DILAS EN VOZ ALTA

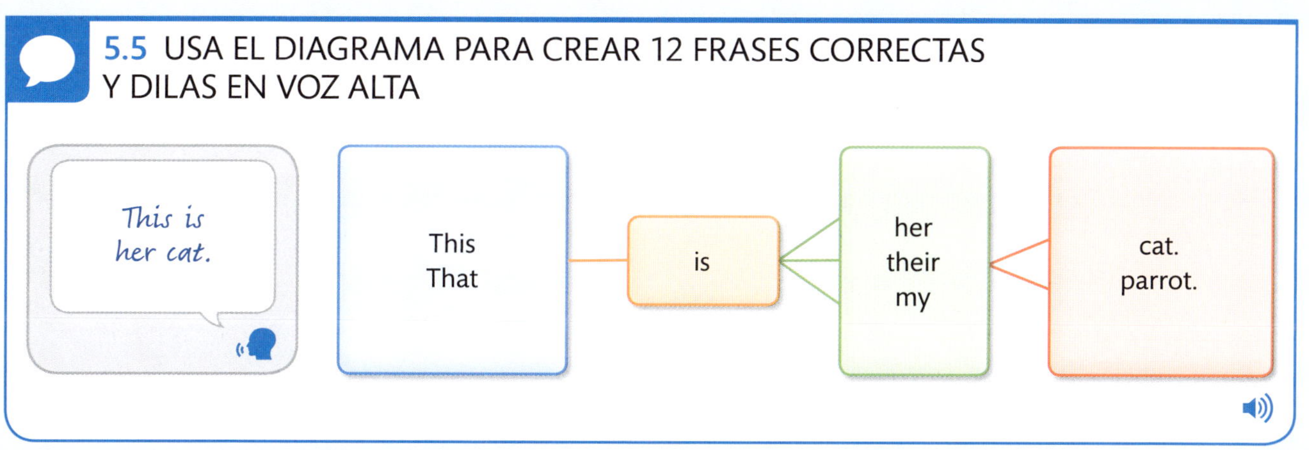

06 Uso del apóstrofo

En inglés se puede utilizar el apóstrofo (') para mostrar pertenencia. Se utiliza para mostrar de quién es algo, como una mascota, y para hablar sobre la familia.

Lenguaje Apóstrofo posesivo
Vocabulario Familia y mascotas
Habilidad Hablar de pertenencia

6.1 VUELVE A ESCRIBIR LAS FRASES USANDO UN APÓSTROFO CON "S"

The son of Christopher = *Christopher's son*

1. The dog of Joe and Greg = ______
2. The granddaughters of Dolly = ______
3. The house of Sue = ______
4. The snake of Pete and Aziz = ______

6.2 ESCUCHA EL AUDIO Y CONECTA LAS PAREJAS

Angela is	Sam's mother.
1 Arthur is	Sam's grandfather.
2 Frank is	Sam's sister.
3 Charlotte is	Sam's grandmother.
4 Micky is	Sam's friend.
5 Sally is	Sam's father.
6 Ronaldo is	Sam's brother.
7 Rebecca is	Sam's cousin.

(Ejemplo: Angela is → Sam's grandmother.)

6.3 LEE EL ARTÍCULO Y CONTESTA LAS PREGUNTAS

Sam lives with seven people.
True ☑ **False** ☐

1. Esme is Sam's grandmother.
   True ☐ **False** ☐
2. Sam's mother is called Helen.
   True ☐ **False** ☐
3. Sam's sisters go to university.
   True ☐ **False** ☐
4. There are two animals in the family's home.
   True ☐ **False** ☐
5. Ted's snake is called Bouncer.
   True ☐ **False** ☐

12 ENTERTAINMENT

TELEVISION

A fascinating look at everyday life with the Douglas family

Sam Douglas lives with seven other people at his home in London. Esme and Alf are Sam's grandparents. They have 14 grandchildren. Sam's mom is called Annie; she works in the pub next to the family's house. Annie's husband is Ralf and he's a mechanic.

Sam has two sisters and one brother. His sisters are called Helen and Rebecca. They go to a school near their house. Ted is Sam's brother. He's 20 and goes to university.

There are two animals in the Douglas family's home. Bouncer is Sam's dog and Hiss is Ted's snake.

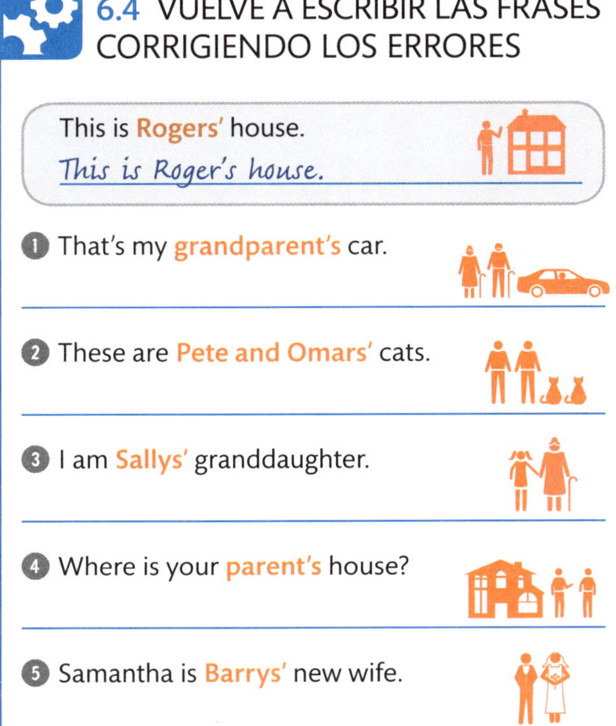

6.4 VUELVE A ESCRIBIR LAS FRASES CORRIGIENDO LOS ERRORES

This is **Rogers'** house.
This is Roger's house.

1. That's my **grandparent's** car.
2. These are **Pete and Omars'** cats.
3. I am **Sallys'** granddaughter.
4. Where is your **parent's** house?
5. Samantha is **Barrys'** new wife.

6.5 DI LAS FRASES EN ALTO, COMPLETANDO LOS ESPACIOS

Sally is *Fred's* **(Fred)** sister.

1. Sooty is ________ **(my brothers)** cat.
2. They are ________ **(Tammy)** parents.
3. This is our ________ **(children)** snake.
4. My ________ **(parents)** house is small.

07 Vocabulario

Aa 7.1 **OBJETOS COTIDIANOS** ESCRIBE LAS PALABRAS DEL RECUADRO DEBAJO DE SUS CORRESPONDIENTES DIBUJOS

1 ______

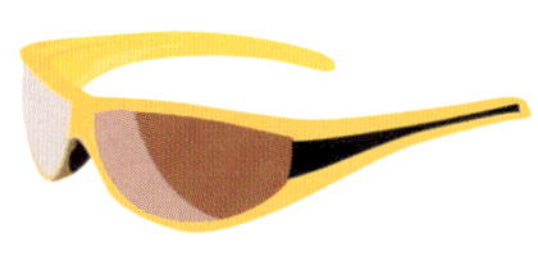

2 ______

3 ______

7 ______

8 ______

9 ______

10 ______

14 ______

15 ______

16 ______

17 ______

21 ______

22 ______

23 ______

24 ______

4 ____ 5 ____ 6 ____

11 ____ 12 ____ 13 ____

18 ____ 19 ____ 20 ____

25 ____ 26 ____ 27 ____

coins dictionary

pencil passport

camera ID card

~~wallet~~ earphones

bottle of water map

apple notebook

tablet toothbrush

sandwich letter

mirror sunglasses

keys newspaper

hairbrush necklace

book glasses

laptop umbrella

magazine pen

08 Hablar de tus cosas

Al referirnos a más de un objeto utilizamos "these" y "those". Para indicar a quién le pertenece algo, podemos utilizar los determinantes o los pronombres posesivos.

Lenguaje "These" y "those"
Aa Vocabulario Pertenencias
Habilidad Usar determinantes y pronombres

8.1 TACHA LA PALABRA INCORRECTA DE CADA FRASE

This / ~~**These**~~ is my phone.

1. **This** / **These** are my mom's glasses.
2. **That** / **Those** are Samantha's keys.
3. **This** / **These** is Tom's umbrella.
4. **This** / **These** is my dog.
5. **That** / **Those** are Pete's books.
6. **That** / **Those** is your newspaper.
7. **This** / **These** are my tickets.
8. **This** / **These** are Marge's earrings.
9. **This** / **These** are his daughters.
10. **That** / **Those** is my teacher.
11. **That** / **Those** is your watch.

8.2 VUELVE A ESCRIBIR LAS FRASES EN SU OTRA FORMA

This is my sister.	*These are my sisters.*
1 ______	These are my letters.
2 This is my purse.	______
3 ______	Those are Greg's keys.
4 That is my cat.	______
5 ______	These are my sister's pencils.
6 That is your dictionary.	______
7 This is Dan's house.	______
8 ______	Those are Stan's books.
9 ______	Those are my brothers.

8.3 ESCRIBE EL PLURAL DE ESTOS NOMBRES

apple = *apples*

1. pencil = ______
2. fish = ______
3. brother = ______
4. diary = ______
5. necklace = ______
6. brush = ______
7. watch = ______
8. box = ______
9. dictionary = ______
10. sister = ______
11. umbrella = ______
12. laptop = ______

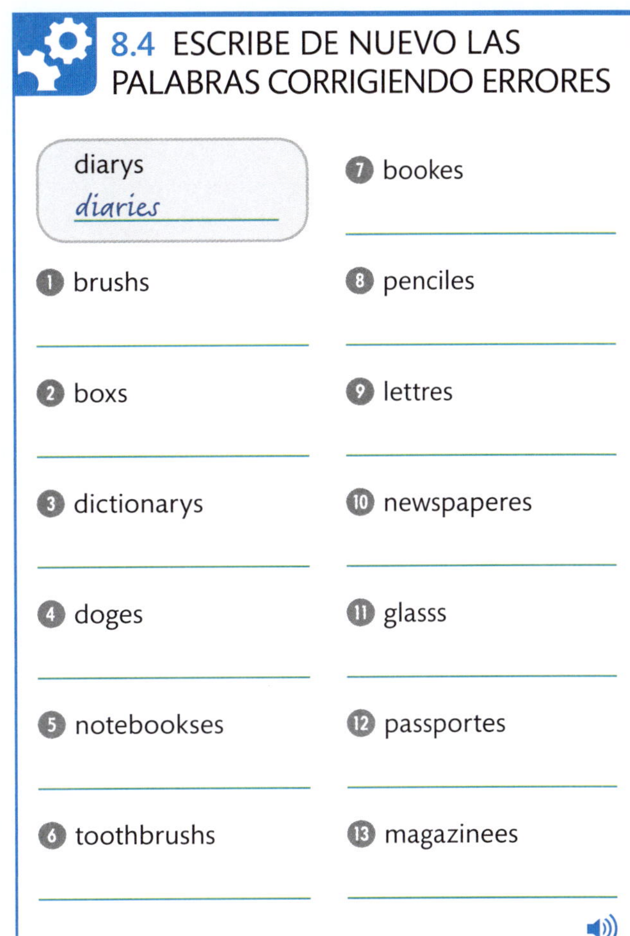

8.4 ESCRIBE DE NUEVO LAS PALABRAS CORRIGIENDO ERRORES

diarys
diaries

1. brushs ______
2. boxs ______
3. dictionarys ______
4. doges ______
5. notebookses ______
6. toothbrushs ______
7. bookes ______
8. penciles ______
9. lettres ______
10. newspaperes ______
11. glasss ______
12. passportes ______
13. magazinees ______

Aa 8.5 ESCRIBE LO QUE MUESTRA CADA IMAGEN

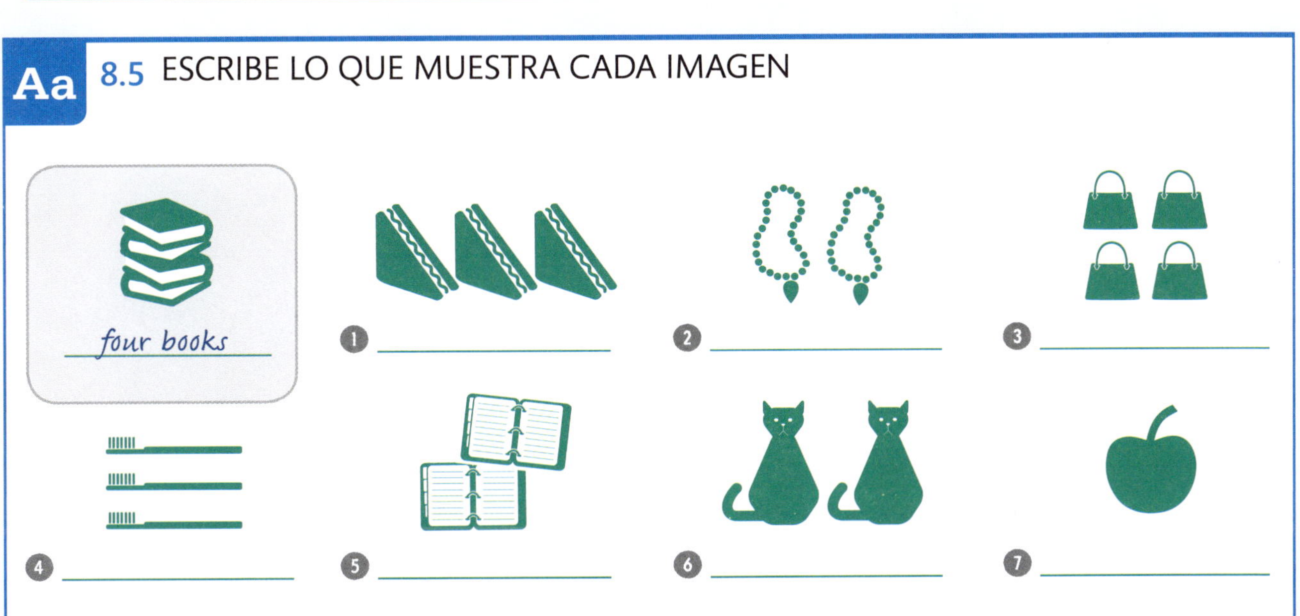

four books

1. ______
2. ______
3. ______
4. ______
5. ______
6. ______
7. ______

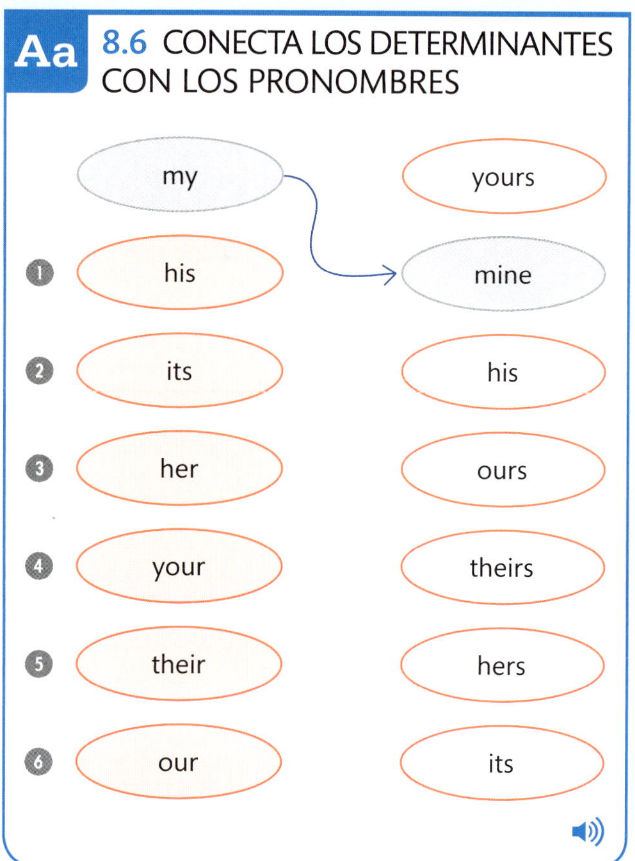

8.6 CONECTA LOS DETERMINANTES CON LOS PRONOMBRES

	my	yours
1	his	mine
2	its	his
3	her	ours
4	your	theirs
5	their	hers
6	our	its

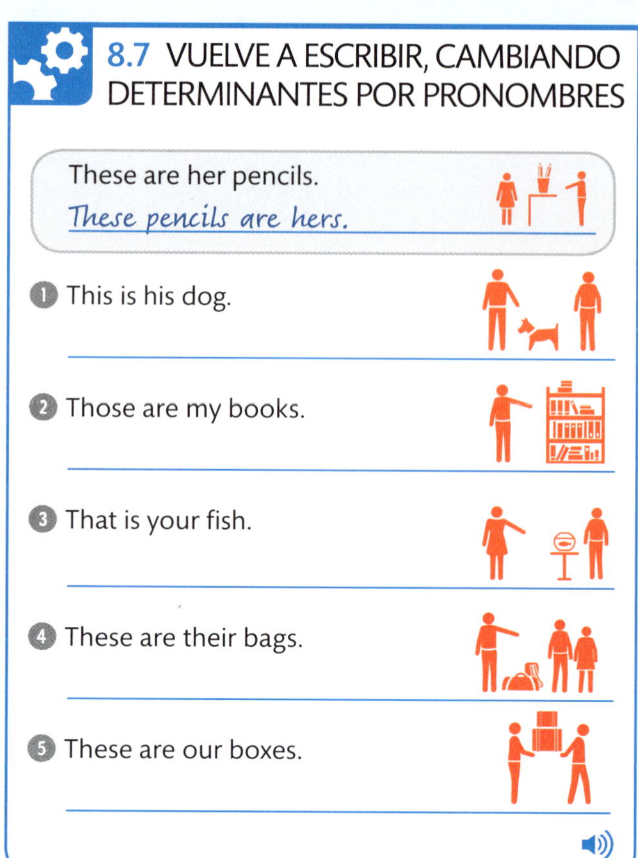

8.7 VUELVE A ESCRIBIR, CAMBIANDO DETERMINANTES POR PRONOMBRES

These are her pencils.
These pencils are hers.

1. This is his dog.
2. Those are my books.
3. That is your fish.
4. These are their bags.
5. These are our boxes.

8.8 ESCUCHA EL AUDIO Y MARCA LAS FRASES QUE ESCUCHES

Those books are mine. ☑
Those books are John's. ☐

1. That dog is yours. ☐
   That dog is Claire's. ☐
2. These sandwiches are theirs. ☐
   These sandwiches are Dan's. ☐
3. That bag is his. ☐
   That bag is hers. ☐
4. Those sandwiches are ours. ☐
   Those sandwiches are Emma's. ☐
5. That purse is hers. ☐
   That purse is Stacey's. ☐
6. This key is his. ☐
   This key is hers. ☐
7. This newspaper is theirs. ☐
   This newspaper is hers. ☐
8. That necklace is Linda's. ☐
   That necklace is hers. ☐
9. Those children are theirs. ☐
   Those children are ours. ☐

8.9 DI LAS FRASES EN VOZ ALTA COMPLETANDO LOS ESPACIOS CON "THIS" Y "THESE"

These are my pencils.

1. ______ are my books.
2. ______ is your dog.
3. ______ are her bags.
4. ______ are their boxes.
5. ______ is my toothbrush.
6. ______ is his diary.
7. ______ is your apple.
8. ______ are my apples.
9. ______ are your glasses.
10. ______ are Kevin's keys.
11. ______ is my dad's car.

8.10 ESCRIBE LOS DETERMINANTES Y LOS PRONOMBRES DEL CORREO ELECTRÓNICO EN EL GRUPO CORRECTO

DETERMINANTES

______

______

______

PRONOMBRES

______

______

To: Samantha

Subject: A new pet

Hi Samantha,

How are you? Thank you for your email. I have some big news: I have a new dog. His name is Rex and he is very big. I take him for a walk in the evening with my girlfriend Jane. Jane has a dog, too, but hers is very small. His name is Fido. Jane's dog likes mine!

We go to the park with our dogs every day. It's fun.

Let's meet soon,

Tim

09 Vocabulario

Aa 9.1 **TRABAJOS** ESCRIBE LAS PALABRAS DEL RECUADRO DEBAJO DE SU CORRESPONDIENTE DIBUJO

1 ____________

2 ____________

3 ____________

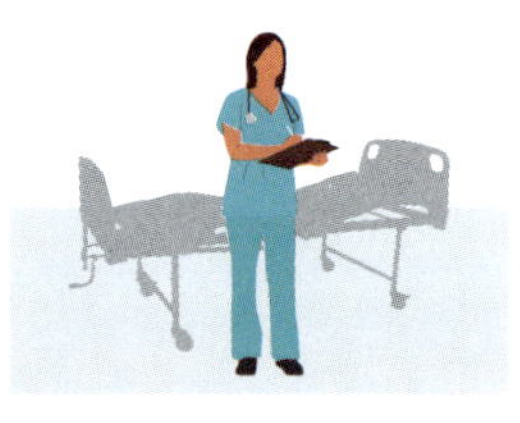

7 ____________

8 ____________

9 ____________

10 ____________

14 ____________

15 ____________

16 ____________

17 ____________

21 ____________

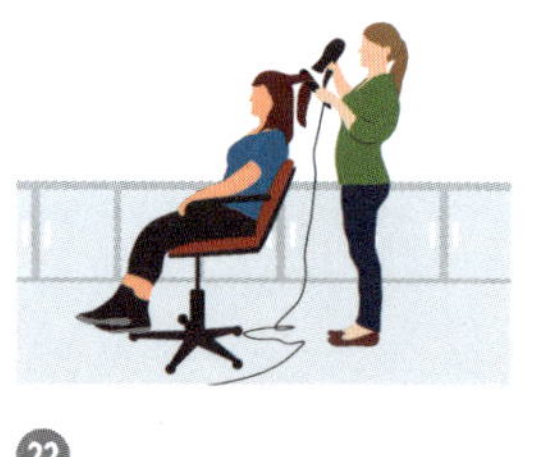

22 ____________

23 ____________

24 ____________

4 ____________

5 ____________

6 ____________

11 ____________

12 ____________

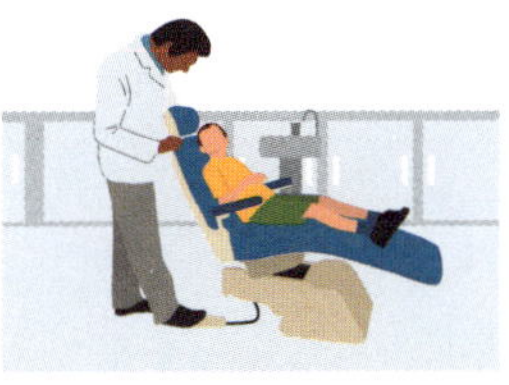

13 ____________

18 ____________

19 ____________

20 ____________

25 ____________

26 ____________

27 ____________

cleaner waiter
artist electrician
businessman
mechanic judge
sales assistant
teacher gardener
receptionist
dentist ~~scientist~~
construction worker
engineer pilot
vet fire fighter
nurse chef
actor hairdresser
businesswoman
doctor farmer
police officer
waitress driver

10 Hablar de tu trabajo

Para describir tu trabajo puedes utilizar el verbo "to be". El verbo "to work" puede dar más información acerca de dónde trabajas y con quién.

Lenguaje Usar "I am" para tu trabajo
Vocabulario Trabajos y lugares de trabajo
Habilidad Describir tu trabajo

10.1 VUELVE A ESCRIBIR LAS FRASES EN SU OTRA FORMA

I am an actor. — *We are actors.*

1. ______ They are doctors.
2. You are a teacher. ______
3. ______ We are hairdressers.
4. I am a mechanic. ______
5. ______ You are cleaners.
6. She is a chef. ______
7. ______ They are actors.
8. He is a vet. ______
9. ______ We are police officers.
10. You are a farmer. ______
11. ______ You are waitresses.
12. I am a gardener. ______
13. ______ We are artists.

10.2 COMPLETA LOS ESPACIOS CON LOS VERBOS Y LOS ARTÍCULOS CORRECTOS

She *is a* doctor.

1. I ______ actor.
2. He ______ teacher.
3. He ______ chef.
4. You ______ engineer.
5. We ______ hairdressers.
6. They ______ farmers.
7. You ______ vet.
8. I ______ waiter.
9. She ______ nurse.

10.3 TACHA LA PALABRA INCORRECTA DE CADA FRASE

They ~~is~~ / are gardeners.

1. I am / is a vet.
2. She is / are a businesswoman.
3. We is / are doctors.
4. They is / are teachers.
5. He is / are a mechanic.
6. I am / is a driver.
7. We am / are receptionists.
8. They are / is waitresses.
9. She is / are a police officer.
10. I am / is a judge.
11. You is / are a nurse.
12. We am / are farmers.
13. She is / are a sales assistant.
14. I am / are a chef.

10.4 UNE CADA IMAGEN CON LA ETIQUETA CORRECTA

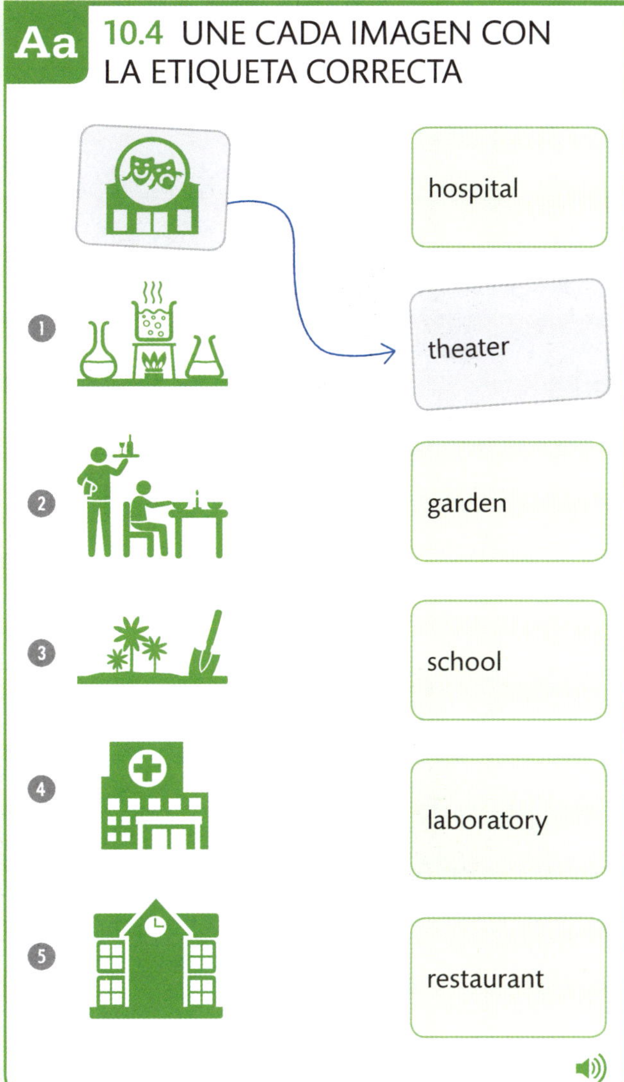

10.5 TACHA LA PALABRA INCORRECTA DE CADA FRASE

I work ~~on~~ / in an office.

1. He works on / in a doctor's office.
2. We work on / in a farm.
3. My dad works on / in a building site.
4. My sister works on / in a café.
5. We work on / in people's gardens.
6. Dan works on / in a hospital.
7. I work on / in a restaurant.
8. We work on / in a school.
9. Chris works on / in a supermarket.

10.6 OBSERVA LAS IMÁGENES Y DI EN VOZ ALTA LAS FRASES USANDO LAS PALABRAS DEL RECUADRO

Eric *is a waiter.*
He *works in a restaurant.*

1. Abby ______________
She ______________

2. Julie ______________
She ______________

3. Simon ______________
He ______________

4. Adam ______________
He ______________

5. Max ______________
He ______________

6. Carol ______________
She ______________

~~waiter~~ police officer park nurse
hairdresser ~~restaurant~~ engineer
police station hospital
beauty salon gardener farm
construction site farmer

Aa

10.7 COMPLETA LOS ESPACIOS CON LAS PALABRAS DEL RECUADRO

Peter is a ___teacher___ ( ) and he works with ___children___ ( ).

1. Sam is a ____________ ( ) and she works with ____________ ( ).
2. Gabriella is a ____________ ( ) and she works with ____________ ( ).
3. Dan is a ____________ ( ) and he works with ____________ ( ).
4. John is a ____________ ( ) and he works with ____________ ( ).
5. Tom is an ____________ ( ) and he works in a ____________ ( ).

doctor	crops	theater	patients	chef	~~children~~
~~teacher~~	animals	food	vet	farmer	actor

10.8 ESCUCHA EL AUDIO Y CONTESTA LAS PREGUNTAS

Pete is a...
farmer. ☑ **contractor.** ☐ **gardener.** ☐

1. Simon is a...
contractor. ☐ **gardener.** ☐ **teacher.** ☐

2. Sue is a...
nurse. ☐ **chef.** ☐ **teacher.** ☐

3. John is a...
scientist. ☐ **businessman.** ☐ **doctor.** ☐

4. Alberto is a...
waiter. ☐ **chef.** ☐ **actor.** ☐

5. Susan and Pam are...
chefs. ☐ **hairdressers.** ☐ **gardeners.** ☐

6. Douglas is an...
actor. ☐ **farmer.** ☐ **police officer.** ☐

7. Danny is a...
contractor. ☐ **architect.** ☐ **farmer.** ☐

11 Decir la hora

En inglés, hay dos maneras de decir la hora. Puedes utilizar las horas y los minutos, o puedes decir primero los minutos y después la relación que se establece con la hora.

Lenguaje Horas del día
Aa Vocabulario Palabras para indicar la hora
Habilidad Decir la hora

11.1 UNE LOS DIBUJOS CON LA HORA CORRECTA

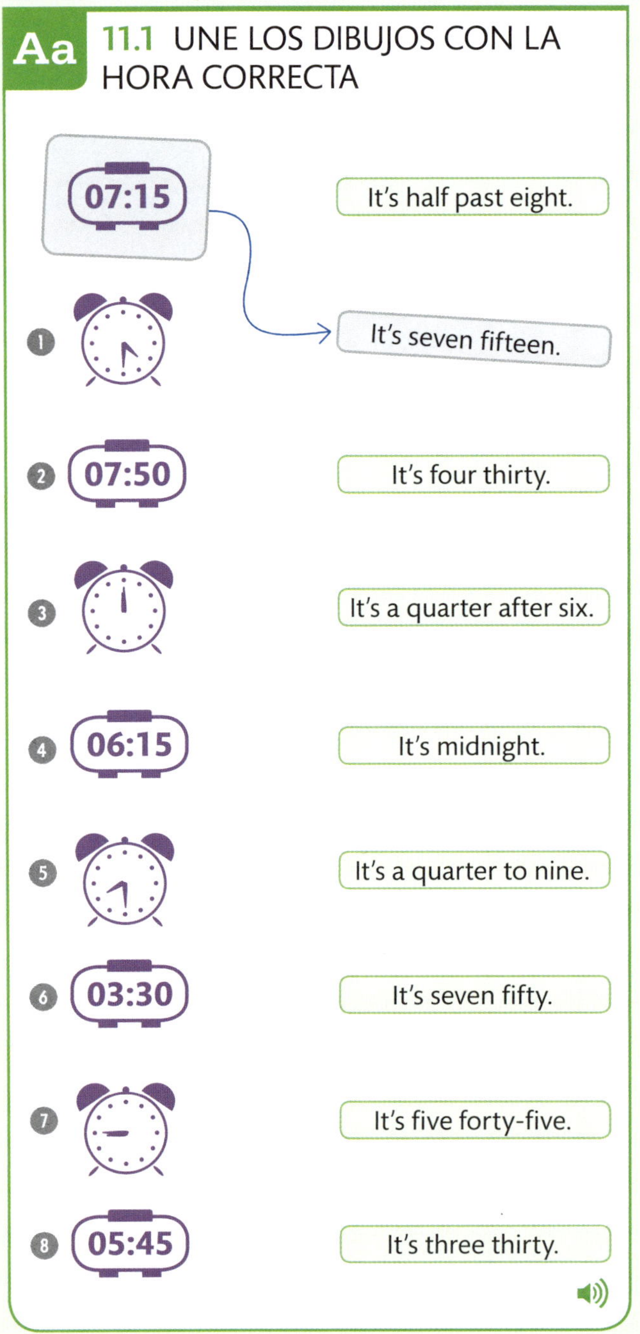

11.2 ESCUCHA EL AUDIO Y SEÑALA LAS HORAS CORRECTAS

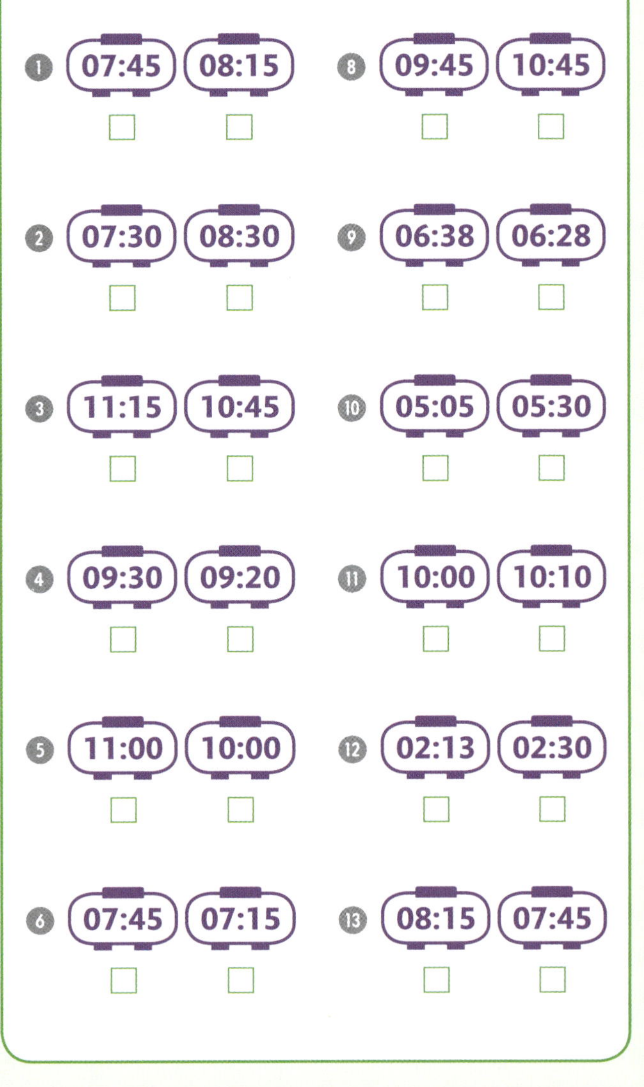

11.3 VUELVE A ESCRIBIR LAS HORAS USANDO NÚMEROS

It's a quarter to six. = *05:45*

1 It's a quarter past eleven. = ______
2 It's eleven o'clock. = ______
3 It's eight twenty-four. = ______
4 It's half past three. = ______
5 It's a quarter to three. = ______
6 It's five twenty-five. = ______
7 It's three forty-nine. = ______
8 It's two fifteen. = ______
9 It's nine o'clock. = ______
10 It's a quarter to eight. = ______
11 It's half past eleven. = ______
12 It's nine twenty-five. = ______
13 It's a quarter after ten. = ______
14 It's eleven twenty. = ______
15 It's one fifty-five. = ______
16 It's quarter to seven. = ______
17 It's six forty-five. = ______

11.4 MIRA LOS DIBUJOS Y DI CADA HORA EN VOZ ALTA

09:15 *It's a quarter past nine.*

1 09:45
2 04:00
3 10:20
4 11:30
5 03:47
6 03:15
7 06:30
8 08:22
9 01:25

12 Vocabulario

Aa 12.1 **ACTIVIDADES DIARIAS** ESCRIBE LAS PALABRAS DEL RECUADRO DEBAJO DE SUS CORRESPONDIENTES DIBUJOS

go to work

1 ______

2 ______

3 ______

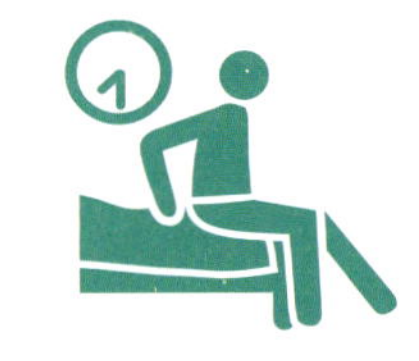

7 ______

8 ______

9 ______

10 ______

14 ______

15 ______

16 ______

17 ______

21 ______

22 ______

23 ______

24 ______

4 ______________

5 ______________

6 ______________

11 ______________

12 ______________

13 ______________

18 ______________

19 ______________

20 ______________

25 ______________

26 ______________

27 ______________

start work | clear the table
wash your face | wake up
go to bed | cook dinner
~~go to work~~ | iron a shirt
leave work | get dressed
do the dishes | have dinner
go to school | walk the dog
buy groceries | take a shower
dawn | have lunch | get up
brush your teeth | go home
day | finish work | dusk
brush your hair | take a bath
have breakfast | night

13 Describir tu jornada

Utiliza el present simple para hablar sobre tus actividades habituales: por ejemplo, cuándo sueles ir a trabajar o a qué hora sueles comer.

Lenguaje Present simple
Aa Vocabulario Actividades diarias
Habilidad Hablar de tus actividades diarias

Aa 13.1 UNE LOS DIBUJOS CON LAS FRASES CORRECTAS

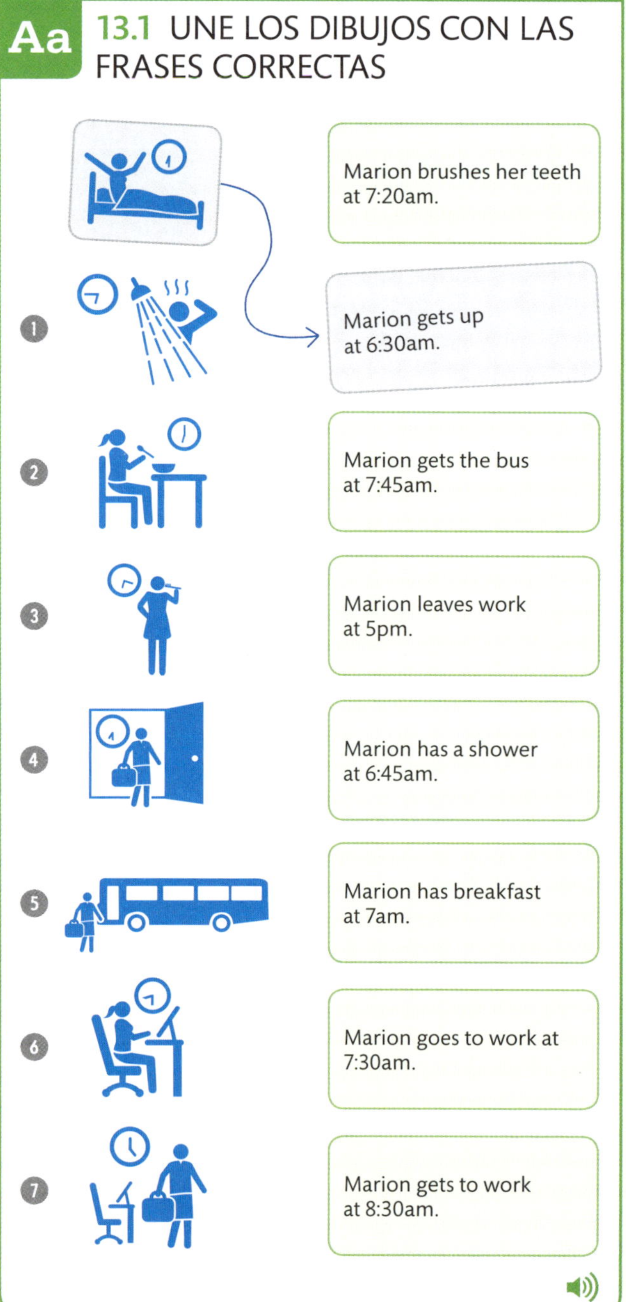

Marion brushes her teeth at 7:20am.

Marion gets up at 6:30am.

Marion gets the bus at 7:45am.

Marion leaves work at 5pm.

Marion has a shower at 6:45am.

Marion has breakfast at 7am.

Marion goes to work at 7:30am.

Marion gets to work at 8:30am.

13.2 TACHA LA PALABRA INCORRECTA DE CADA FRASE

She eats / ~~eat~~ dinner in the evening.

1. I wake / wakes up at 6:30am.
2. He gets / get up at 6am.
3. She have / has a shower at 7am.
4. They have / has cereal for breakfast.
5. He have / has a shower before breakfast.
6. She leaves / leave home at 7:15am.
7. The bus go / goes every half hour.
8. I get / gets to work at 8:30am.
9. He start / starts work at 9am.
10. She take / takes an hour for lunch.
11. I go / goes to the sandwich shop for lunch.
12. They eat / eats lunch in the canteen.
13. He finish / finishes work at 5pm.
14. They go / goes home on the bus.
15. He wash / washes his car every weekend.
16. I watch / watches TV after dinner.
17. They go / goes to bed at 11pm.
18. He sleep / sleeps for eight hours.

13.3 COMPLETA LOS ESPACIOS CON LOS VERBOS EN SU FORMA CORRECTA

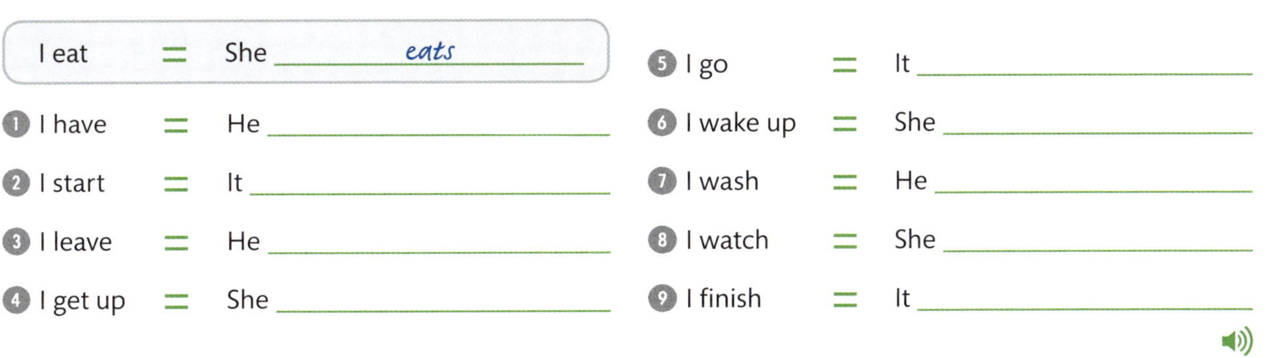

I eat = She *eats*

1. I have = He ______
2. I start = It ______
3. I leave = He ______
4. I get up = She ______
5. I go = It ______
6. I wake up = She ______
7. I wash = He ______
8. I watch = She ______
9. I finish = It ______

13.4 COMPLETA LOS ESPACIOS CON LOS VERBOS EN SU FORMA CORRECTA

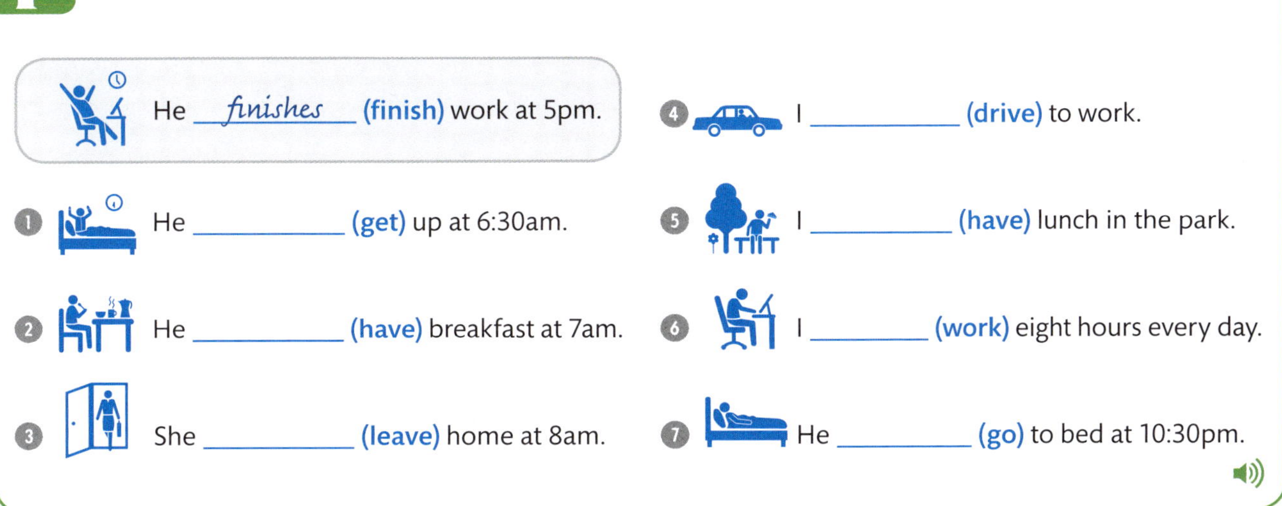

He *finishes* **(finish)** work at 5pm.

1. He ______ **(get)** up at 6:30am.
2. He ______ **(have)** breakfast at 7am.
3. She ______ **(leave)** home at 8am.
4. I ______ **(drive)** to work.
5. I ______ **(have)** lunch in the park.
6. I ______ **(work)** eight hours every day.
7. He ______ **(go)** to bed at 10:30pm.

13.5 DI ESTOS VERBOS EN VOZ ALTA

starts

1. goes
2. washes
3. wakes
4. gets
5. watches
6. leaves
7. has
8. finishes

14 Describir tu semana

Puedes hablar sobre lo que haces cada semana utilizando el presente y expresiones temporales. Estas, normalmente, se forman utilizando preposiciones y los días de la semana.

Lenguaje Días y preposiciones
Vocabulario Días de la semana
Habilidad Hablar de tus rutinas semanales

14.1 COMPLETA LOS ESPACIOS CON LAS PALABRAS "ON" E "IN"

Peter plays soccer _on_ Sundays.

1. I go to the movies ______ the weekend.
2. Joe starts work at 6pm ______ Mondays.
3. You watch TV ______ the afternoon.
4. Harry plays tennis ______ Wednesdays.
5. Lin goes swimming ______ the evening.
6. Alex goes fishing ______ the weekend.
7. He eats lunch at 1pm ______ Fridays.
8. Sam goes to the gym ______ the morning.

14.2 SEÑALA LAS FRASES QUE SEAN CORRECTAS

I play soccer on Mondays. ☑
I play soccer at Mondays. ☐

1. I work from Monday to Thursday. ☐
   I work of Monday to Thursday. ☐
2. My sister go swimming every day. ☐
   My sister goes swimming every day. ☐
3. We go to the gym on Saturdays. ☐
   We go to the gym at Saturdays. ☐
4. You read the newspaper in Sundays. ☐
   You read the newspaper on Sundays. ☐
5. Peter goes to work on the weekend. ☐
   Peter goes to work from the weekend. ☐
6. Jennifer goes to a café for Fridays. ☐
   Jennifer goes to a café on Fridays. ☐
7. Sam and Pete work to 9am from 5pm. ☐
   Sam and Pete work from 9am to 5pm. ☐

14.3 DI LAS FRASES EN VOZ ALTA COMPLETANDO LOS ESPACIOS

I leave early for work _on_ Mondays.

1. Pam works ____ Monday ____ Friday.
2. I work at home ____ Thursdays.
3. Tom goes to the cinema ____ Fridays.
4. I play soccer ____ the weekend.
5. They work ____ Monday ____ Thursday.
6. We go to bed at 9pm ____ Mondays.
7. Laura goes shopping ____ Tuesdays.
8. Peter gets up at 8am ____ Mondays.
9. We go to the gym ____ Thursdays.
10. Gerald reads a book ____ the weekend.
11. Jane swims ____ Monday ____ Friday.
12. John takes a bath ____ Fridays.
13. Lizzy starts work at 9am ____ Fridays.

14.4 VUELVE A ESCRIBIR LAS FRASES PONIENDO LAS PALABRAS EN SU ORDEN CORRECTO

every day. | has | She | breakfast

She has breakfast every day.

1. goes to | Dan | three times a week. | the gym
2. twice a week. | goes to | the cinema | Sam
3. every day. | We | at 11:30pm | go to bed
4. goes to | Joe | college | five times a week.
5. once a week. | washes her | Clarice | clothes
6. Jennifer | twice a week. | at 10am | gets up
7. at 7pm | every day. | eat dinner | We

14.5 VUELVE A ESCRIBIR LAS FRASES CORRIGIENDO LOS ERRORES

I **wakes up** at 6:30am.
I wake up at 6:30am.

1. Bob **go swimming** on Thursdays.
2. I play tennis **on weekend**.
3. Jane and Tom go to the gym **three time** a week.
4. Angus works from **Monday on Thursday**.
5. I go to the movies **on weekend**.
6. Sam goes to **college Wednesdays**.
7. Jenny gets up **in 7am** every day.
8. Peter **work from** Monday to Friday.
9. Nina **go to bed** at 11pm every day.

14.6 LEE EL CORREO ELECTRÓNICO Y CONTESTA LAS PREGUNTAS

Jim goes to the gym three times a week.
True ☐ **False** ☑

1. Jim goes to work at 6am.
True ☐ **False** ☐
2. Jim goes to the gym on Mondays and Tuesdays.
True ☐ **False** ☐
3. He plays soccer on Fridays.
True ☐ **False** ☐
4. Jim and his wife get up at 10am on the weekend.
True ☐ **False** ☐
5. They go to the theater on Saturdays.
True ☐ **False** ☐
6. They go to a restaurant on Sundays.
True ☐ **False** ☐

To: Pete
Subject: My week

Hi Pete,
Let me tell you about my typical week. From Monday to Thursday, I get up early, at 6am. I eat breakfast, then I go to work at 8:30am. On Fridays, I work at home. I like Fridays. I like sports a lot. I go to the gym twice a week, on Mondays and Tuesdays, and I go swimming on Wednesdays. I play soccer on Thursdays, but I relax on Friday and read a newspaper.

On the weekend, my wife and I get up at 10am. We go to the movies on Saturdays, and on Sundays, we go to a good restaurant. Tell me about your weekend!

Jim

14.7 ESCUCHA EL AUDIO Y NUMERA DESPUÉS LAS IMÁGENES EN EL ORDEN EN QUE SE DESCRIBEN

A ☐

B ☐

C ☐

D ☐

E 1

F ☐

14.8 VUELVE A ESCUCHAR 14.7 Y CONTESTA LAS PREGUNTAS

Kate goes to the gym on...
Monday ☐ **Tuesday** ☐ **Friday** ☑

1. Paul is a...
farmer ☐ **teacher** ☐ **doctor** ☐

2. Jane is a...
nurse ☐ **doctor** ☐ **teacher** ☐

3. On the weekend, Jane goes to...
a restaurant ☐ **the movies** ☐ **a gym** ☐

4. Sally gets up at...
6am ☐ **7am** ☐ **8am** ☐

5. Sally goes swimming on...
Saturday ☐ **Sunday** ☐ **Thursday** ☐

6. Eric works at the...
school ☐ **theater** ☐ **restaurant** ☐

7. Eric works... a week.
twice ☐ **three days** ☐ **four days** ☐

8. Claire is a...
waitress ☐ **carpenter** ☐ **farmer** ☐

9. Claire starts work at...
6am ☐ **4pm** ☐ **6pm** ☐

15 Frases negativas con "to be"

Para hacer una frase negativa se utiliza "not" o la forma contraída "n't". Las frases negativas con el verbo "to be" siguen reglas diferentes que las formadas con otros verbos.

Lenguaje Frases negativas con "to be"
Vocabulario "Not"
Habilidad Decir lo que las cosas no son

15.1 VUELVE A ESCRIBIR LAS FRASES PONIENDO LAS PALABRAS EN SU ORDEN CORRECTO

o'clock. | 5 | not | is | It

It is not 5 o'clock.

1. teacher. | Paula | not | is | a
2. are | not | England. | We | from
3. my | This | phone. | not | is
4. years | Kirsty | not | old. | 18 | is
5. is | not | Frank | my | father.
6. This | my | not | purse. | is
7. not | They | are | engineers.
8. is | That | salon. | not | a
9. Kim | a | teacher. | is | not

15.2 COMPLETA LOS ESPACIOS PARA CONSTRUIR FRASES NEGATIVAS

They *are not* hairdressers.

1. That ______ a castle.
2. They ______ at school.
3. He ______ a grandfather.
4. We ______ engineers.
5. She ______ 70 years old.
6. You ______ French.
7. This ______ my dog.
8. I ______ a doctor.
9. It ______ 11 o'clock.

15.3 ESCUCHA EL AUDIO Y NUMERA DESPUÉS LAS IMÁGENES EN EL ORDEN EN QUE SE DESCRIBEN

A ☐

B 1

C ☐

D ☐

15.4 COMPLETA LOS ESPACIOS PARA ESCRIBIR CADA FRASE DE TRES MANERAS DISTINTAS

She is not a nurse.	*She's not a nurse.*	*She isn't a nurse.*
1 ______	Fredo's not a chef.	______
2 Susie is not my cat.	______	______
3 ______	______	My dad isn't at work.
4 ______	They're not at the theater.	______

15.5 LEE EL BLOG Y CONTESTA LAS PREGUNTAS

Mia is 45 years old.	True ☐	False ☑
1 She lives in California.	True ☐	False ☐
2 She's a waitress in a restaurant.	True ☐	False ☐
3 She isn't Mexican.	True ☐	False ☐
4 Franco isn't an engineer.	True ☐	False ☐
5 They have a daughter in college.	True ☐	False ☐

Mia's blog

HOME | ENTRIES | ABOUT | CONTACT

POSTED MONDAY, APRIL 20

My life

Hi! I'm Mia and I'm 47 years old. I live in Los Angeles, California, and I'm a chef. I work in a Mexican restaurant. A lot of people think I'm from Mexico, but I'm not. I'm from Colombia. I'm married to Franco. He's a carpenter. We have a son, Sam. He studies at a local college.

15.6 VUELVE A ESCRIBIR LAS FRASES CORRIGIENDO LOS ERRORES

This **aren't** your cat.
This isn't your cat.

1. This **aren't** his umbrella.
2. Pedro **aren't** Spanish.
3. Pete and Terry **isn't** hairdressers.
4. It **aren't** a snake.
5. My cousins **isn't** 21 years old.
6. It **aren't** half past six.
7. **I isn't** your friend.

15.7 LEE EL BLOG Y CONTESTA LAS PREGUNTAS

Theresa is not from Germany.
True ☐ **False** ☑

1. Lucia is not 41 years old.
   True ☐ **False** ☐
2. There isn't a learner from Spain.
   True ☐ **False** ☐
3. Pablo is not a teacher.
   True ☐ **False** ☐
4. Theresa is not a teacher.
   True ☐ **False** ☐
5. Xi is not a chef.
   True ☐ **False** ☐
6. Xi does not live in China.
   True ☐ **False** ☐

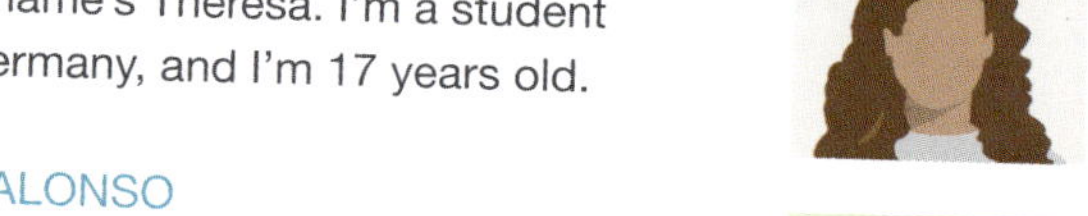

THERESA GEISSLER
Hi, my name's Theresa. I'm a student from Germany, and I'm 17 years old.

LUCIA ALONSO
Hello, everyone. I am from Italy, and my name is Lucia. I am 42, and I am an engineer.

PABLO MONTOYA
I am a teacher called Pablo. I come from Argentina. I am 51, and I have been learning English for the last six months.

XI LIU
Hello, my name is Xi. I am 32 years old. I am a doctor, and I live with my wife and son in China.

15.8 CONVIERTE LAS FRASES CON "YOU" EN FRASES CON "I"

You're a nurse. You're not a doctor.
I'm a nurse. I'm not a doctor.

1. You're a student. You're not a teacher.
2. You're 30 years old. You're not 40.
3. You're a farmer. You're not a police officer.
4. You're French. You're not English.
5. You're an uncle. You're not a father.
6. You're 18. You're not 21.
7. You're a waitress. You're not a chef.
8. You're Spanish. You're not Italian.

15.9 CONVIERTE LAS FRASES CON "I" EN FRASES CON "YOU"

I'm French. I'm not German.
You're French. You're not German.

1. I'm 28. I'm not 29.
2. I'm a scientist. I'm not a gardener.
3. I'm Austrian. I'm not English.
4. I'm a contractor. I'm not an actor.
5. I'm 16. I'm not 18.
6. I'm an uncle. I'm not a grandfather.
7. I'm a mechanic. I'm not an engineer.
8. I'm a police officer. I'm not a firefighter.

15.10 USA EL DIAGRAMA PARA CREAR 12 FRASES CORRECTAS Y DILAS EN VOZ ALTA

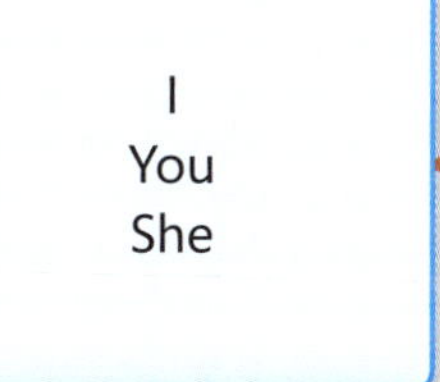

'm not
isn't
aren't

at work.
an actor.
American.
40 years old.

16 Más frases negativas

Añade "do not" o "does not" antes de la mayoría de los verbos para hacer su forma negativa. Es habitual acortar estas formas escribiendo "don't" o "doesn't".

Lenguaje Present simple negativo
Vocabulario Actividades diarias
Habilidad Decir lo que no haces

16.1 COMPLETA LOS ESPACIOS CON "DO NOT" O "DOES NOT"

She *does not* play tennis on Wednesdays.

1. Jane ______ walk to work.
2. My brother ______ watch TV.
3. I ______ read a book in the evening.
4. Frank ______ work at the museum.
5. They ______ go dancing on the weekend.
6. We ______ go to work on Fridays.
7. I ______ get up at 7:30am.
8. You ______ have a car.
9. My dad ______ work in an office.
10. You ______ have a dog.
11. My sister ______ work with children.
12. They ______ live in the country.
13. Freddie ______ eat meat.

16.2 VUELVE A ESCRIBIR LAS FRASES PONIENDO LAS PALABRAS EN SU ORDEN CORRECTO

go | Mick | on Wednesdays. | to work | doesn't

Mick doesn't go to work on Wednesdays.

1. in New York. | live | doesn't | Tony
2. doesn't | a farm. | work | on | Sebastian
3. a factory. | doesn't | uncle | My | in | work
4. on Thursdays. | soccer | play | We | don't
5. German | don't | at school. | I | learn
6. work | Carlo | on Mondays. | doesn't
7. don't | at | You | take | a bath | night.

16.3 ESCRIBE DOS FORMAS NEGATIVAS DE CADA FRASE

I get up at 7am.	*I do not get up at 7am.*	*I don't get up at 7am.*
1 Tim plays tennis.		
2 You have a black cat.		
3 Jules reads a book every day.		
4 Sam works in a restaurant.		
5 They play soccer.		
6 Emily works with animals.		
7 Mel and Greg have a car.		
8 You work in a factory.		

16.4 VUELVE A ESCRIBIR LAS FRASES CORRIGIENDO LOS ERRORES

He don't go swimming on Wednesdays.
He doesn't go swimming on Wednesdays.

1. Chloe don't play tennis with her friends.
2. You doesn't work outside.
3. Sal and Doug doesn't have a car.
4. We doesn't watch TV at home.
5. Mrs. O'Brien don't work in an office.
6. You doesn't wake up at 6am.
7. They doesn't eat lunch at 1pm.
8. Virginia don't speak good English.
9. Trevor don't live near here.
10. My dad don't live in Los Angeles.
11. David don't play chess.

Aa 16.5 MARCA LAS FRASES QUE SON CORRECTAS

Jenny doesn't work in a bank. ☑
Jenny don't work in a bank. ☐

1. Jean don't cycle to work. ☐
   Jean doesn't cycle to work. ☐
2. They don't live in the city. ☐
   They doesn't live in the city. ☐
3. Mr. James don't go to the theater. ☐
   Mr. James doesn't go to the theater. ☐
4. He doesn't read a newspaper. ☐
   He don't read a newspaper. ☐
5. My cousins don't have tickets. ☐
   My cousins doesn't have tickets. ☐
6. Sally doesn't go to the gym. ☐
   Sally don't go to the gym. ☐
7. Our dog don't have a ball. ☐
   Our dog doesn't have a ball. ☐
8. I don't have a laptop. ☐
   I doesn't have a laptop. ☐
9. My mom doesn't get up at 7:30am. ☐
   My mom don't get up at 7:30am. ☐
10. You doesn't live in the country. ☐
    You don't live in the country. ☐
11. Claude don't have a dictionary. ☐
    Claude doesn't have a dictionary. ☐

16.6 ESCUCHA EL AUDIO Y RESPONDE A LAS PREGUNTAS

Julie habla acerca de cosas que hace durante la semana.

Julie works in the museum.
True ☑ **False** ☐

1. Julie gets up at 7am.
   True ☐ **False** ☐
2. Julie doesn't work on Fridays.
   True ☐ **False** ☐
3. Julie has lunch with her friends.
   True ☐ **False** ☐
4. Julie plays tennis on Wednesday evenings.
   True ☐ **False** ☐
5. Julie gets home at 8pm.
   True ☐ **False** ☐
6. Julie doesn't eat dinner.
   True ☐ **False** ☐
7. Julie watches TV before she goes to bed.
   True ☐ **False** ☐

16.7 LEE EL ARTÍCULO Y RESPONDE A LAS PREGUNTAS

Who doesn't live in a city?
Sam ☐ **Carla** ☐ **Greg** ☑

1. Who plays a sport on Thursdays?
Sam ☐ **Carla** ☐ **Greg** ☐

2. Who works in the evenings?
Sam ☐ **Carla** ☐ **Greg** ☐

3. Who doesn't have lunch?
Sam ☐ **Carla** ☐ **Greg** ☐

4. Who works in an office?
Sam ☐ **Carla** ☐ **Greg** ☐

5. Who doesn't work on Mondays?
Sam ☐ **Carla** ☐ **Greg** ☐

6. Who starts work at 5am?
Sam ☐ **Carla** ☐ **Greg** ☐

7. Who plays basketball on Mondays?
Sam ☐ **Carla** ☐ **Greg** ☐

8. Who plays soccer?
Sam ☐ **Carla** ☐ **Greg** ☐

What I do

Sam

I'm a waiter from New York. I like my job. I work evenings and the food is fantastic. I work from Tuesday to Sunday, and I don't work on Mondays. On Mondays I play basketball in the afternoon.

Carla

I work in an office in Dublin. I start work at 9am and have lunch at 1pm. I love sports. I play soccer with my colleagues on Thursday evenings.

Greg

I live in the country in South Australia. I work on a farm and start work at 5am. I have a big breakfast and a big dinner, but I don't have lunch. Every weekend, I play golf.

16.8 UTILIZA EL DIAGRAMA PARA CREAR NUEVE FRASES CORRECTAS Y DILAS EN VOZ ALTA

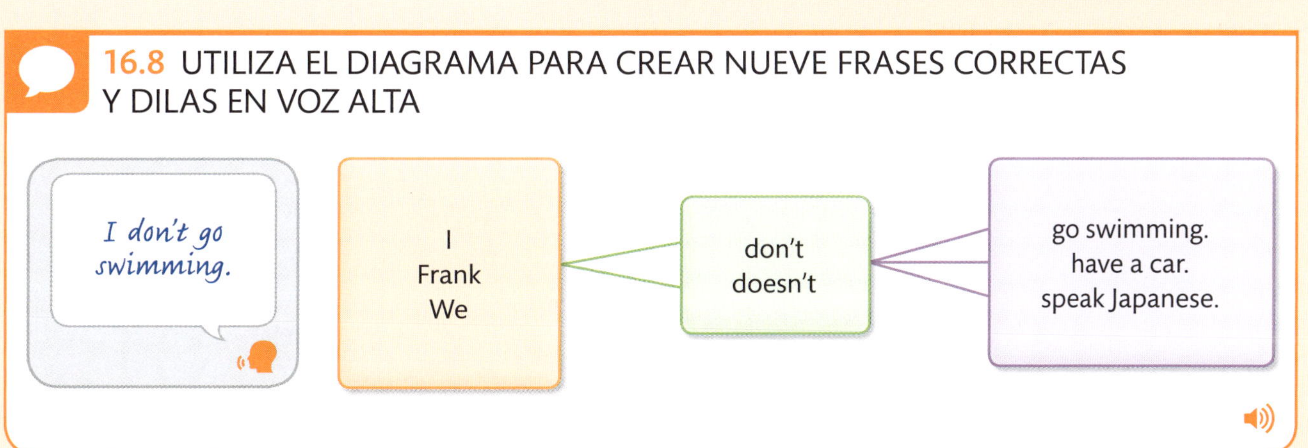

17 Preguntas simples

Para hacer preguntas simples con el verbo "to be", basta con cambiar el orden de sujeto y verbo. Normalmente, la respuesta a una pregunta simple empieza con "yes" o "no".

Lenguaje Preguntas simples
Vocabulario Trabajos y actividades habituales
Habilidad Hacer preguntas simples

17.1 REESCRIBE LAS AFIRMACIONES COMO PREGUNTAS

She is an engineer.
Is she an engineer?

1. This is his passport.
2. It is 6 o'clock.
3. Doug and Jim are hairdressers.
4. These are my glasses.
5. Sally is his sister.
6. Those are your letters.
7. She is a nurse.
8. This is your snake.
9. It is 3pm.
10. His wife is a chef.
11. Katie and Jess are my friends.

17.2 UTILIZA EL DIAGRAMA PARA CREAR SEIS PREGUNTAS DISTINTAS Y DILAS EN VOZ ALTA

Are you an actor?

Are Is	you she they	an actor? a teacher? engineers?

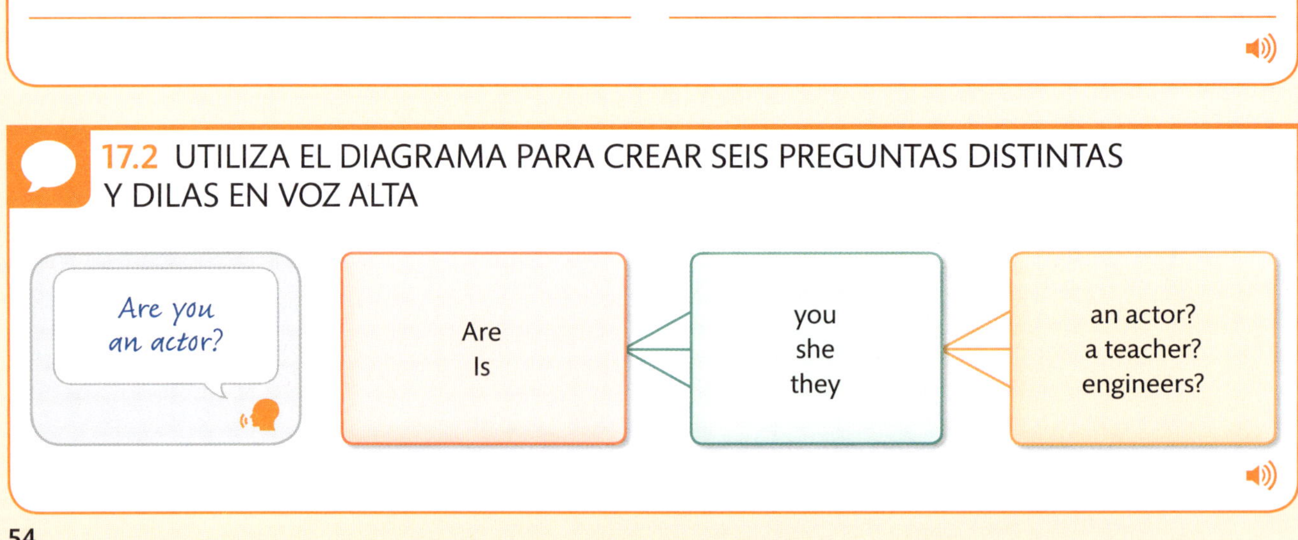

17.3 COMPLETA LOS ESPACIOS UTILIZANDO "IS" O "ARE"

Is he a police officer?

1.  ______ Dorota at school?
2.  ______ this your parrot?
3.  ______ there a bank near here?
4.  ______ you a gardener?
5.  ______ these Jean's keys?
6.  ______ there a castle in your town?
7.  ______ that your bag?
8.  ______ they your cousins?
9.  ______ they from France?
10.  ______ she Sam's sister?
11.  ______ this my burger?
12.  ______ there a church in this town?
13.  ______ those Brooke's shirts?

17.4 VUELVE A ESCRIBIR LAS PREGUNTAS PONIENDO LAS PALABRAS EN SU ORDEN CORRECTO

Are | a | doctor? | you

Are you a doctor?

1. Is | Italy? | from | Paula
2. past | two? | it | Is | half
3. your | Ronaldo | father? | Is
4. on | there | Is | bank | your | a | street?
5. your | Are | these | glasses? | dad's
6. this | Is | laptop? | your
7. books? | those | Katherine's | Are

17.5 COMPLETA LOS ESPACIOS CON "DO" O "DOES"

Does Maria go swimming?

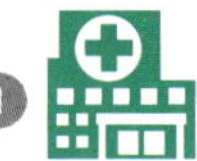

1 ______ you work in a hospital?

2 ______ your dog like children?

3 ______ you get up at 10am on Sundays?

4 ______ Simone work with children?

5 ______ they live in the town?

6 ______ we finish work at 3pm today?

7 ______ Frank play tennis with Pete?

17.6 TACHA LA PALABRA INCORRECTA DE CADA PREGUNTA

Do / ~~Does~~ they play tennis together?

1 Do / Does you read a newspaper every day?

2 Do / Does he go to bed at 11pm?

3 Do / Does they live in a castle?

4 Do / Does Pedro come from Bolivia?

5 Do / Does she work with children?

6 Do / Does Claire and Sam eat lunch at 2pm?

7 Do / Does your brother work with animals?

8 Do / Does Tim play soccer on Mondays?

9 Do / Does they work in a café?

10 Do / Does you have a shower in the evening?

11 Do / Does we start work at 10am on Thursdays?

12 Do / Does Pamela work in a bank?

17.7 REESCRIBE LAS AFIRMACIONES COMO PREGUNTAS

Bill gets up at 7am.
Does Bill get up at 7am?

1 They work in a museum.

____

2 You work with children.

____

3 Shane lives in Sydney.

____

4 John plays tennis on Wednesdays.

____

5 Yves and Marie eat dinner at 6pm.

____

6 Seth works in a post office.

____

17.8 LEE EL CORREO ELECTRÓNICO Y RESPONDE A LAS PREGUNTAS

Does Sam get up at 7:30am?
Yes ☐ No ☑

1. Does Sam have a bath?
Yes ☐ No ☐

2. Does he eat breakfast at home?
Yes ☐ No ☐

3. Does he eat some fruit at work?
Yes ☐ No ☐

4. Does he work in a bank?
Yes ☐ No ☐

5. Does Sam's work finish at 6pm?
Yes ☐ No ☐

6. Does he have lunch at 2:30pm?
Yes ☐ No ☐

7. Does he watch TV in the evening?
Yes ☐ No ☐

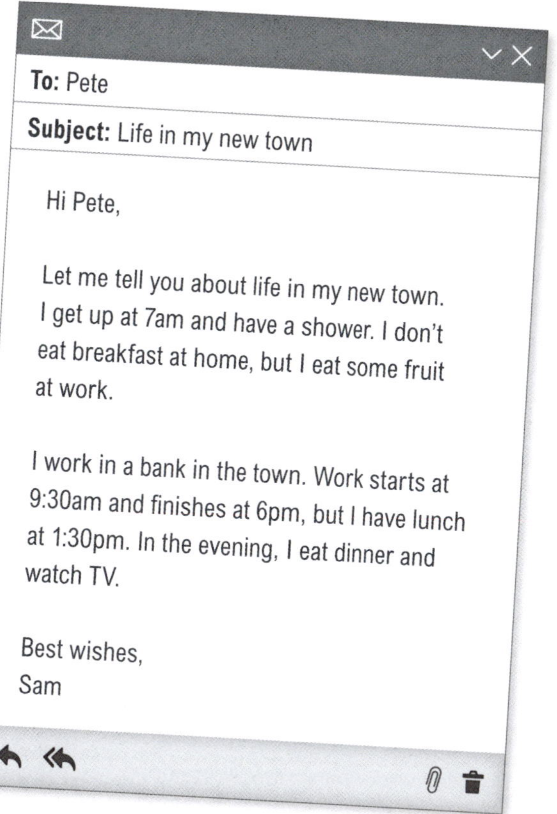

To: Pete

Subject: Life in my new town

Hi Pete,

Let me tell you about life in my new town. I get up at 7am and have a shower. I don't eat breakfast at home, but I eat some fruit at work.

I work in a bank in the town. Work starts at 9:30am and finishes at 6pm, but I have lunch at 1:30pm. In the evening, I eat dinner and watch TV.

Best wishes,
Sam

17.9 DI LAS FRASES EN VOZ ALTA COMPLETANDO LOS ESPACIOS

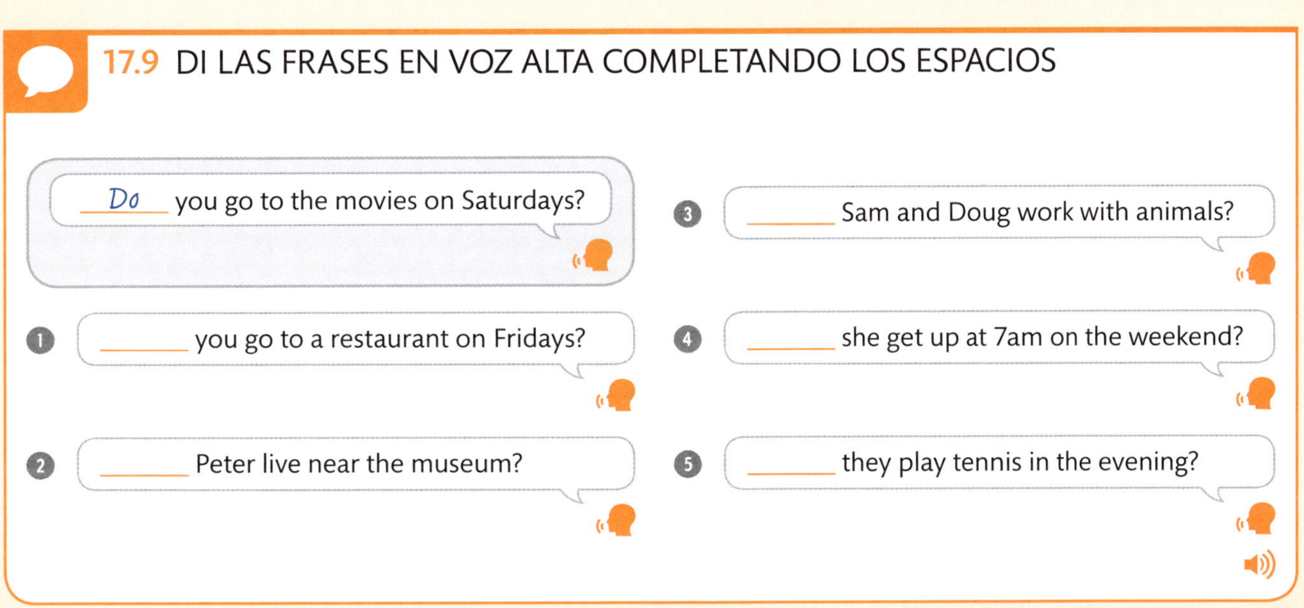

Do you go to the movies on Saturdays?

1. ______ you go to a restaurant on Fridays?
2. ______ Peter live near the museum?
3. ______ Sam and Doug work with animals?
4. ______ she get up at 7am on the weekend?
5. ______ they play tennis in the evening?

18 Responder preguntas

Cuando en inglés respondes a una pregunta, es habitual prescindir de palabras para acortar la respuesta. Las respuestas cortas se utilizan con frecuencia en el lenguaje hablado.

Lenguaje Respuestas cortas
Vocabulario Trabajos y rutinas
Habilidad Responder preguntas orales

18.1 MARCA LA MEJOR RESPUESTA A CADA PREGUNTA

18.2 COMPLETA LOS ESPACIOS CON LA RESPUESTA CORTA CORRECTA

Is this your cat?
Yes, *it is.*

1 Do you play golf?
No, ____________________

2 Is Paula your wife?
Yes, ____________________

3 Does Peter speak French?
No, ____________________

4 Do they work at the factory?
No, ____________________

5 Is Mario from Italy?
Yes, ____________________

18.3 LEE EL CORREO ELECTRÓNICO Y RESPONDE A LAS PREGUNTAS CON FRASES COMPLETAS

Does Helen have a new job?

Yes, she does.

1. Is Helen a German teacher?

2. Does Helen start work at 8am?

3. Is Helen's school small?

4. Does Helen finish at 4pm?

5. Does Helen read a book in the evening?

To: Kim

Subject: My new job

Hi Kim,

I have some great news! I have a new job. I'm a French teacher at the school on Palm Avenue. Let me tell you about my typical day.

I get up at 8am and I walk to work. The school is big and has 800 children. I start work at 9am and I have lunch at 1pm. My students are very nice! I finish work at 4pm, and then I walk home. In the evening, I mark up my students' homework, then drink a glass of wine and watch a movie.

Say hello to Bob!

Helen

18.4 ESCUCHA EL AUDIO Y RESPONDE A LAS PREGUNTAS

Jane comienza a trabajar como profesora. Se encuentra con Bob, otro profesor de la escuela.

Jane is a teacher.

True ☑ **False** ☐ **Not given** ☐

1. Bob is an English teacher.

   True ☐ **False** ☐ **Not given** ☐

2. Jane is from Dublin.

   True ☐ **False** ☐ **Not given** ☐

3. Jane's husband is a teacher too.

   True ☐ **False** ☐ **Not given** ☐

4. Jane's husband works near their house.

   True ☐ **False** ☐ **Not given** ☐

5. Jane's husband starts work at 8:30am.

   True ☐ **False** ☐ **Not given** ☐

6. Bob plays tennis every weekend.

   True ☐ **False** ☐ **Not given** ☐

7. Jane goes to the movies a lot.

   True ☐ **False** ☐ **Not given** ☐

19 Hacer preguntas

Utiliza las palabras interrogativas "what", "who", "when" y "where" para hacer preguntas abiertas que no se pueden responder con "yes" o "no".

Lenguaje Preguntas abiertas
Aa Vocabulario Palabras interrogativas
Habilidad Preguntar sobre detalles

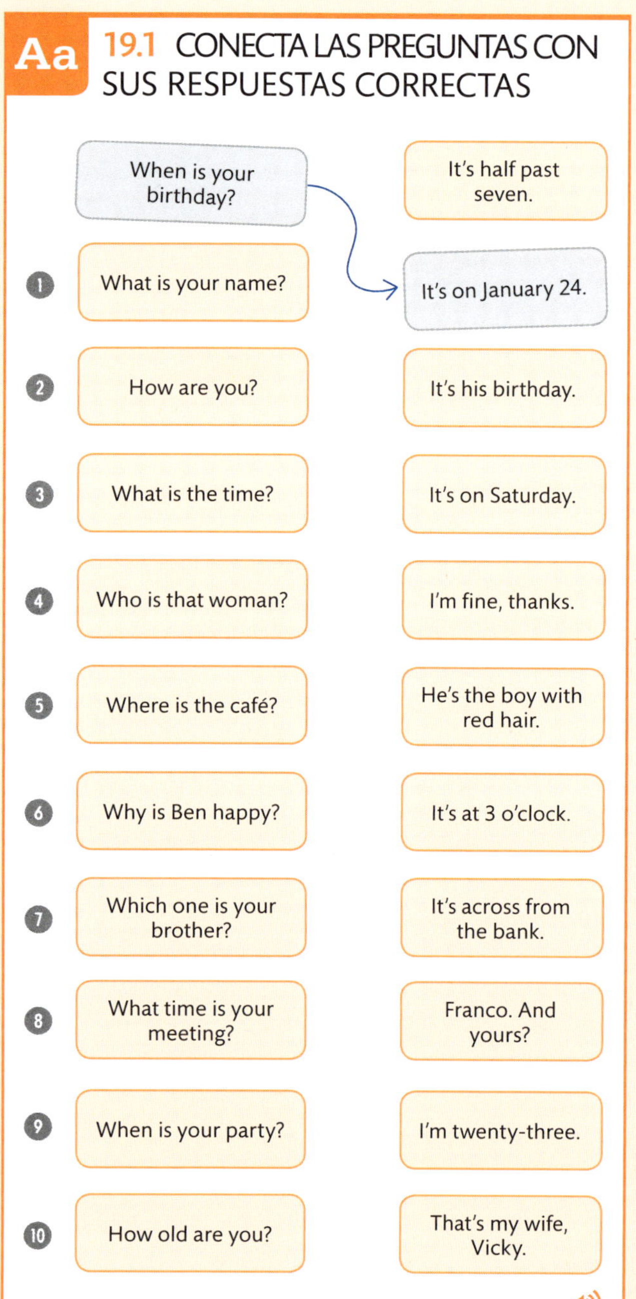

19.1 CONECTA LAS PREGUNTAS CON SUS RESPUESTAS CORRECTAS

When is your birthday? → It's on January 24.

1. What is your name?
2. How are you?
3. What is the time?
4. Who is that woman?
5. Where is the café?
6. Why is Ben happy?
7. Which one is your brother?
8. What time is your meeting?
9. When is your party?
10. How old are you?

- It's half past seven.
- It's on January 24.
- It's his birthday.
- It's on Saturday.
- I'm fine, thanks.
- He's the boy with red hair.
- It's at 3 o'clock.
- It's across from the bank.
- Franco. And yours?
- I'm twenty-three.
- That's my wife, Vicky.

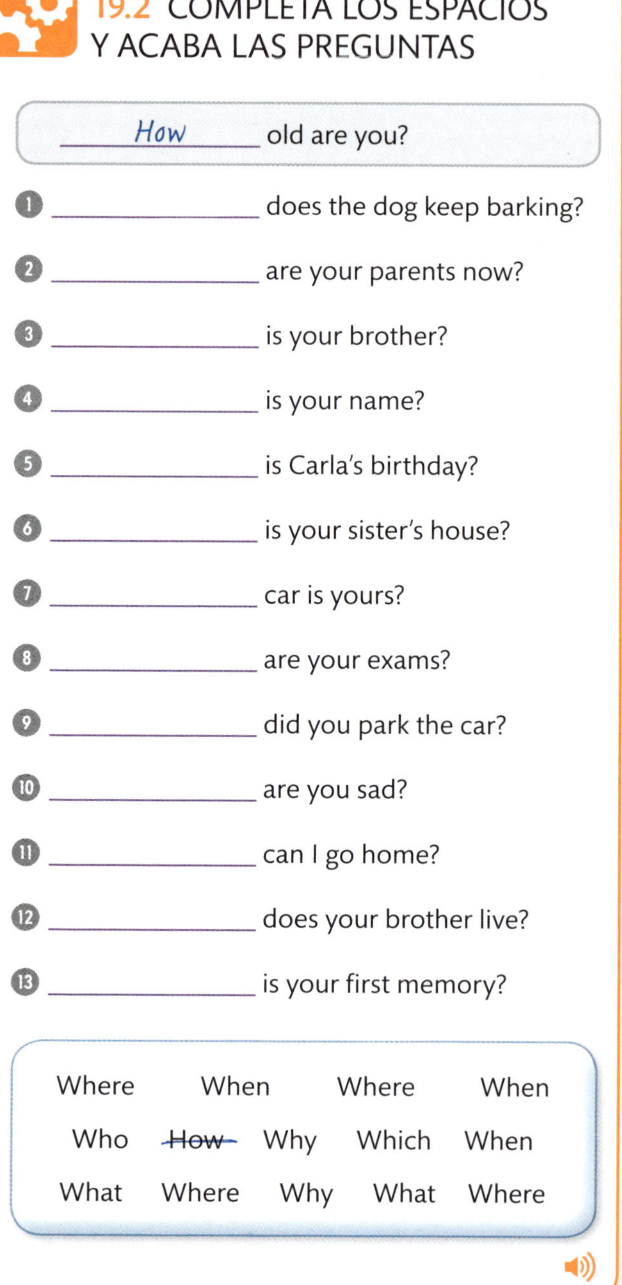

19.2 COMPLETA LOS ESPACIOS Y ACABA LAS PREGUNTAS

How old are you?

1. ________ does the dog keep barking?
2. ________ are your parents now?
3. ________ is your brother?
4. ________ is your name?
5. ________ is Carla's birthday?
6. ________ is your sister's house?
7. ________ car is yours?
8. ________ are your exams?
9. ________ did you park the car?
10. ________ are you sad?
11. ________ can I go home?
12. ________ does your brother live?
13. ________ is your first memory?

Where When Where When
Who ~~How~~ Why Which When
What Where Why What Where

19.3 ESCUCHA EL AUDIO Y RESPONDE A LAS PREGUNTAS

Greg habla de distintos miembros de su familia.

What is Greg's grandmother's name?
- Shelley ☐
- Ellie ☑
- Emma ☐

1. How old is Greg's grandmother?
   - 84 years old ☐
   - 82 years old ☐
   - 83 years old ☐

2. Where does she live?
   - Near the church ☐
   - Near the cathedral ☐
   - Near the supermarket ☐

3. Where does Greg's mother work?
   - At a school ☐
   - At a museum ☐
   - At a theater ☐

4. What does Greg's mother do?
   - She's a cleaner ☐
   - She's a receptionist ☐
   - She's a teacher ☐

5. How old is Samantha?
   - 21 ☐
   - 19 ☐
   - 23 ☐

19.4 VUELVE A ESCRIBIR LAS FRASES PONIENDO LAS PALABRAS EN SU ORDEN CORRECTO

wake / do / you / up? / When

When do you wake up?

1. you / shirt / do / Which / prefer?

   ____

2. son / does / go / your / to / college? / Where

   ____

3. get / How / do / you / to / work?

   ____

4. go / you / Where / swimming? / do

   ____

5. bed? / you / What / do / time / go / to

   ____

6. start / does / When / work? / Jane

   ____

7. for / do / What / you / eat / breakfast?

   ____

19.5 DI LAS FRASES EN VOZ ALTA COMPLETANDO LOS ESPACIOS CON LAS PALABRAS DEL RECUADRO

What do you do?

1. ______ do you study?
2. ______ do you want?
3. ______ building is your college?
4. ______ do you live?
5. ______ time do you wake up?
6. ______ many shirts do you own?
7. ______ do you want for lunch?
8. ______ does the course finish?
9. ______ do you do in the evening?

What | What | Which | ~~What~~ | When | How | Which | What | What | Where

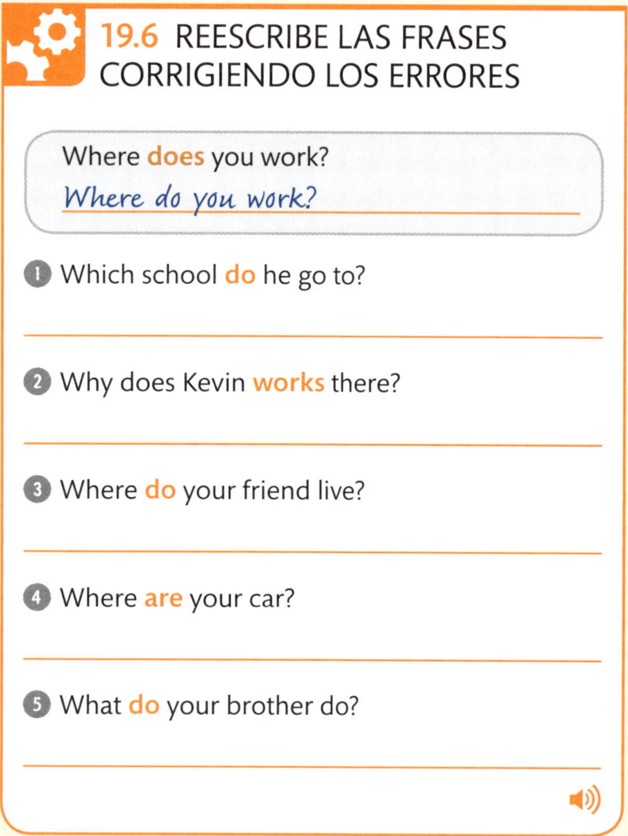

19.6 REESCRIBE LAS FRASES CORRIGIENDO LOS ERRORES

Where **does** you work?
Where do you work?

1. Which school **do** he go to?
______
2. Why does Kevin **works** there?
______
3. Where **do** your friend live?
______
4. Where **are** your car?
______
5. What **do** your brother do?
______

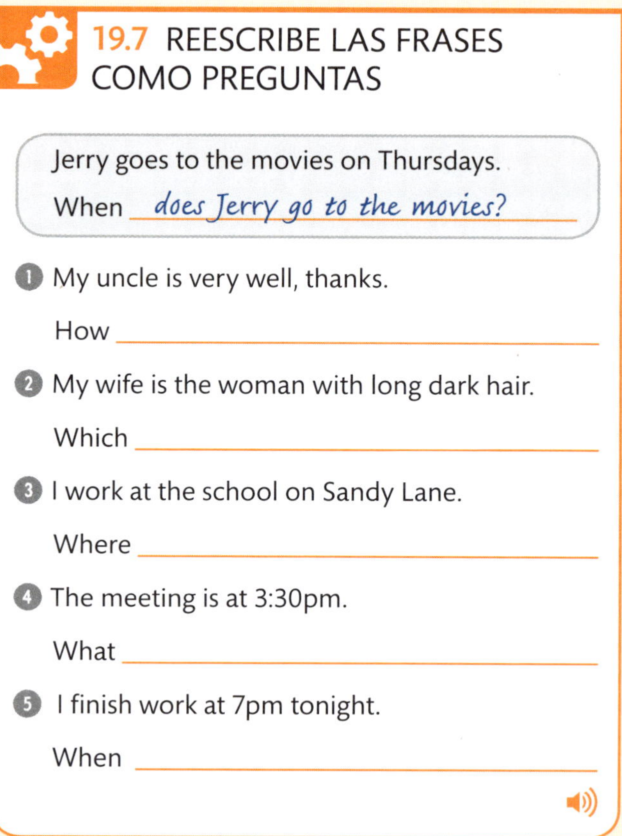

19.7 REESCRIBE LAS FRASES COMO PREGUNTAS

Jerry goes to the movies on Thursdays.
When *does Jerry go to the movies?*

1. My uncle is very well, thanks.
How ______
2. My wife is the woman with long dark hair.
Which ______
3. I work at the school on Sandy Lane.
Where ______
4. The meeting is at 3:30pm.
What ______
5. I finish work at 7pm tonight.
When ______

19.8 USA EL DIAGRAMA PARA CREAR 12 FRASES CORRECTAS Y DILAS EN VOZ ALTA

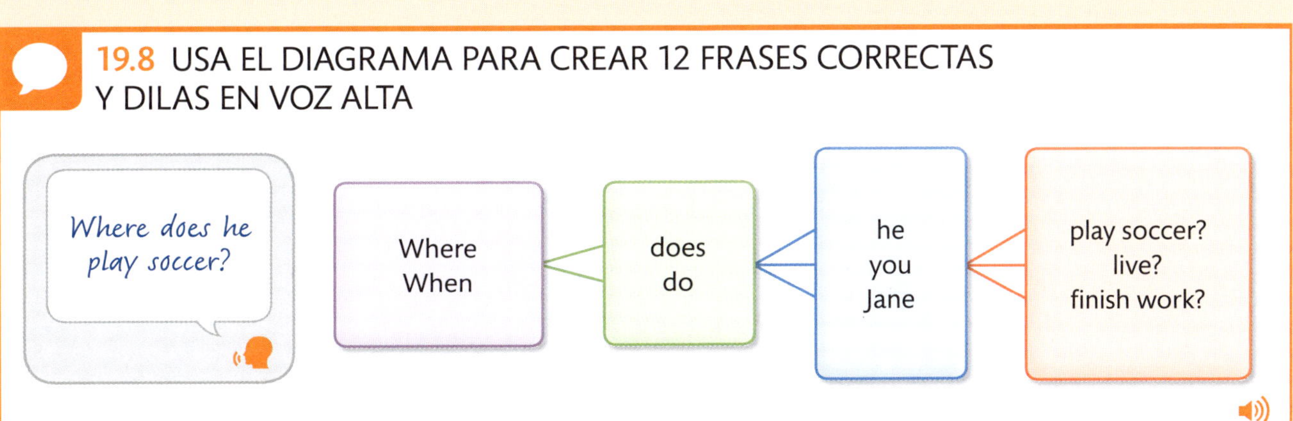

19.9 LEE EL CORREO Y RESPONDE A LAS PREGUNTAS

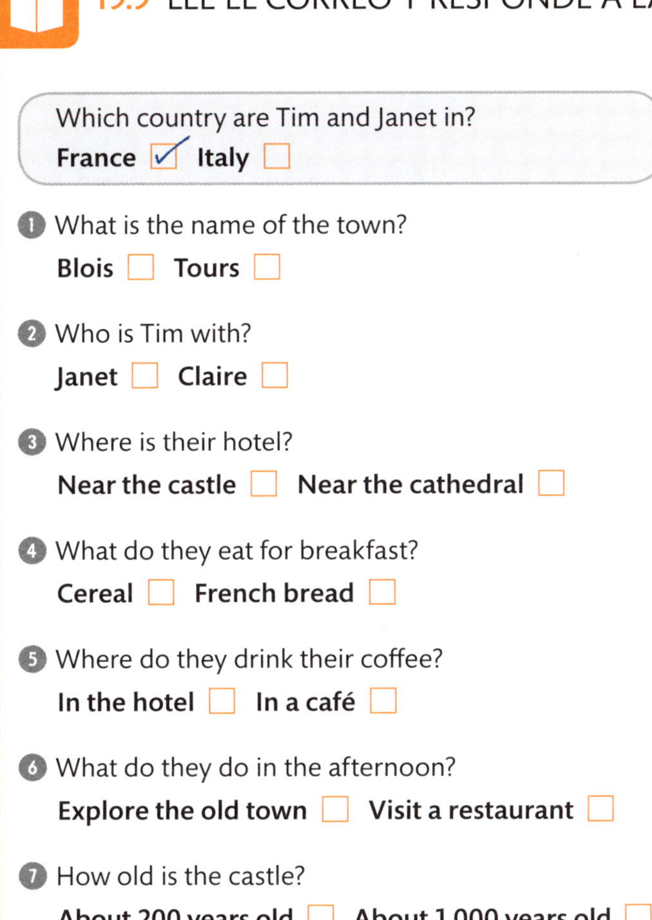

Which country are Tim and Janet in?
France ☑ **Italy** ☐

1. What is the name of the town?
   Blois ☐ **Tours** ☐
2. Who is Tim with?
   Janet ☐ **Claire** ☐
3. Where is their hotel?
   Near the castle ☐ **Near the cathedral** ☐
4. What do they eat for breakfast?
   Cereal ☐ **French bread** ☐
5. Where do they drink their coffee?
   In the hotel ☐ **In a café** ☐
6. What do they do in the afternoon?
   Explore the old town ☐ **Visit a restaurant** ☐
7. How old is the castle?
   About 200 years old ☐ **About 1,000 years old** ☐
8. What can you see at the castle?
   Some beautiful paintings ☐ **Historic furniture** ☐

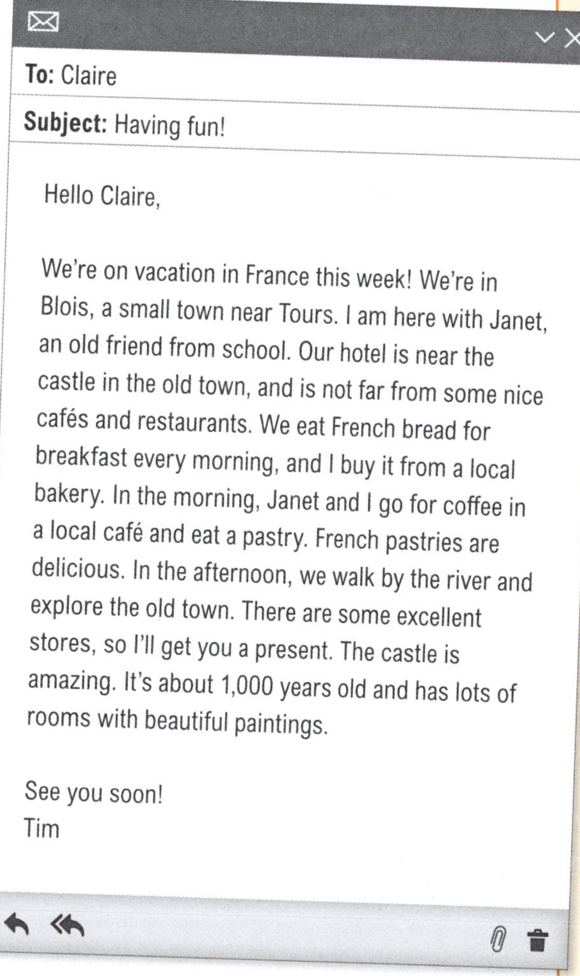

To: Claire

Subject: Having fun!

Hello Claire,

We're on vacation in France this week! We're in Blois, a small town near Tours. I am here with Janet, an old friend from school. Our hotel is near the castle in the old town, and is not far from some nice cafés and restaurants. We eat French bread for breakfast every morning, and I buy it from a local bakery. In the morning, Janet and I go for coffee in a local café and eat a pastry. French pastries are delicious. In the afternoon, we walk by the river and explore the old town. There are some excellent stores, so I'll get you a present. The castle is amazing. It's about 1,000 years old and has lots of rooms with beautiful paintings.

See you soon!
Tim

20 Vocabulario

Aa 20.1 **LA CIUDAD** ESCRIBE LAS PALABRAS DEL RECUADRO DEBAJO DE SU CORRESPONDIENTE DIBUJO

village

1 ______

2 ______

3 ______

4 ______

7 ______

8 ______

9 ______

10 ______

11 ______

14 ______

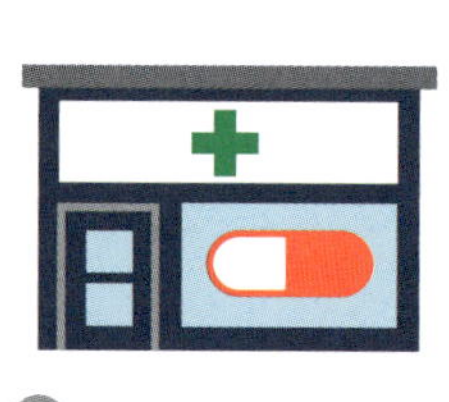

15 ______

16 ______

17 ______

18 ______

21 ______

22 ______

23 ______

24 ______

25 ______

5 ______

6 ______

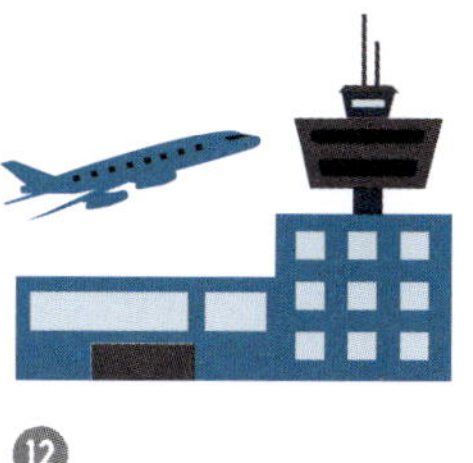

12 ______

13 ______

19 ______

20 ______

26 ______

27 ______

supermarket pharmacy

far hospital bus station

library café post office

here ~~village~~ town

park castle airport

police station there bank

bridge factory bar

mosque train station near

hotel school office building

swimming pool restaurant

21 Hablar sobre tu ciudad

Cuando hablas sobre objetos, puedes utilizar "there is" para uno solo y "there are" para más de uno. "There isn't" y "there aren't" son las respectivas formas negativas.

Lenguaje "There is" y "there are"
Vocabulario Ciudades y edificios
Habilidad Describir una ciudad

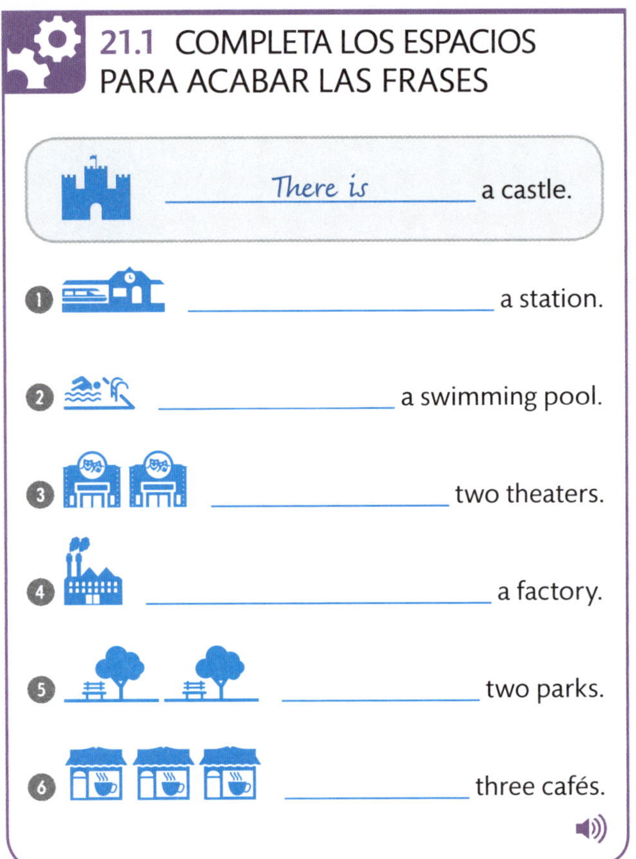

21.1 COMPLETA LOS ESPACIOS PARA ACABAR LAS FRASES

There is a castle.

1. ______ a station.
2. ______ a swimming pool.
3. ______ two theaters.
4. ______ a factory.
5. ______ two parks.
6. ______ three cafés.

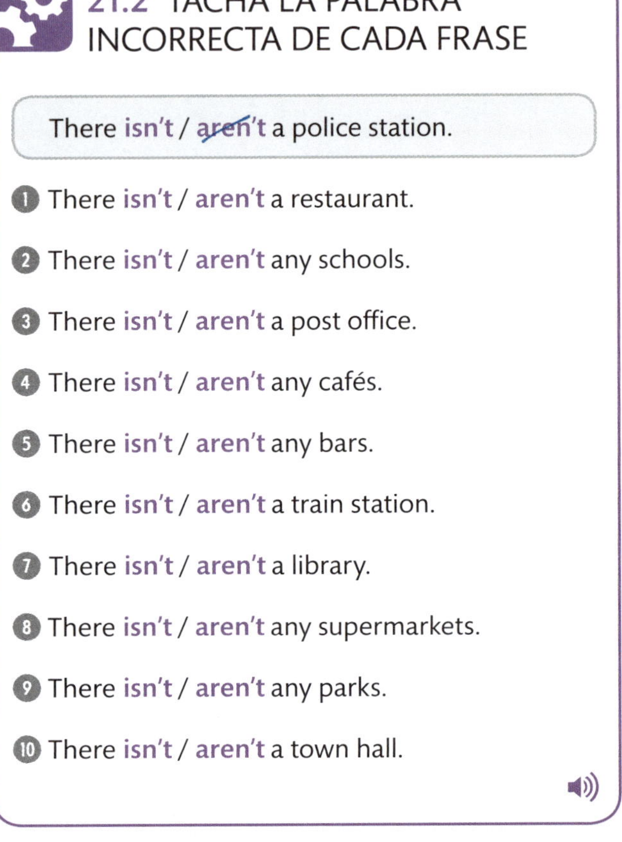

21.2 TACHA LA PALABRA INCORRECTA DE CADA FRASE

There isn't / ~~aren't~~ a police station.

1. There isn't / aren't a restaurant.
2. There isn't / aren't any schools.
3. There isn't / aren't a post office.
4. There isn't / aren't any cafés.
5. There isn't / aren't any bars.
6. There isn't / aren't a train station.
7. There isn't / aren't a library.
8. There isn't / aren't any supermarkets.
9. There isn't / aren't any parks.
10. There isn't / aren't a town hall.

21.3 DI OCHO FRASES CORRECTAS UTILIZANDO LAS PALABRAS DEL DIAGRAMA

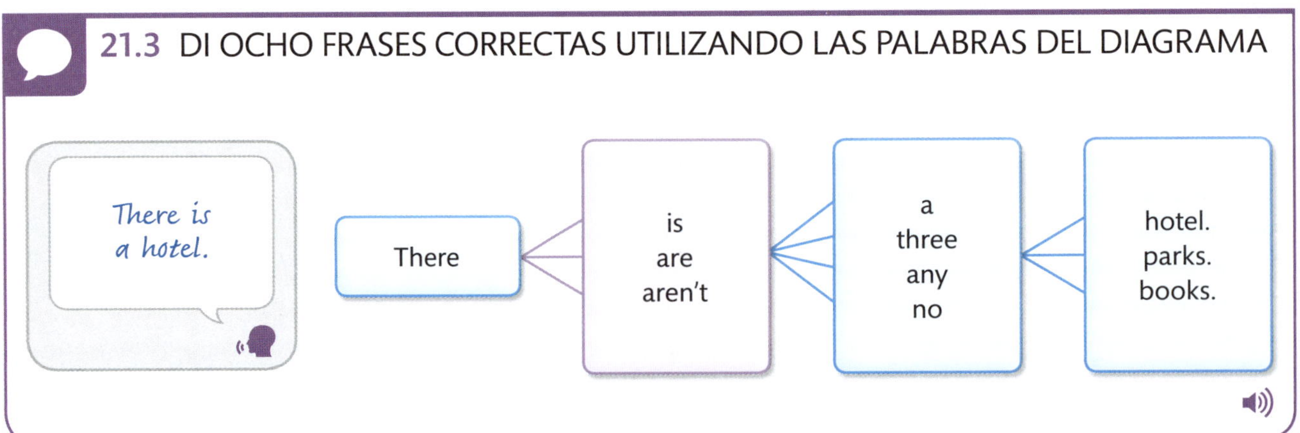

21.4 ESCUCHA EL AUDIO Y NUMERA LAS IMÁGENES EN EL ORDEN EN QUE SE DESCRIBEN

A ☐

B ☐

C 1

D ☐

E ☐

21.5 VUELVE A ESCRIBIR CADA FRASE EN FORMA NEGATIVA

There is a theater. = *There isn't a theater.*

1. There is a school. = ______
2. There are two churches. = ______
3. There is a café. = ______
4. There is a library. = ______
5. There are two airports. = ______
6. There are three hotels. = ______
7. There are two parks. = ______
8. There is a town hall. = ______

21.6 ESCUCHA EL AUDIO Y MARCA LAS RESPUESTAS CORRECTAS

Gordon describe la ciudad en la que vive con su familia.

Melcome is in...
Scotland. ☐
Canada. ☑
England. ☐
New Zealand. ☐

1 There are two ...... in Melcome.
post offices ☐
banks ☐
churches ☐
offices ☐

2 Gordon works in a...
museum. ☐
café. ☐
factory. ☐
primary school. ☐

3 In the evening Gordon goes to a...
library. ☐
café. ☐
restaurant. ☐
swimming pool. ☐

4 Gordon's wife works in a...
hospital. ☐
theater. ☐
store. ☐
post office. ☐

5 Gordon's son is a...
teacher. ☐
doctor. ☐
police officer. ☐
actor. ☐

21.7 VUELVE A ESCRIBIR LAS FRASES PONIENDO LAS PALABRAS EN SU ORDEN CORRECTO

are | three | cafés. | There

There are three cafés.

1 supermarket. | is | a | There

2 restaurants. | There | any | aren't

3 hotels. | are | There | no

4 There | three | are | schools.

5 is | station. | a | There | bus

21.8 LEE EL CORREO Y RESPONDE A LAS PREGUNTAS

There are two beaches.
True ☐ **False** ☑

1. There isn't a castle.
True ☐ **False** ☐

2. There is a park.
True ☐ **False** ☐

3. There is a supermarket.
True ☐ **False** ☐

4. There aren't any stores.
True ☐ **False** ☐

5. There is a big restaurant.
True ☐ **False** ☐

6. There are four cafés.
True ☐ **False** ☐

7. There is an airport.
True ☐ **False** ☐

To: Christine

Subject: Visiting Westport

Hi Christine,

We are on vacation in Westport and it's beautiful! There's lots to do here for all the family. There aren't any beaches, but there's a castle and a big park. The castle is very old and really interesting. And the children go to the park every day. There isn't a supermarket here, but there are lots of small stores in the center. Anne loves them.

In the evening, I walk with Anne and the children in the center. There is a big fish restaurant here. I like fish a lot! There are also three cafés where we relax. It's easy to get to Westport. The airport is not far from the center and there's a bus station near our hotel.

Wish you were here!

See you soon!

Tom

21.9 OBSERVA EL DIBUJO Y DI LAS FRASES EN VOZ ALTA, COMPLETANDO LOS ESPACIOS

There is a library.

1. ______ stores.

2. ______ castles.

3. ______ a church.

4. ______ a hospital.

5. ______ a post office.

22 Utilizar "a" y "the"

Utiliza el artículo definido ("the") o el artículo indefinido ("a", "an") para hablar de cosas de manera específica o general. Utiliza "some" para hablar de más de una cosa.

Lenguaje Artículos definidos e indefinidos
Aa Vocabulario Lugares en la ciudad
Habilidad Utilizar los artículos

22.1 TACHA LAS PALABRAS INCORRECTAS DE CADA FRASE

Alex is a / ~~an~~ / ~~the~~ teacher.

1  A / An / The new doctor is called Hilary.

2  Sammy is a / an / the nurse.

3  There is a / an / the bank downtown.

4  Is there a / an / the hospital near here?

5  A / An / The gym is near Sam's house.

6  There is a / an / the new café in town.

7  A / An / The hotel on Elm Lane is nice.

8  A / An / The new teacher is good.

9  There's a / an / the old theater in town.

22.2 VUELVE A ESCRIBIR LAS FRASES CORRIGIENDO LOS ERRORES

A new teacher is called Mr. Smith.
The new teacher is called Mr. Smith.

1 I have the sister and the brother.

____

2 There is the library on Queens Road.

____

3 I bought a apple and a orange.

____

4 Is there the bank near here?

____

5 There is an café at the bus station.

____

6 My dad is a engineer.

____

7 There is the cell phone on the table.

____

22.3 COMPLETA LOS ESPACIOS UTILIZANDO "A", "AN", "SOME" O "THE"

Dear Bob and Sally,

We are in Glenmuir, ______ quiet town in Scotland. There's ______ castle and ______ cathedral here. They're beautiful and ______ castle is really old. There are ______ interesting stores, which we visit every day. We also have ______ new friend here. He's called Alfonso and he works as ______ waiter in ______ Italian restaurant next to ______ shopping mall. He's great!

Jane

22.4 TACHA LAS PALABRAS INCORRECTAS DE CADA FRASE

Is there a / ~~an~~ / ~~any~~ museum in Littleton?

1. Are there a / an / any factories in your town?
2. Is there a / an / any gym downtown?
3. Are there a / an / any pencils in your bag?
4. Is there a / an / any old church on Station Road?
5. Is there a / an / any hospital in the town?
6. Is there a / an / any salon near here?
7. Is there a / an / any apple in the basket?
8. Are there a / an / any restaurants in your town?
9. Is there a / an / any library downtown?
10. Are there a / an / any books on the table?
11. Is there a / an / any café nearby?
12. Is there a / an / any cathedral in that town?
13. Is there a / an / any bank near the supermarket?
14. Are there a / an / any kittens here?
15. Is there a / an / any school in this neighborhood?

22.5 VUELVE A ESCRIBIR LAS FRASES PONIENDO LAS PALABRAS EN SU ORDEN CORRECTO

some | in | town. | are | my | There | banks

There are some banks in my town.

1. Is | here? | supermarket | there | near | a

2. There | cafés | Beech Road. | some | are | on

3. horses | on | farm. | There | Frank's | are | some

4. airport. | near | There | some | the | are | hotels

22.6 DI LAS FRASES EN VOZ ALTA, COMPLETANDO LOS ESPACIOS

Are *there any* stores?

1. Is ______ museum?
2. Are ______ cafés?
3. Are ______ parks near here?
4. Is ______ mosque in the town?
5. Is ______ airport in Saltforth?
6. Are ______ factories in Halford?
7. Is ______ castle in your town?

22.7 RESPONDE AL AUDIO EN VOZ ALTA COMPLETANDO LOS ESPACIOS

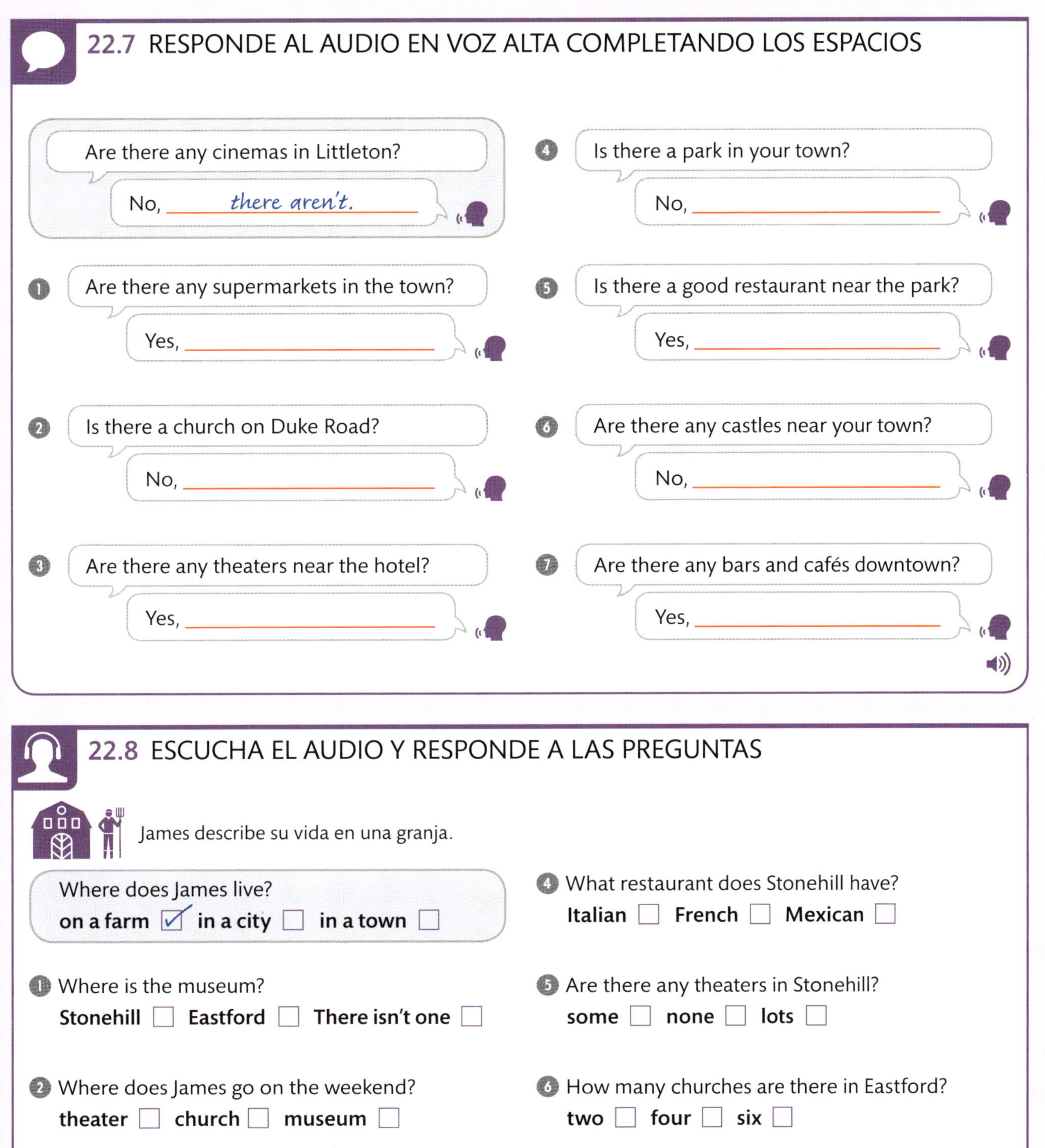

Are there any cinemas in Littleton?
No, *there aren't.*

1. Are there any supermarkets in the town?
Yes, ________________

2. Is there a church on Duke Road?
No, ________________

3. Are there any theaters near the hotel?
Yes, ________________

4. Is there a park in your town?
No, ________________

5. Is there a good restaurant near the park?
Yes, ________________

6. Are there any castles near your town?
No, ________________

7. Are there any bars and cafés downtown?
Yes, ________________

22.8 ESCUCHA EL AUDIO Y RESPONDE A LAS PREGUNTAS

James describe su vida en una granja.

Where does James live?
on a farm ☑ **in a city** ☐ **in a town** ☐

1. Where is the museum?
Stonehill ☐ **Eastford** ☐ **There isn't one** ☐

2. Where does James go on the weekend?
theater ☐ **church** ☐ **museum** ☐

3. Are there any stores in Stonehill?
some ☐ **none** ☐ **lots** ☐

4. What restaurant does Stonehill have?
Italian ☐ **French** ☐ **Mexican** ☐

5. Are there any theaters in Stonehill?
some ☐ **none** ☐ **lots** ☐

6. How many churches are there in Eastford?
two ☐ **four** ☐ **six** ☐

7. Are there any stores in Eastford?
some ☐ **none** ☐ **lots** ☐

23 Órdenes y direcciones

Utiliza el imperativo para decirle a alguien que haga algo. También se usa para hacer una advertencia, o para indicar una dirección a alguien.

Lenguaje Imperativo
Vocabulario Direcciones
Habilidad Orientarse

23.1 ESCRIBE LOS IMPERATIVOS DE CADA INFINITIVO

he takes = *take*

1. to put = ______
2. I read = ______
3. she works = ______
4. to start = ______
5. you eat = ______
6. they have = ______
7. it stops = ______
8. to wake up = ______
9. we run = ______
10. they come = ______
11. you are = ______

23.2 MARCA SI CADA FRASE ESTÁ EN IMPERATIVO O EN PRESENT SIMPLE

Eat your breakfast.
imperativo ☑ **present simple** ☐

1. I eat my dinner at 6pm.
imperativo ☐ **present simple** ☐

2. Come with me.
imperativo ☐ **present simple** ☐

3. You read your book every day.
imperativo ☐ **present simple** ☐

4. Give that to me.
imperativo ☐ **present simple** ☐

5. Read this book.
imperativo ☐ **present simple** ☐

6. Eat your dinner.
imperativo ☐ **present simple** ☐

7. She goes to bed at 9pm.
imperativo ☐ **present simple** ☐

8. I start school at 9am.
imperativo ☐ **present simple** ☐

9. Go to bed.
imperativo ☐ **present simple** ☐

23.3 MARCA LAS DIRECCIONES QUE TE LLEVAN A LOS LUGARES CORRECTOS

For the hospital...

Take the first left. The hospital is on the left ☑

Take the first left. The hospital is on the right. ☐

1. For the swimming pool...

   Go straight ahead. The swimming pool is opposite the castle. ☐

   Go straight ahead. The swimming pool is opposite the station. ☐

2. For the school...

   Take the second left. The school is opposite the factory. ☐

   Take the third left. The school is next to the factory. ☐

3. For the church...

   Turn right and take the second right. The church is opposite the hotel. ☐

   Turn right and take the first left. The church is opposite the hotel. ☐

4. For the theater...

   Take the third left and go straight ahead. The theater is on the right. ☐

   Take the third right and go straight ahead. The theater is on the left. ☐

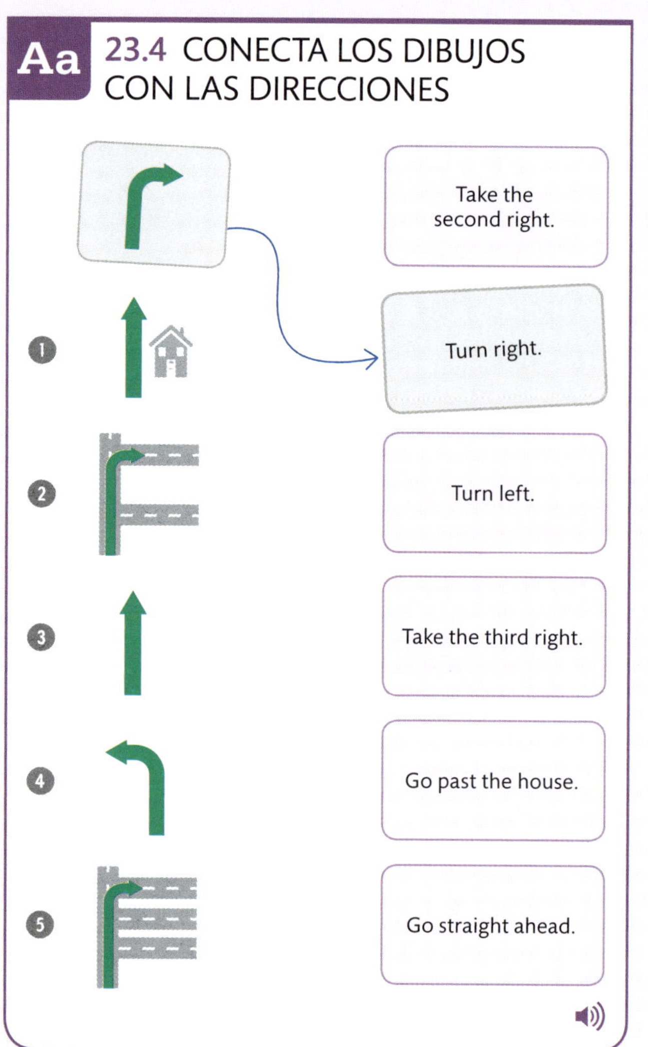

23.4 CONECTA LOS DIBUJOS CON LAS DIRECCIONES

Take the second right.

Turn right.

Turn left.

Take the third right.

Go past the house.

Go straight ahead.

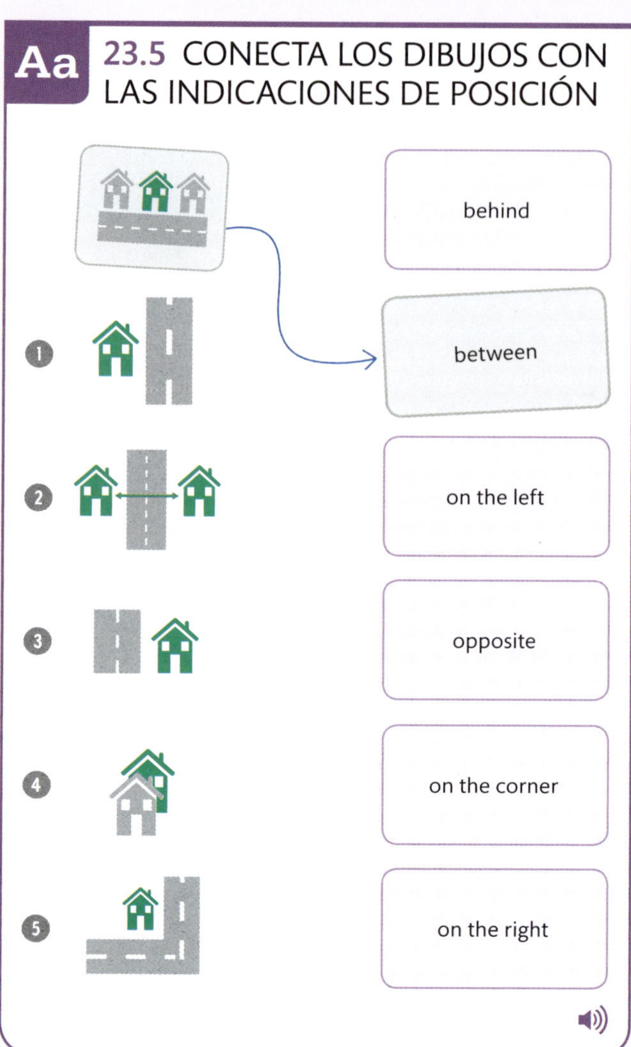

23.5 CONECTA LOS DIBUJOS CON LAS INDICACIONES DE POSICIÓN

behind

between

on the left

opposite

on the corner

on the right

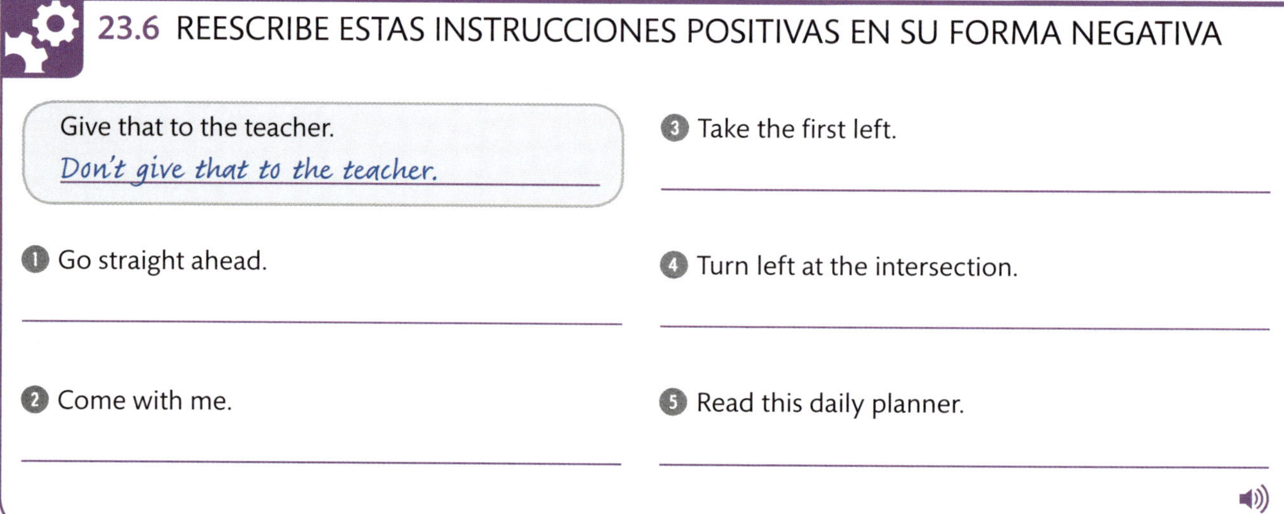

23.6 REESCRIBE ESTAS INSTRUCCIONES POSITIVAS EN SU FORMA NEGATIVA

Give that to the teacher.
Don't give that to the teacher.

1. Go straight ahead.

2. Come with me.

3. Take the first left.

4. Turn left at the intersection.

5. Read this daily planner.

23.7 ESCUCHA EL AUDIO Y NUMERA LAS DIRECCIONES EN EL ORDEN EN QUE LAS ESCUCHES

Turn left and the theater is on your right across from the church. [1]

- **A** The café is on the corner next to the church. [ ]
- **B** The restaurant is on the right next to the bank. [ ]
- **C** Go straight ahead and take the second road on your right. [ ]
- **D** Turn right, then take the first left. [ ]
- **E** Go past the hotel and the café is on the left. [ ]
- **F** The hospital is on the corner on the left. [ ]
- **G** Go straight ahead and it's the fourth road on the right. [ ]
- **H** Go straight ahead and take the third left. [ ]

23.8 MIRA LOS DIBUJOS Y UTILIZA LAS INDICACIONES DE LUGAR PARA COMPLETAR LOS ESPACIOS

The supermarket is *next to* the hotel.

1. The museum is ______________ the library.

2. The restaurant is ______________ the store.

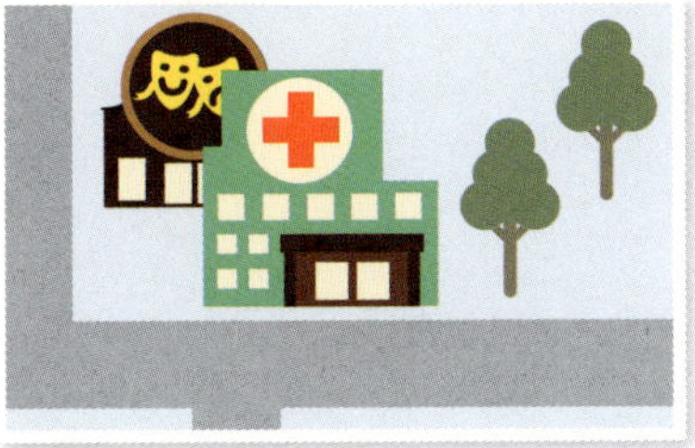

3. The hospital is ______________ the theater.

4. The post office is ______________ the school.

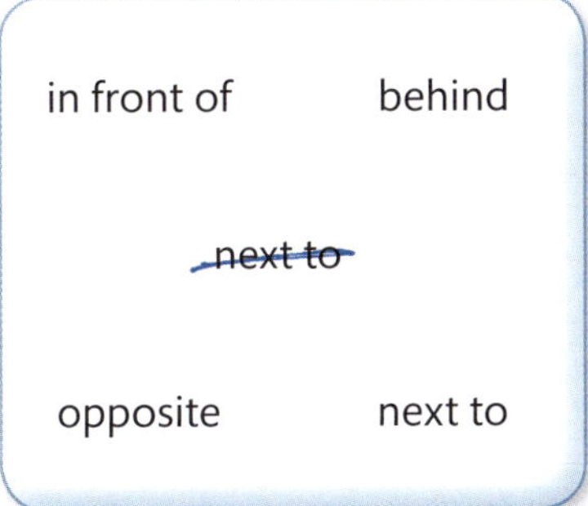

24 Unir frases

"And" y "but" son conjunciones: palabras que unen frases. "And" añade elementos a una frase o une varias en una sola. "But" introduce un contraste en una frase.

Lenguaje Utilizar "and" y "but"
Vocabulario Ciudad, trabajos y familia
Habilidad Unir frases

24.1 CONECTA EL COMIENZO Y EL FINAL DE CADA FRASE

There is a market and → a theater in Heswall.

1. My cousin lives and
2. I play soccer and
3. There's a library and
4. I eat two eggs and
5. Pete's uncle and
6. I read a book and

- a bookstore in my town.
- aunt live in Arizona.
- works in Los Angeles.
- a theater in Heswall.
- basketball in the evening.
- watch TV on the weekend.
- a banana for breakfast.

24.2 ESCUCHA EL AUDIO Y CONECTA LOS DOS LUGARES QUE SE DESCRIBEN

1 2 3 4 5

restaurant | mosque | movie theater | church | hospital | supermarket

Aa 24.3 MARCA LAS FRASES QUE SON CORRECTAS

There's a library, a store, and a museum. ☑
There's a library, and a store, a museum. ☐

1. Three chefs, four waiters work in my hotel. ☐
   Three chefs and four waiters work in my hotel. ☐

2. There's a park, a café, and a theater in Pella. ☐
   There's a park, a café, a theater in Pella. ☐

3. I have one aunt, and two sisters, and a niece. ☐
   I have one aunt, two sisters, and a niece. ☐

4. Ben eats breakfast, and lunch and dinner. ☐
   Ben eats breakfast, lunch, and dinner. ☐

5. I play and tennis and soccer. ☐
   I play tennis and soccer. ☐

6. We have and dog and a cat. ☐
   We have a dog and a cat. ☐

7. I read a book, take a bath on Sundays. ☐
   I read a book and take a bath on Sundays. ☐

8. Jen speaks French, Spanish, Japanese. ☐
   Jen speaks French, Spanish, and Japanese. ☐

9. Pete has two dogs and a cat. ☐
   Pete has two dogs, a cat. ☐

24.4 UTILIZA "AND" PARA ESCRIBIR UNA ÚNICA FRASE CON LAS DOS AFIRMACIONES PROPUESTAS

I get up. I take a shower.
I get up and take a shower.

1. This is my brother. These are my sisters.
   ____

2. I speak English. I don't speak French.
   ____

3. I play video games. I watch TV.
   ____

4. I have one uncle. I don't have any aunts.
   ____

5. There are two stores. There are three hotels.
   ____

6. I eat lunch every day. I don't eat breakfast.
   ____

7. There's a hotel. There isn't a store.
   ____

8. I have a sandwich. I have an apple.
   ____

9. This is my house. These aren't my keys.
   ____

10. Those are Sarah's magazines. That is her ID card.
    ____

11. This phone is Joe's. This laptop isn't Joe's.
    ____

24.5 TACHA LA PALABRA INCORRECTA DE CADA FRASE

I work every weekday ~~and~~ / but not on weekends. 

1. There's a library, a store, and / but a café.   
2. There's a castle and a church and / but there isn't a museum. 
3. Pete eats apples and / but doesn't eat bananas. 
4. Greg reads magazines and / but a newspaper. 
5. I have a calendar and / but a notebook. 
6. He goes swimming and / but he doesn't play soccer. 

24.6 DI LAS FRASES EN VOZ ALTA, COMPLETANDO LOS ESPACIOS

My mom ___and___ dad work as doctors in the hospital.

1. Meg likes this restaurant ______ she doesn't like that café.
2. There are two schools ______ there isn't a library in my town.
3. I have a pen, a notebook, ______ a calendar in my bag.
4. My sister goes to the gym on Mondays ______ Thursdays.
5. Pedro works in a school ______ he isn't a teacher.

25 Describir lugares

Utiliza los adjetivos para dar más información sobre los sustantivos, por ejemplo, para describir una persona, edificio o lugar.

Lenguaje Adjetivos
Vocabulario Adjetivos y nombres de lugares
Habilidad Describir lugares

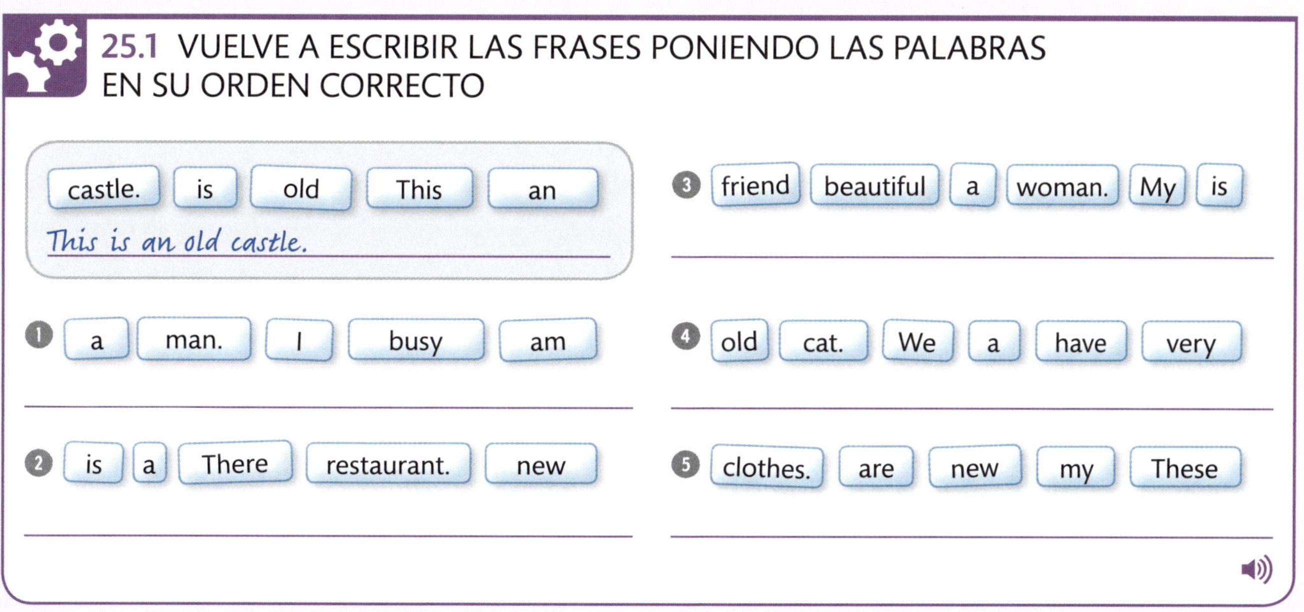

25.1 VUELVE A ESCRIBIR LAS FRASES PONIENDO LAS PALABRAS EN SU ORDEN CORRECTO

castle. | is | old | This | an
This is an old castle.

1. a | man. | I | busy | am

2. is | a | There | restaurant. | new

3. friend | beautiful | a | woman. | My | is

4. old | cat. | We | a | have | very

5. clothes. | are | new | my | These

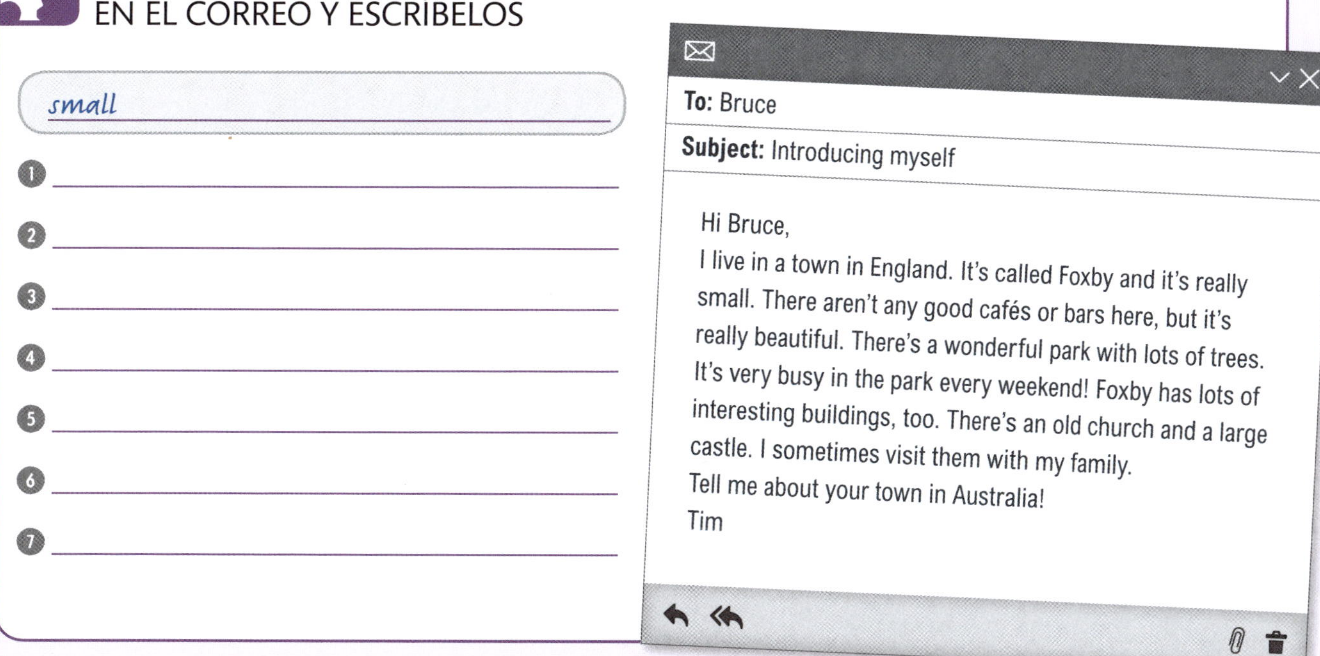

25.2 BUSCA OCHO ADJETIVOS EN EL CORREO Y ESCRÍBELOS

small

1. ___
2. ___
3. ___
4. ___
5. ___
6. ___
7. ___

To: Bruce
Subject: Introducing myself

Hi Bruce,
I live in a town in England. It's called Foxby and it's really small. There aren't any good cafés or bars here, but it's really beautiful. There's a wonderful park with lots of trees. It's very busy in the park every weekend! Foxby has lots of interesting buildings, too. There's an old church and a large castle. I sometimes visit them with my family.
Tell me about your town in Australia!
Tim

25.3 COMPLETA LOS ESPACIOS Y ESCRIBE CADA FRASE DE DOS MANERAS DISTINTAS

Paris is a beautiful city. *The city is beautiful.* *It is beautiful.*

1. They are small children. ______ ______
2. Peter is a good waiter. ______ ______
3. Fido is a big dog. ______ ______
4. Melby is a quiet town. ______ ______

Aa 25.4 CONECTA LOS ADJETIVOS CON SUS OPUESTOS

	busy	easy
1	old	quiet
2	small	bad
3	good	old
4	horrible	slow
5	young	large
6	fast	beautiful
7	difficult	new

25.5 ESCUCHA EL AUDIO Y RESPONDE A LAS PREGUNTAS

Braemore is a large town in Scotland.
True ☐ **False** ☑ **Not given** ☐

1. There are lots of lakes near Braemore.
True ☐ **False** ☐ **Not given** ☐
2. There are a few old buildings.
True ☐ **False** ☐ **Not given** ☐
3. Braemore has only a few hotels.
True ☐ **False** ☐ **Not given** ☐
4. Kirsty works in a large hotel.
True ☐ **False** ☐ **Not given** ☐
5. Kirsty is not very busy on weekends.
True ☐ **False** ☐ **Not given** ☐
6. Kirsty goes to a café with her friends.
True ☐ **False** ☐ **Not given** ☐

25.6 DI LAS FRASES EN VOZ ALTA, COMPLETANDO LOS ESPACIOS

The lakes *are* beautiful *and the* beaches *are* quiet.

1. ______ sea ______ blue ______ sun ______ hot.
2. ______ beach ______ busy ______ hotels ______ ugly.
3. ______ city ______ old ______ buildings ______ beautiful.
4. ______ restaurant ______ good ______ waiter ______ friendly.
5. ______ countryside ______ beautiful ______ mountains ______ large.
6. ______ town ______ small ______ shops ______ quiet.

25.7 COMPLETA LOS ESPACIOS CON LAS PALABRAS DEL RECUADRO

There are lots of buildings.

1. ______ shops.
2. ______ trees.
3. ______ cars.
4. ______ churches.
5. ______ flowers.
6. ______ cafés.
7. ______ parks.

~~lots of~~ some lots of a few some a few some a few

26 Dar razones

Utiliza la conjunción "because" para explicar la causa de algo. También puedes utilizar "because" para responder a la pregunta "why?".

Lenguaje "Because"
Aa Vocabulario Lugares y trabajos
Habilidad Dar razones

Aa 26.1 CONECTA EL COMIENZO Y EL FINAL DE CADA FRASE

I work at night because → I'm a night nurse.

1. Fred works outside because
2. Mick travels to Switzerland because
3. Saul goes to bed late because
4. I get up at 5am because
5. Marion goes to the library because
6. Colin works with children because

- he's a teacher.
- she's a student.
- I'm a mailman.
- I'm a night nurse.
- he goes skiing there.
- he works in a restaurant.
- he's a farmer.

26.2 ESCUCHA EL AUDIO Y RESPONDE A LAS PREGUNTAS

Leo uses a computer because...
he works in an office ☑ **he works on a farm** ☐

1. Rick works outside because...
he's a gardener ☐ **he's a farmer** ☐

2. Mary Lou works with children because...
she's a teacher ☐ **she's a nurse** ☐

3. Carl goes to the library because...
he's a student ☐ **he's a professor** ☐

4. Sally gets up at 6am because...
she goes running ☐ **she goes to the gym** ☐

5. Pete works at the theater because...
he's an actor ☐ **he's a receptionist** ☐

6. Michael has not come to work because...
he's out of town ☐ **he has the flu** ☐

7. Sana works in a restaurant because...
she's a chef ☐ **she's a waitress** ☐

26.3 COMPLETA LOS ESPACIOS CON LAS FRASES DEL RECUADRO

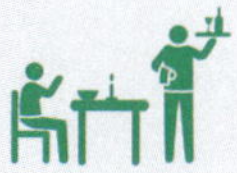

John goes to the restaurant because *it has delicious food*.

1. Aziz lives in the countryside because ______________________.
2. We don't have breakfast because ______________________.
3. Mr. Aspinall gets up early because ______________________.
4. Arnold wears a suit because ______________________.
5. Vicky works outside because ______________________.
6. I work in a hospital because ______________________.

he thinks it's beautiful | ~~it has delicious food~~ | we're very busy | I'm a doctor
he takes his dog for a walk | he works in a bank | she is a gardener

26.4 UTILIZA EL DIAGRAMA PARA CREAR SEIS FRASES CORRECTAS Y DILAS EN VOZ ALTA

Clara works in a theater because she is an actor.

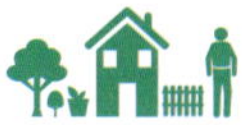

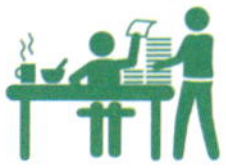

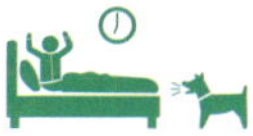

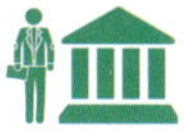

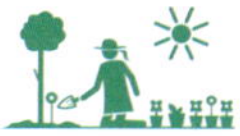

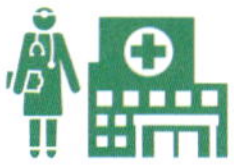

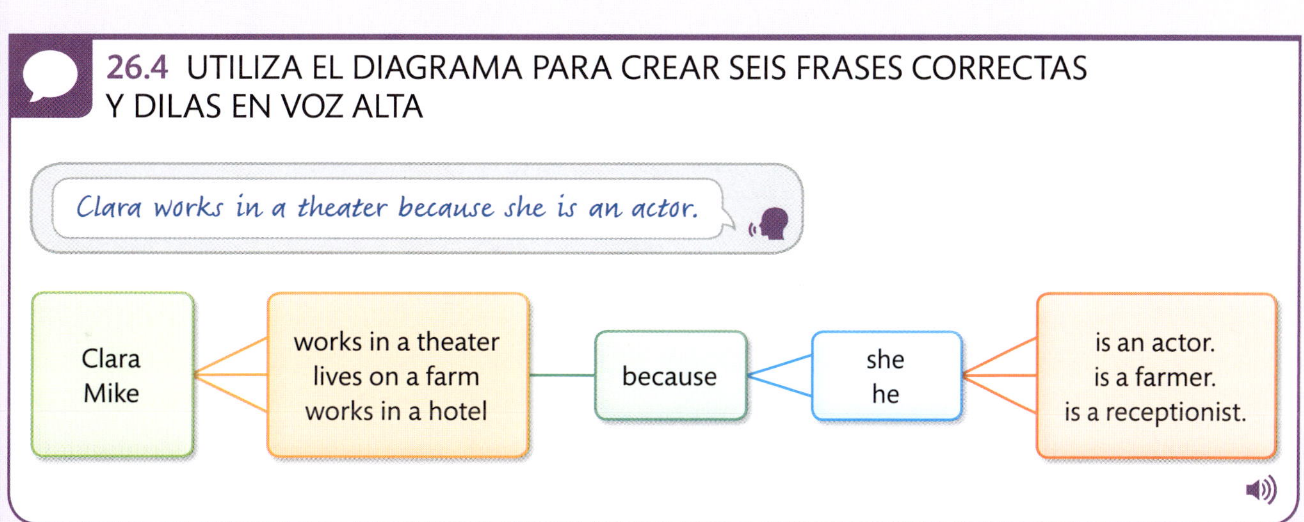

27 Vocabulario

Aa 27.1 **LA CASA** ESCRIBE LAS PALABRAS DEL RECUADRO DEBAJO DE LA IMAGEN CORRECTA

desk

1 ______

2 ______

3 ______

8 ______

9 ______

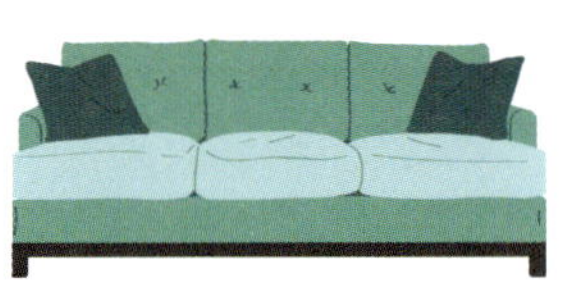

10 ______

11 ______

16 ______

17 ______

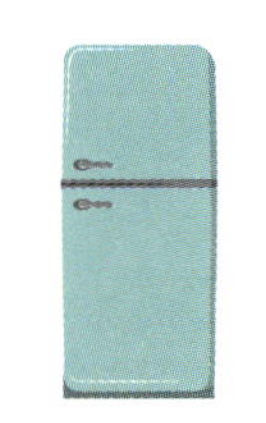

18 ______

19 ______

couch (US) / sofa (UK) dining room toilet house closet (US) / wardrobe (UK)

bathroom bedroom ~~desk~~ chair bathtub table bookcase

4 ____________

5 ____________

6 ____________

7 ____________

12 ____________

13 ____________

14 ____________

15 ____________

20 ____________

21 ____________

22 ____________

23 ____________

kitchen · door · armchair · study · garage · apartment block (US) / block of flats (UK)

lamp · television · bed · shower · window · refrigerator (US) / fridge (UK)

28 Mis cosas

Cuando hables de tus cosas, como por ejemplo muebles o mascotas, puedes utilizar el verbo "have". También lo puedes usar para referirte a tus cualidades y a los electrodomésticos y habitaciones de tu casa.

Lenguaje Utilizar "have"
Aa Vocabulario Objetos de la casa
Habilidad Hablar de las pertenencias

28.1 TACHA LA PALABRA INCORRECTA DE CADA FRASE

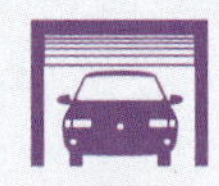

We **have** / ~~**has**~~ a car in the garage.

1.  My friend **have** / **has** new glasses.
2.  John **have** / **has** two dogs.
3.  We **have** / **has** an old castle in our city.
4.  They **have** / **has** a lot of parks in their town.
5.  I **have** / **has** a beautiful necklace.
6.  Alex **have** / **has** a new camera.
7.  Our house **have** / **has** a lovely yard.
8.  Phil and Sue **have** / **has** four daughters.
9.  Pete **have** / **has** a new cell phone.
10.  Your town **have** / **has** a big hotel.
11.  I **have** / **has** a lot of friends.

28.2 COMPLETA LOS ESPACIOS CON "HAS" O "HAVE"

They ___have___ two daughters.

1. Bob and Shirley ________ a big dog.
2. She ________ some new friends.
3. We ________ two sons at home.
4. James ________ two cars.
5. His house ________ three bedrooms.
6. Pam ________ lots of books at home.
7. He ________ two cats.
8. Sally's house ________ a new kitchen.
9. You ________ a beautiful house.
10. I ________ three sisters.
11. Kelly and Mark ________ a microwave.
12. We ________ a castle in our town.
13. Sanjay ________ a cat and a dog.
14. You ________ three brothers.
15. Ross ________ a new cell phone.
16. Our house ________ two bathrooms.
17. I ________ a couch in my room.
18. Washington ________ some lovely parks.

28.3 MARCA LAS FRASES CORRECTAS

We have apples and oranges. ☑
We apples and oranges have. ☐

1. I have two sisters. ☐
   I has two sisters. ☐

2. You has a beautiful house. ☐
   You have a beautiful house. ☐

3. We a garden have. ☐
   We have a garden. ☐

4. Sam and Greg have a dog. ☐
   Sam and Greg has a dog. ☐

5. Marlon a brother has. ☐
   Marlon has a brother. ☐

6. Fardale have an old castle. ☐
   Fardale has an old castle. ☐

7. They have a new car. ☐
   They has a new car. ☐

28.4 LEE EL ANUNCIO Y RESPONDE A LAS PREGUNTAS

Ocean View has two bedrooms.
True ☐ **False** ☑

1. Ocean View has a garage.
   True ☐ **False** ☐

2. Sunny Bank has two bathrooms.
   True ☐ **False** ☐

3. There isn't a garage at Sunny Bank.
   True ☐ **False** ☐

4. Belle Vue Manor has six bedrooms.
   True ☐ **False** ☐

5. Belle Vue Manor has a small yard.
   True ☐ **False** ☐

6. Mossfield Cottage has an old kitchen.
   True ☐ **False** ☐

7. Mossfield Cottage has a small yard.
   True ☐ **False** ☐

34 ACCOMMODATION

PROPERTY

Ocean View **$2,000/month**
This beautiful house is right on the ocean. There are three bedrooms and a big kitchen. It also has a lovely yard, but there is no garage.

Sunny Bank **$1,500/month**
This modern apartment has two bedrooms and one bathroom with a bath and a shower. All the furniture is new. There isn't a yard, but there is a garage.

Belle Vue Manor
This large house is in the center of Sunset Cove. It has six bedrooms, three bathrooms, and two garages. There is a big yard with lots of trees and a lake.

Mossfield Cottage **$1300/month**
This small house is in the old part of Summerwood. It has two bedrooms, a bathroom, and a new kitchen. There is a small yard with lots of beautiful flowers.

28.5 VUELVE A ESCRIBIR LAS FRASES UTILIZANDO CONTRACCIONES

Sam **does not** have a car.
Sam doesn't have a car.

1. We **do not** have a computer at home.
2. My city **does not** have a castle.
3. Rob's house **does not** have a garage.
4. You **do not** have any sisters.
5. The village **does not** have any stores.

28.6 REESCRIBE LAS FRASES SIN CONTRACCIONES

I **haven't** got a dog.
I have not got a dog.

1. **You've** got a beautiful necklace.
2. She **hasn't** got any sisters.
3. We **haven't** got a microwave.
4. Greg **hasn't** got a bike.
5. My **town's** got two theaters.
6. Chloe **hasn't** got a cat.
7. **They've** got a new house.

28.7 ESCUCHA EL AUDIO Y RELACIONA LOS OBJETOS CON SUS PROPIETARIOS

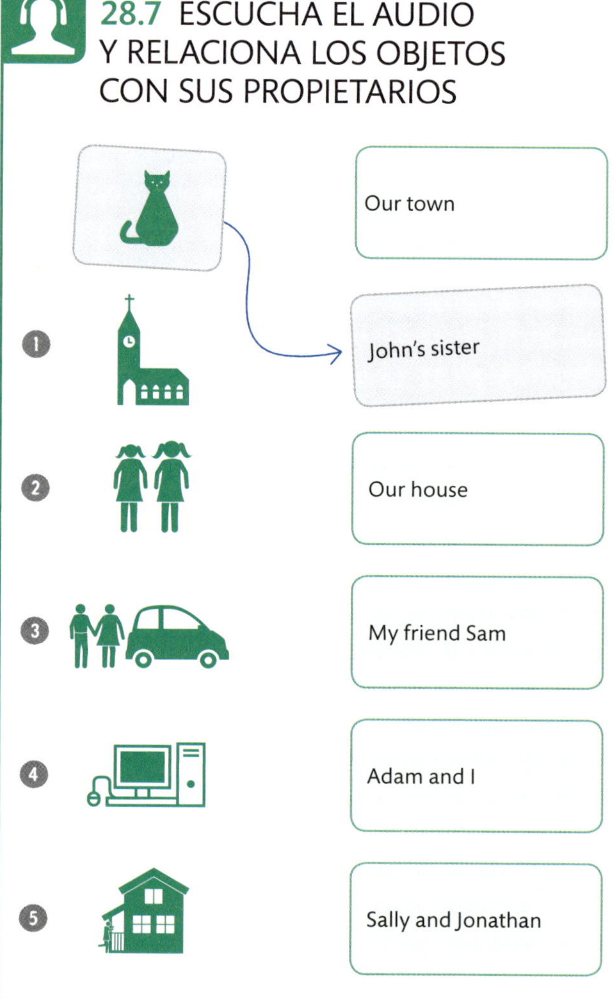

28.8 UTILIZA EL DIAGRAMA PARA CREAR 11 FRASES CORRECTAS Y DILAS EN VOZ ALTA

I have a computer.

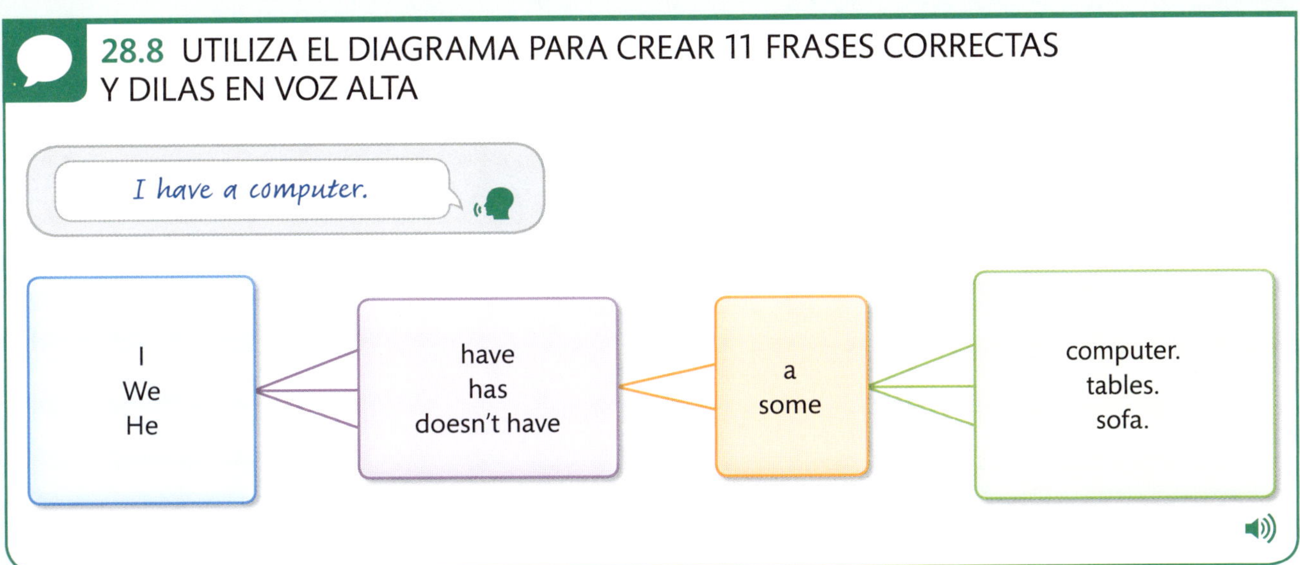

28.9 COMPLETA LOS ESPACIOS PARA ESCRIBIR LAS FRASES DE TRES FORMAS DISTINTAS

	I **have** a car.	*I have got a car.*	*I've got a car.*
1		She **has got** two bedrooms.	
2	They **don't have** a dog.		
3			We've **got** some chairs.
4		He **has got** a brother.	
5	Carla **doesn't have** a sister.		
6		You **have got** a car.	
7			Phil's **got** a dog.
8	You **have** a yard.		
9			Jamal **hasn't got** a sofa.
10		They **have got** a shower.	
11			May's **got** a couch.
12	He **doesn't have** a cat.		

29 ¿Qué tienes?

Haz preguntas con "have" para averiguar las cosas que posee alguien. Los auxiliares "do" o "does" ayudan a formar la pregunta.

Lenguaje Preguntas con "have"
Aa Vocabulario La casa y los muebles
Habilidad Preguntar sobre objetos de casa

Aa 29.1 CONECTA LOS DIBUJOS CON LAS PALABRAS

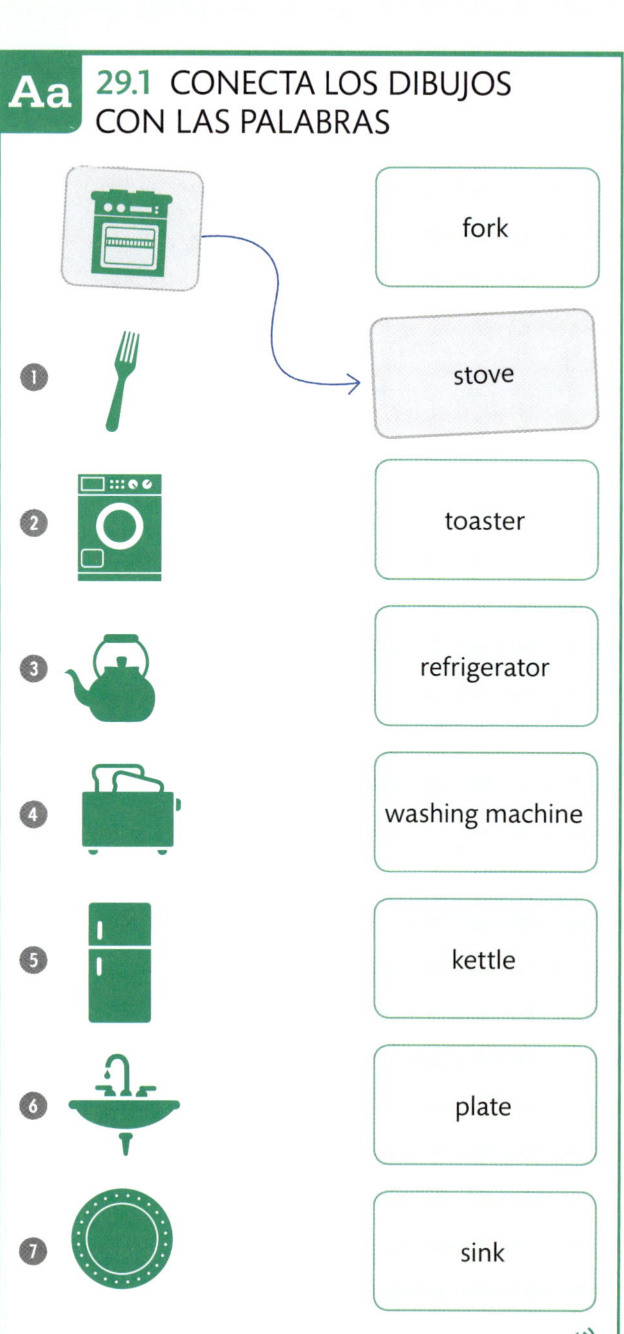

29.2 REESCRIBE LAS AFIRMACIONES COMO PREGUNTAS

She has a toaster.
Does she have a toaster?

1. The house has a yard.

____

2. Their kitchen has a refrigerator.

____

3. Bill's house has a big garage.

____

4. You have a sofa.

____

5. Barry has a kettle.

____

6. She has a barbecue at her house.

____

7. Marge has a new washing machine.

____

8. Jack and Marienne have a TV.

____

9. Leela's brother has a knife and fork.

____

29.3 ESCUCHA Y CONECTA LAS PERSONAS CON SUS COSAS

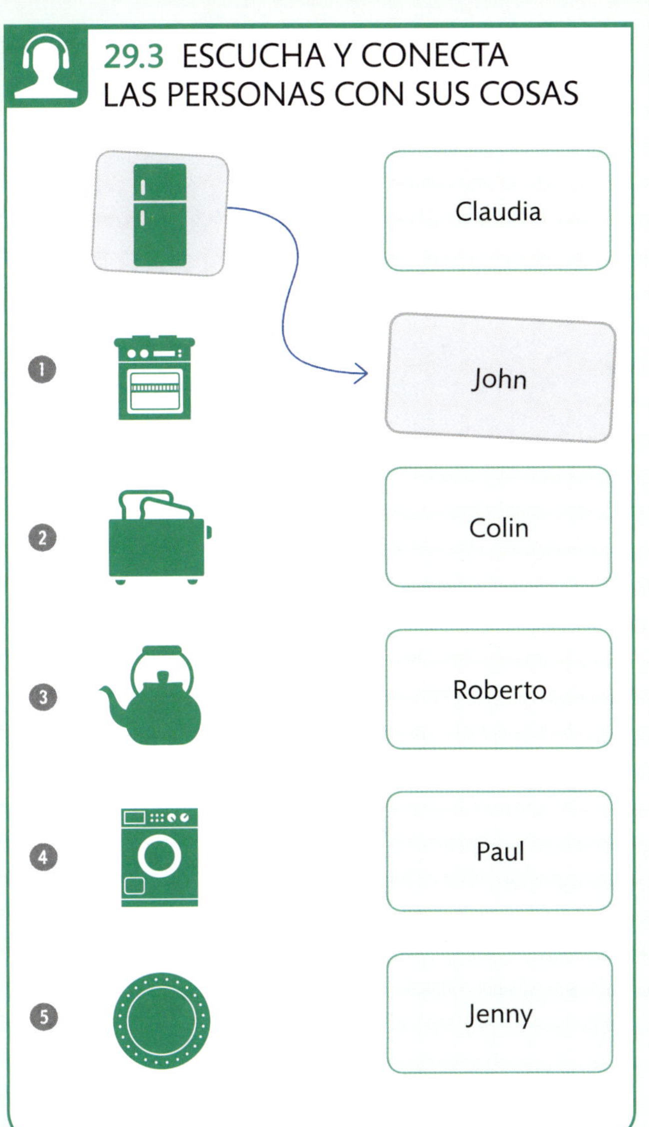

29.4 MIRA EL DIBUJO Y ESCRIBE RESPUESTAS CORTAS

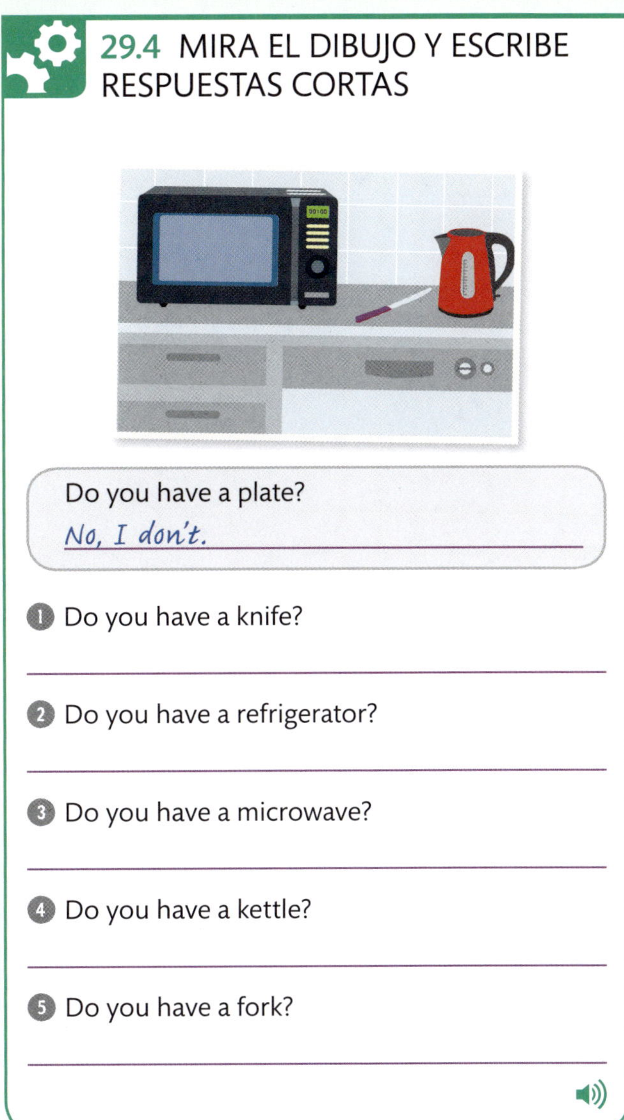

29.5 USA EL DIAGRAMA PARA CREAR NUEVE FRASES CORRECTAS Y DILAS EN VOZ ALTA

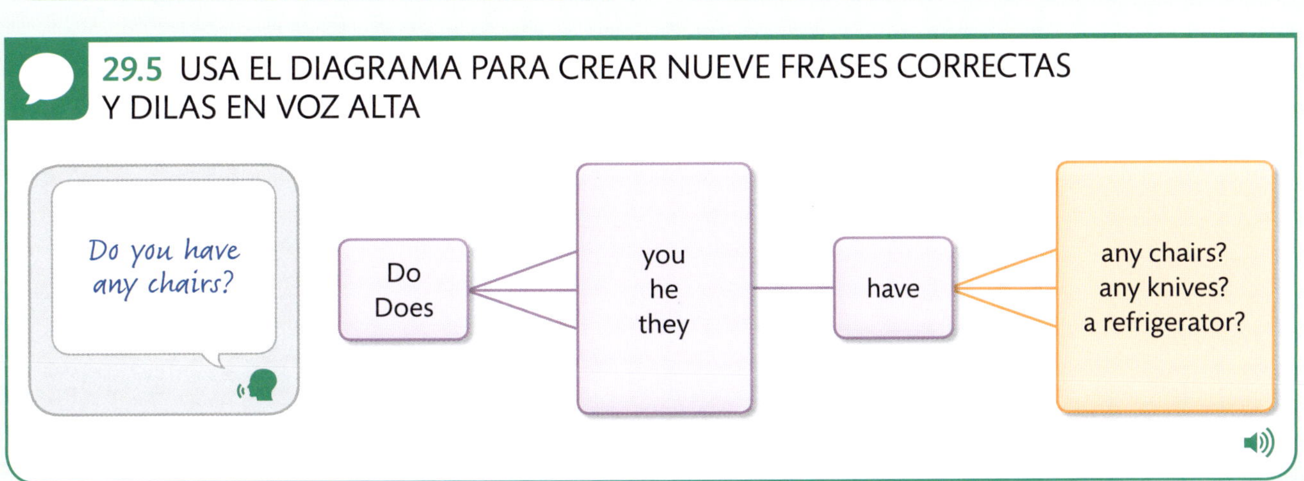

29.6 RESPONDE AL AUDIO EN VOZ ALTA, COMPLETANDO LOS ESPACIOS

Does Kate have a necklace?
No, *she doesn't*.

1. Does Paula have a sofa?
   Yes, ______.

2. Does James have a snake?
   Yes, ______.

3. Does Keith have an umbrella?
   No, ______.

4. Does your town have a library?
   Yes, ______.

5. Do your parents have a car?
   No, ______.

6. Does your mom have a microwave?
   No, ______.

7. Does Gerald have a bottle?
   Yes, ______.

29.7 ESCRIBE UNA PREGUNTA QUE CORRESPONDA A CADA FRASE

She has got a car.
Has she got a car?

1. They have got a microwave.
2. Shaun and Shania have got a pet snake.
3. Charles has got a camera.
4. Clarissa has got a new laptop.
5. Carol's house has got a big yard.
6. Your friends have got my book.
7. Brian has got a new TV.

29.8 REESCRIBE LAS PREGUNTAS CON "HAVE" COMO PREGUNTAS CON "HAVE GOT"

Do you have a dog?
Have you got a dog?

1. Does the kitchen have a microwave?
2. Does your house have a yard?
3. Do the Hendersons have a car?
4. Does Claire have my glasses?
5. Do your parents have a computer?
6. Does Paul have my book?
7. Does Brian have a magazine?
8. Do your neighbors have a basement?
9. Does your cell phone have a camera?
10. Does Sam have any money?
11. Does your town have a supermarket?
12. Does Brian have a sister?
13. Do your children have a cat?
14. Does your husband have a camera?
15. Does your school have a library?
16. Does Jane have a cell phone?
17. Do the kids have their bikes?

29.9 UTILIZA EL DIAGRAMA PARA CREAR SIETE FRASES CORRECTAS Y DILAS EN VOZ ALTA

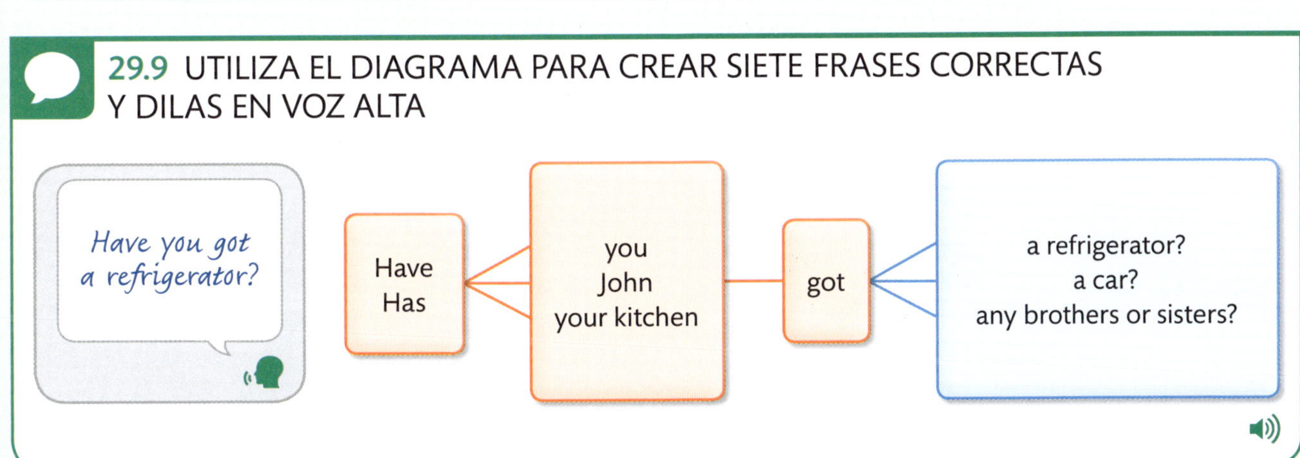

30 Vocabulario

30.1 **COMIDA Y BEBIDA** ESCRIBE LAS PALABRAS DEL RECUADRO DEBAJO DE LAS IMÁGENES CORRESPONDIENTES

food

1 ____________
2 ____________
3 ____________
4 ____________

8 ____________
9 ____________
10 ____________
11 ____________
12 ____________

16 ____________
17 ____________
18 ____________
19 ____________
20 ____________

24 ____________
25 ____________
26 ____________
27 ____________
28 ____________

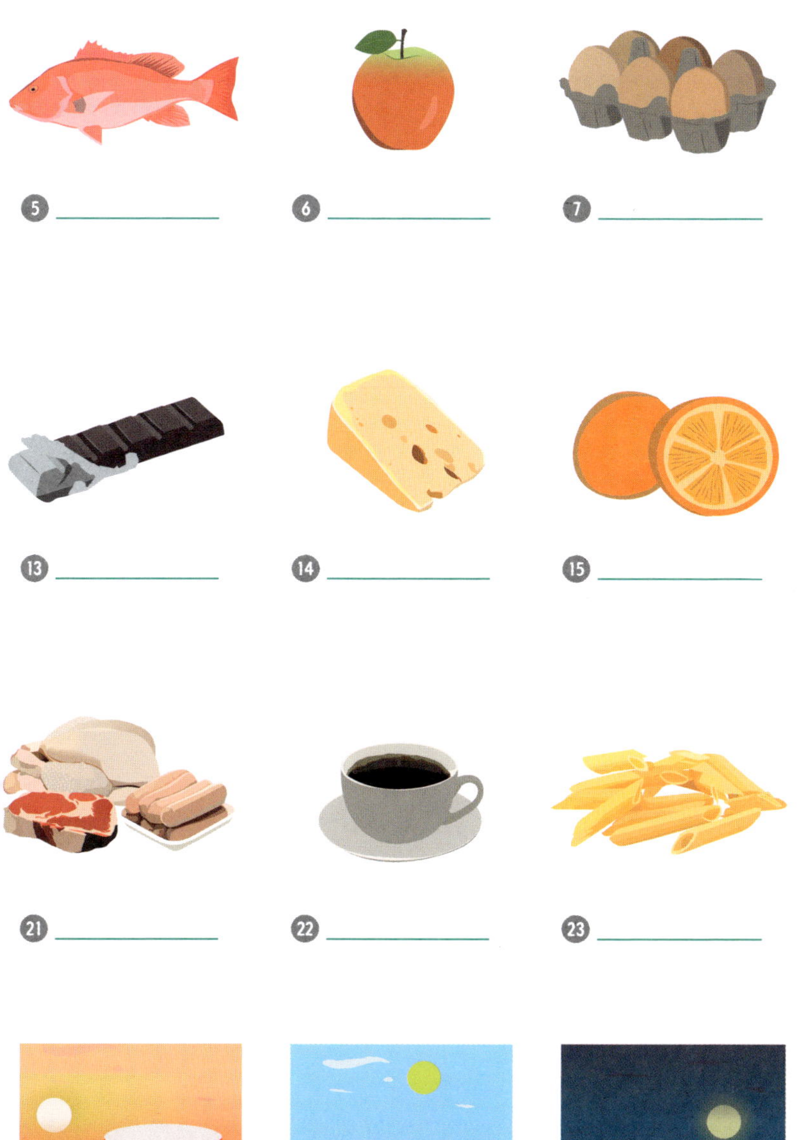

5 ____________ 6 ____________ 7 ____________

13 ____________ 14 ____________ 15 ____________

21 ____________ 22 ____________ 23 ____________

29 ____________ 30 ____________ 31 ____________

meat breakfast
sugar potatoes
bread fruit cheese
vegetables drinks
strawberry juice
apple seafood
butter chocolate
spaghetti orange
water coffee
pasta milk
lunch burger
eggs ~~food~~
rice fish dinner
salad cereal
banana cake

31 Contar

En inglés, los sustantivos pueden ser contables e incontables. Los contables se pueden contar individualmente. Los objetos que no se pueden contar por separado se llaman incontables.

Lenguaje Sustantivos incontables
Vocabulario Contenedores de comida
Habilidad Hablar sobre la comida

31.1 ESCRIBE LAS PALABRAS DEL RECUADRO EN LA LISTA CORRECTA

CONTABLES	INCONTABLES
sandwich	*water*

coffee · ~~water~~ · burger · rice · egg · juice · apple · ~~sandwich~~

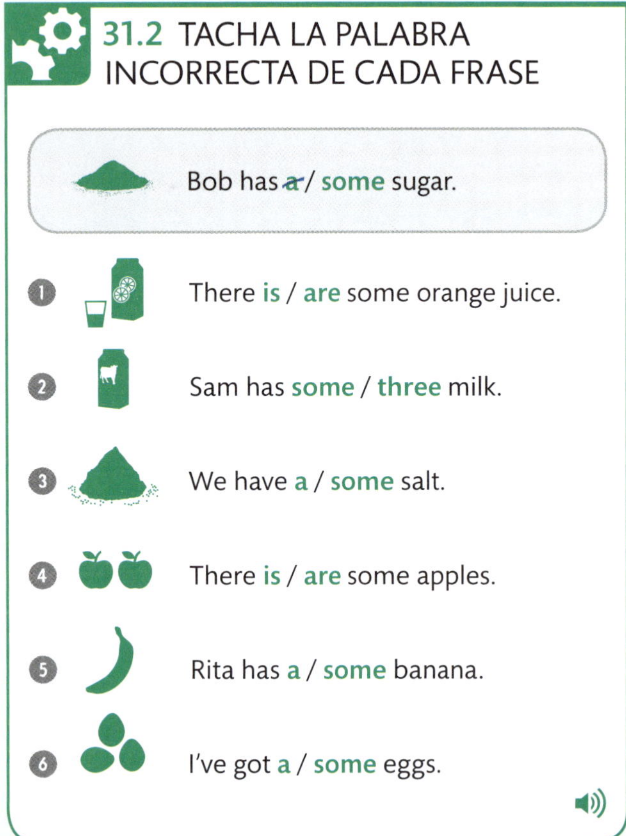

31.2 TACHA LA PALABRA INCORRECTA DE CADA FRASE

Bob has ~~a~~ / some sugar.

1. There is / are some orange juice.
2. Sam has some / three milk.
3. We have a / some salt.
4. There is / are some apples.
5. Rita has a / some banana.
6. I've got a / some eggs.

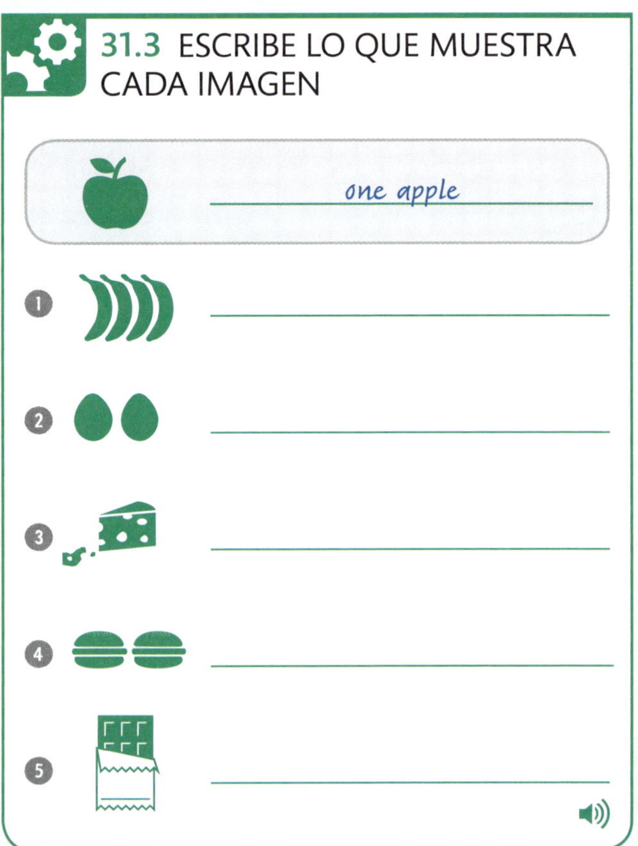

31.3 ESCRIBE LO QUE MUESTRA CADA IMAGEN

one apple

1. ______
2. ______
3. ______
4. ______
5. ______

31.4 COMPLETA LOS ESPACIOS ESCRIBIENDO CADA FRASE DE TRES MANERAS DISTINTAS

	Are there any apples?	*There are some apples.*	*There aren't any apples.*
1	Is there any salt?		
2		There is some wine.	
3	Are there any burgers?		
4		There are some cookies.	
5			There aren't any pastries.
6	Is there any bread?		
7		There is some rice.	
8			There isn't any butter.
9	Are there any pizzas?		
10		There is some cheese.	

31.5 ESCUCHA EL AUDIO Y RESPONDE A LAS PREGUNTAS

Steve and Kate have three bags of flour.
True ☑ **False** ☐

1. They have three bags of sugar in their cupboard.
True ☐ **False** ☐

2. Steve and Kate haven't got any tomatoes.
True ☐ **False** ☐

3. They have two blocks of cheese.
True ☐ **False** ☐

4. Steve and Kate have got two oranges.
True ☐ **False** ☐

5. They haven't got any apples.
True ☐ **False** ☐

6. Steve and Kate don't have any coffee.
True ☐ **False** ☐

7. Kate doesn't have any chocolate.
True ☐ **False** ☐

8. Steve and Kate don't have any onions.
True ☐ **False** ☐

9. They have some rice.
True ☐ **False** ☐

31.6 COMPLETA LOS ESPACIOS UTILIZANDO LAS PALABRAS DEL RECUADRO

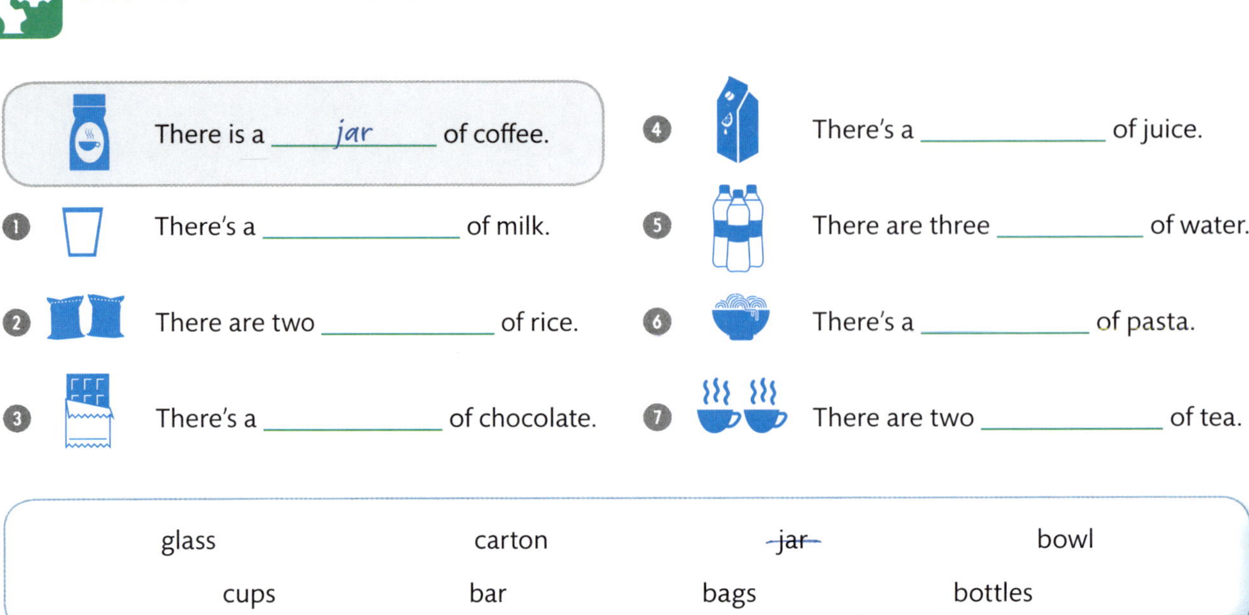

There is a ___jar___ of coffee.

1. There's a ______________ of milk.
2. There are two ______________ of rice.
3. There's a ______________ of chocolate.
4. There's a ______________ of juice.
5. There are three ______________ of water.
6. There's a ______________ of pasta.
7. There are two ______________ of tea.

glass | carton | ~~jar~~ | bowl | cups | bar | bags | bottles

31.7 TACHA LA PALABRA INCORRECTA DE CADA FRASE

There ~~is~~ / **are** three cartons of milk. 

1. There **is** / **are** a jar of coffee. 
2. There **isn't** / **aren't** any rice.
3. There **is** / **are** two cartons of juice. 
4. There **is** / **are** some meat. 
5. There **is** / **are** two bottles of wine. 
6. There **isn't** / **aren't** any bread.
7. There **is** / **are** a bag of flour. 
8. There **is** / **are** some pasta. 
9. There **is** / **are** two bars of chocolate. 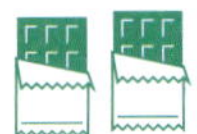
10. There **isn't** / **aren't** any sugar.
11. There **is** / **are** some butter. 

31.8 BUSCA EN LA TABLA NUEVE CONTENEDORES DE COMIDA

K P D B O W L Y M T
W O K O N S S J N E
A C Y T P S B O E E
J Y M T A L T G J H
V A K L U R A S G E
G A G E A B Z I B S
R Y D C D E E H N Q
N W F G L D B Z E E
A T L P X I M T O E
E A L R Y T K C S S
R S C I D Q S J A R
A Q U Y E Z D W T E
N H P X O E C N N C
K B T I B A R K D J
Y R W N G R M S L O

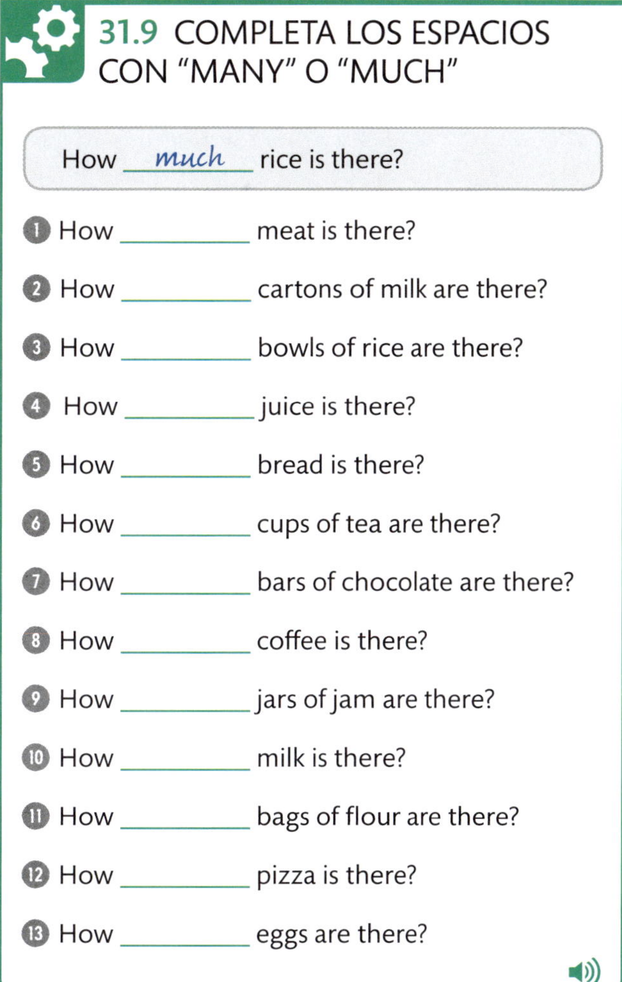

31.9 COMPLETA LOS ESPACIOS CON "MANY" O "MUCH"

How *much* rice is there?

1. How ________ meat is there?
2. How ________ cartons of milk are there?
3. How ________ bowls of rice are there?
4. How ________ juice is there?
5. How ________ bread is there?
6. How ________ cups of tea are there?
7. How ________ bars of chocolate are there?
8. How ________ coffee is there?
9. How ________ jars of jam are there?
10. How ________ milk is there?
11. How ________ bags of flour are there?
12. How ________ pizza is there?
13. How ________ eggs are there?

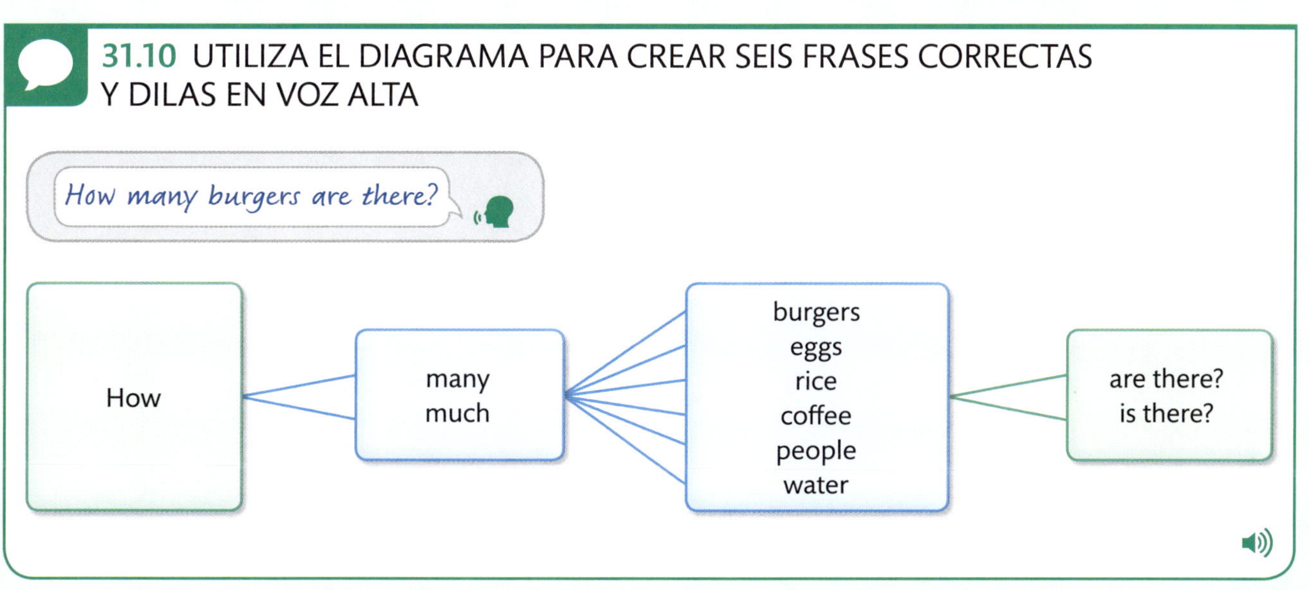

31.10 UTILIZA EL DIAGRAMA PARA CREAR SEIS FRASES CORRECTAS Y DILAS EN VOZ ALTA

How many burgers are there?

32 Medir

Utiliza "enough" cuando tengas la cantidad correcta de algún objeto. Utiliza "too many" o "too much" cuando tengas más que suficiente.

Lenguaje Medidas
Vocabulario Ingredientes y cantidades
Habilidad Hablar de cantidades

32.1 TACHA LAS PALABRAS INCORRECTAS DE CADA FRASE

We have too many / ~~too much~~ eggs.

1. There are too many / too much pears.
2. There is too many / too much milk.
3. She has too many / too much pasta.
4. We have too many / too much bananas.
5. There is too many / too much butter.
6. There are too many / too much apples.
7. There are too many / too much tomatoes.
8. I have too many / too much juice.
9. There are too many / too much mushrooms.
10. They have too many / too much burgers.
11. Sue owns too many / too much shoes.

32.2 COMPLETA LOS ESPACIOS CON "IS ENOUGH" O "ARE ENOUGH"

There *is enough* flour.

1. There ______________ pineapples.
2. There ______________ mangoes.
3. There ______________ sugar.
4. There ______________ bread.
5. There ______________ milk.
6. There ______________ pasta.
7. There ______________ apples.
8. There ______________ oranges.
9. There ______________ bananas.
10. There ______________ chocolate.
11. There ______________ eggs.
12. There ______________ cheese.
13. There ______________ tomatoes.
14. There ______________ butter.
15. There ______________ juice.

32.3 COMPLETA LOS ESPACIOS ESCRIBIENDO CADA FRASE DE TRES MANERAS DISTINTAS

	We don't have enough salt.	*We have enough salt.*	*We have too much salt.*
1	You don't have enough oranges.		
2		There's enough sugar.	
3			We have too much butter.
4		There are enough eggs.	
5	There isn't enough flour.		
6			There are too many potatoes.
7		You have enough melons.	
8	He doesn't have enough bread.		
9			There is too much tea.
10		We have enough milk.	
11	You don't have enough rice.		
12			There are too many mangoes.
13		Martha has enough onions.	
14	You don't have enough carrots.		

32.4 ESCUCHA EL AUDIO Y RESPONDE A LAS PREGUNTAS

Bruce and Shelley don't have any bread.
True ☐ **False** ☑

1. They don't have enough butter.
True ☐ **False** ☐

2. They have too many bags of flour.
True ☐ **False** ☐

3. They don't have enough salt.
True ☐ **False** ☐

4. They have enough tomatoes.
True ☐ **False** ☐

5. They don't have enough cheese.
True ☐ **False** ☐

32.5 COMPLETA LOS ESPACIOS CON "ENOUGH", "NOT ENOUGH", "TOO MANY" O "TOO MUCH"

Vegetable pasta soup

1 onion
3 carrots
2 potatoes
4 tomatoes
15 oz pasta
3 fl oz oil
1 loaf of bread

Fruit cake

6 oz butter
9 oz flour
6 oz sugar
2 oranges
2 bananas
3 eggs
1 glass of milk

There are *too many* onions.

1. There are ______________ carrots.
2. There are ______________ potatoes.
3. There are ______________ tomatoes.
4. There is ______________ pasta.
5. There is ______________ oil.
6. There is ______________ bread.
7. There is ______________ butter.
8. There is ______________ flour.
9. There is ______________ sugar.
10. There are ______________ oranges.
11. There are ______________ bananas.
12. There are ______________ eggs.
13. There is ______________ milk.

32.6 ESCRIBE DE NUEVO LAS FRASES CORRIGIENDO LOS ERRORES

There **are** enough corn to make the soup.
There is enough corn to make the soup.

1. There **aren't** enough butter.
2. There **isn't** enough tomatoes.
3. There **isn't** enough mangoes.
4. You have too **money** bananas.
5. They don't have **enoug** butter.
6. There **is** enough onions.
7. There **aren't** enough sugar.
8. You have **to** many pineapples.
9. They have too **moch** bread.
10. You **dont** have enough apples.
11. They have **enogh** flour.
12. There **is** too many potatoes.
13. There **are** too much salt.
14. There **are** too much chocolate.
15. There **is** too many mangoes.
16. You have **enugh** eggs.
17. There **is** enough oranges.

32.7 UTILIZA EL DIAGRAMA PARA CREAR NUEVE FRASES CORRECTAS Y DILAS EN VOZ ALTA

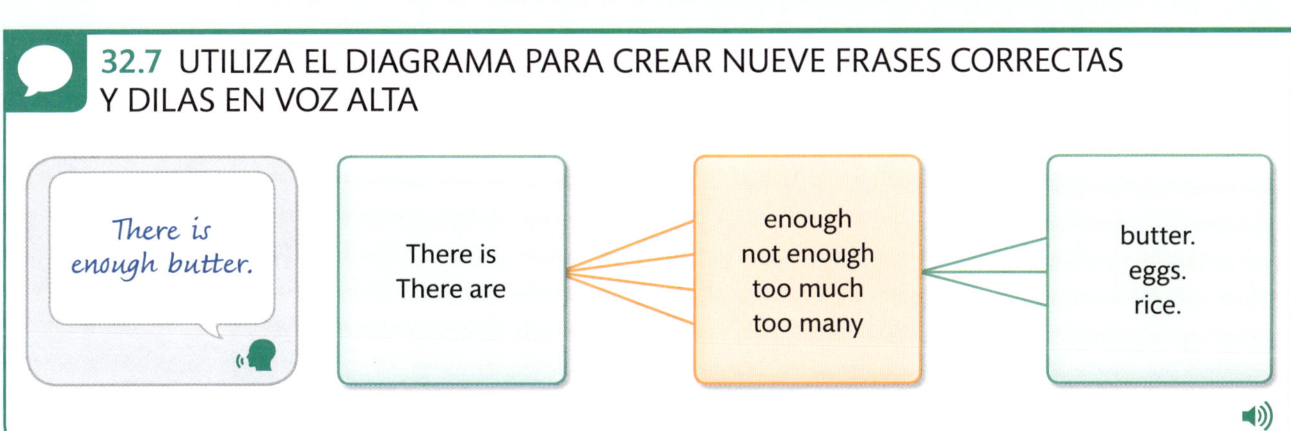

33 Vocabulario

Aa 33.1 ROPA, ACCESORIOS Y COLORES ESCRIBE LAS PALABRAS DEL RECUADRO DEBAJO DE SU IMAGEN

1 ______________

2 ______________

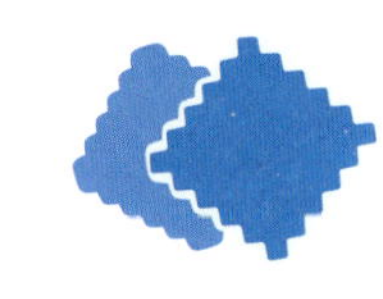

3 ______________

4 ______________

7 ______________

8 ______________

9 ______________

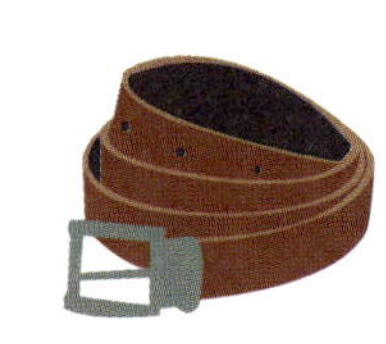

10 ______________

11 ______________

14 ______________

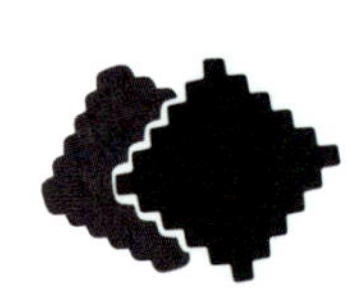

15 ______________

16 ______________

17 ______________

18 ______________

21 ______________

22 ______________

23 ______________

24 ______________

25 ______________

5 ____________

6 ____________

12 ____________

13 ____________

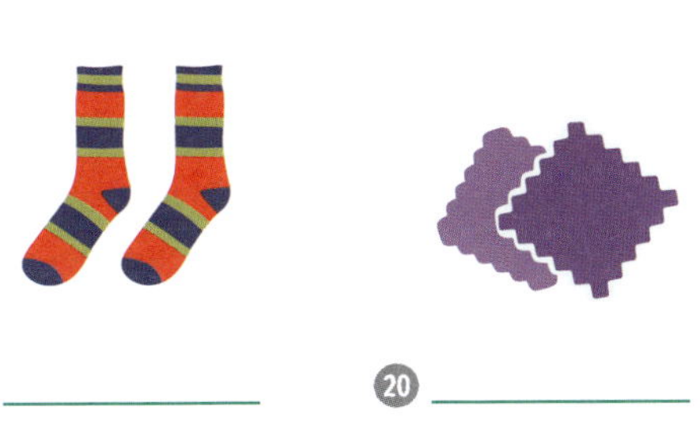

19 ____________

20 ____________

26 ____________

27 ____________

34 De compras

Puedes utilizar varios verbos para hablar sobre lo que pasa cuando vas de compras. Utiliza "too" y "enough" para describir cómo te queda la ropa.

Lenguaje Utilizar "too" y "fit"
Vocabulario Compras y ropa
Habilidad Describir la ropa

34.1 COMPLETA LOS ESPACIOS CON LAS PALABRAS DEL RECUADRO

Jane *owns* a red motorcycle.

1. That sweater ______ you. It's the right size.
2. My mom always ______ my dad's clothes.
3. These jeans don't ______. They're too small.
4. I ______ 30 pairs of shoes.
5. I always ______ clothes before I buy them.
6. Those shops ______ very fashionable clothes.
7. We ______ fruit at the market.
8. I ______ some shoes for my birthday.
9. I sometimes ______ by credit card.

chooses | fits | ~~owns~~ | sell | pay | want | buy | fit | try on | own

34.2 ESCRIBE DE NUEVO LAS FRASES CORRIGIENDO LOS ERRORES

Sally always choose her husband's clothes.
Sally always chooses her husband's clothes.

1. Ruth do a lot of her shopping on the internet.
2. The shop don't sell my size of clothes.
3. She wear short skirts.
4. Greg's jeans doesn't fit him.
5. Amy own a lot of fashionable clothes.
6. We pays for our shopping with cash.
7. Duncan never try on clothes before he buys them.
8. My parents usually pays for my clothes.
9. Peter don't own many clothes.

34.3 ESCRIBE DE NUEVO LAS FRASES CORRIGIENDO LOS ERRORES

Kim **want** a blue skirt.
Kim wants a blue skirt.

1. That blouse **don't** fit you.
2. Sue always **try** on her new clothes.
3. Rob **want** a new tie for Christmas.
4. Peter **buy** his meat at the butcher's shop.
5. Jose **own** a beautiful house in France.
6. My jeans **doesn't** fit me. They're too big.
7. Samantha **choose** high-quality clothes.
8. They **sells** vegetables in the market.
9. Do you **wants** a new shirt for your birthday?

34.4 TACHA EL ADJETIVO INCORRECTO DE CADA FRASE

This is a **long** / ~~**short**~~ dress.

1.  This is a **new** / **old** T-shirt.
2.  These are **short** / **long** jeans.
3.  This is an **cheap** / **expensive** tie.
4.  This is a **large** / **small** sweater.
5.  This is a **pink** / **blue** dress.
6.   This is an **new** / **old** T-shirt.
7.   These are **old** / **cheap** shoes.
8.   This is a **long** / **short** skirt.
9.   This is a **red** / **blue** shirt.
10.  These are **big** / **small** shoes.
11.  This is a **large** / **small** sweater.

34.5 ESCUCHA EL AUDIO Y RESPONDE A LAS PREGUNTAS

Jane y Ruth describen las prendas que quieren comprar.

What type of cardigan does Jane buy?
- **red and short** ☐
- **blue and long** ☐
- **black and long** ☑

1. What does Jane want to buy?
   - **a red shirt** ☐
   - **a red skirt** ☐
   - **a blue skirt** ☐

2. What does Ruth want to buy for her mother?
   - **a red scarf** ☐
   - **yellow gloves** ☐
   - **a red hat** ☐

3. What does Ruth want to buy?
   - **brown shoes** ☐
   - **black shoes** ☐
   - **brown boots** ☐

4. What does Jane want next?
   - **blue jeans** ☐
   - **black jeans** ☐
   - **purple jeans** ☐

5. Jane then tries on the...
   - **black coat.** ☐
   - **red coat.** ☐
   - **green coat.** ☐

34.6 BUSCA CINCO ADJETIVOS EN LA TABLA

D	F	S	P	F	Q	A	T	E	H
C	E	S	T	L	S	S	T	F	Y
H	S	S	C	O	H	Y	C	Z	N
E	X	L	G	N	S	I	M	E	L
A	T	E	P	G	H	X	U	R	H
P	I	W	S	R	O	G	X	E	E
B	P	A	H	A	R	D	R	P	I
N	C	S	O	F	T	E	I	H	R

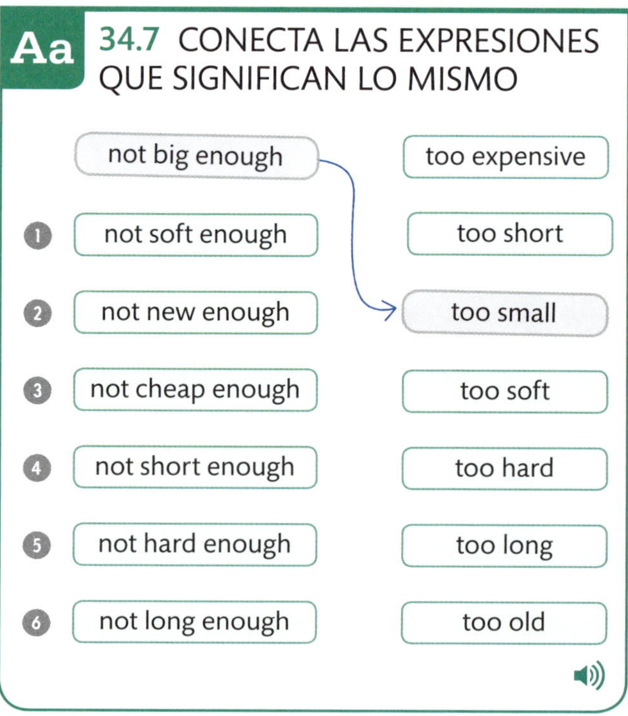

34.7 CONECTA LAS EXPRESIONES QUE SIGNIFICAN LO MISMO

	not big enough	too expensive
1	not soft enough	too short
2	not new enough	too small
3	not cheap enough	too soft
4	not short enough	too hard
5	not hard enough	too long
6	not long enough	too old

34.8 DI LAS FRASES EN VOZ ALTA, COMPLETANDO LOS ESPACIOS CON LAS EXPRESIONES DEL RECUADRO

Sharon's dress is *too long* .

1 Claire's hat is ______ .

2 These shoes are ______ .

3 Sophie's pullover is ______ .

4 Corrine's coat is ______ .

5 Emma's sweater is ______ .

6 Chloe's scarf is ______ .

7 Phoebe's shoes are ______ .

8 Joshua's jacket is ______ .

too big ~~too long~~ too small big enough too long
too small too big too expensive too small

35 Describir cosas

Para dar tu opinión sobre alguna cosa o bien para facilitar información se pueden utilizar adjetivos. Antes de un sustantivo se puede colocar más de un adjetivo.

Lenguaje Adjetivos para opinar
Vocabulario Ir de compras y materiales
Habilidad Dar opiniones

35.1 LEE EL BLOG Y RESPONDE A LAS PREGUNTAS

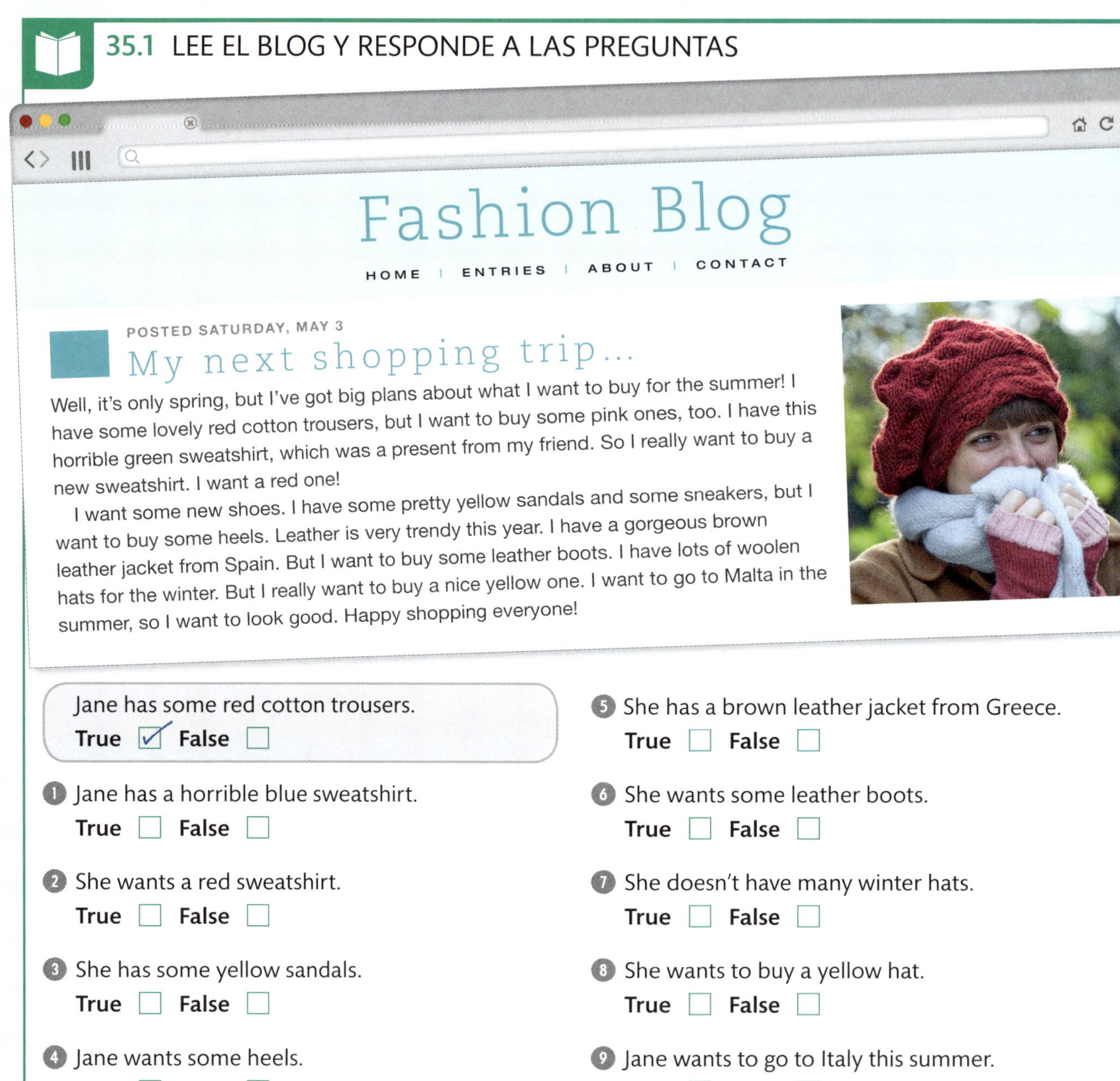

Fashion Blog

HOME | ENTRIES | ABOUT | CONTACT

POSTED SATURDAY, MAY 3

My next shopping trip...

Well, it's only spring, but I've got big plans about what I want to buy for the summer! I have some lovely red cotton trousers, but I want to buy some pink ones, too. I have this horrible green sweatshirt, which was a present from my friend. So I really want to buy a new sweatshirt. I want a red one!

I want some new shoes. I have some pretty yellow sandals and some sneakers, but I want to buy some heels. Leather is very trendy this year. I have a gorgeous brown leather jacket from Spain. But I want to buy some leather boots. I have lots of woolen hats for the winter. But I really want to buy a nice yellow one. I want to go to Malta in the summer, so I want to look good. Happy shopping everyone!

Jane has some red cotton trousers.
True ☑ **False** ☐

1. Jane has a horrible blue sweatshirt.
True ☐ **False** ☐

2. She wants a red sweatshirt.
True ☐ **False** ☐

3. She has some yellow sandals.
True ☐ **False** ☐

4. Jane wants some heels.
True ☐ **False** ☐

5. She has a brown leather jacket from Greece.
True ☐ **False** ☐

6. She wants some leather boots.
True ☐ **False** ☐

7. She doesn't have many winter hats.
True ☐ **False** ☐

8. She wants to buy a yellow hat.
True ☐ **False** ☐

9. Jane wants to go to Italy this summer.
True ☐ **False** ☐

35.2 MARCA LAS FRASES CORRECTAS

This is a beautiful green blouse. ☑
This is a green beautiful blouse. ☐

1. Our house has a pretty little yard. ☐
   Our house has a little pretty yard. ☐
2. James has a leather ugly jacket. ☐
   James has an ugly leather jacket. ☐
3. Pete has a wooden old table. ☐
   Pete has an old wooden table. ☐
4. This is a brilliant new book. ☐
   This is a new brilliant book. ☐
5. Shelley's got a beautiful glass bottle. ☐
   Shelley's got a glass beautiful bottle. ☐
6. That was such a boring old film. ☐
   That was such an old boring film. ☐
7. That's an ugly woolen sweater. ☐
   That's a woolen ugly sweater. ☐
8. Those are black boring shoes. ☐
   Those are boring black shoes. ☐
9. I've got a horrible old car. ☐
   I've got an old horrible car. ☐
10. Simone has a beautiful gray parrot. ☐
    Simone has a gray beautiful parrot. ☐
11. That's an old horrible house! ☐
    That's a horrible old house! ☐
12. You've got a red nice shirt. ☐
    You've got a nice red shirt. ☐

Aa 35.3 ESCRIBE DE NUEVO LAS FRASES PONIENDO LAS PALABRAS EN SU ORDEN CORRECTO

a | It's | green | hat. | lovely

It's a lovely green hat.

1. beautiful | Jill's | got | dog. | a | black

   ____

2. new | nice | has | house. | a | Simon

   ____

3. ugly | have | old | an | car. | They

   ____

4. red | pretty | are | shoes. | Those

   ____

5. pink | an | ugly | hat. | That's

   ____

6. a | has | brown | horrible | snake. | Greg

   ____

7. got | You've | black | a | bag. | beautiful

   ____

8. new | is | great | a | book. | This

   ____

35.4 BUSCA SIETE PALABRAS QUE DESCRIBAN DE QUÉ ESTÁN HECHAS LAS COSAS

S	H	C	G	A	I	R	C	C	A	L	C	W
Q	M	E	T	A	L	K	V	O	Q	E	V	O
A	E	D	E	M	J	S	D	T	K	A	D	O
P	L	A	S	T	I	C	G	T	T	T	I	D
B	T	B	C	X	W	D	L	O	X	H	B	N
E	E	P	A	P	E	R	A	N	A	E	D	R
R	M	Z	W	O	O	L	S	R	O	R	Z	O
K	S	X	A	E	B	R	S	L	S	X	U	X

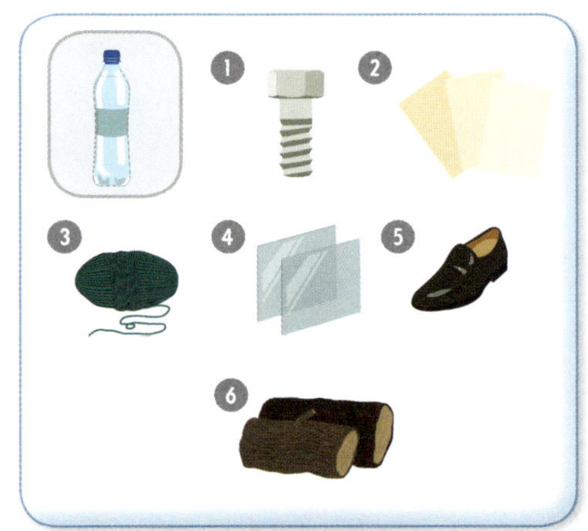

35.5 ESCUCHA EL AUDIO Y RESPONDE A LAS PREGUNTAS

The shoes are...
cotton ☐ **leather** ☑ **plastic** ☐

1. The cups are...
metal ☐ **glass** ☐ **plastic** ☐

2. The table is...
wooden ☐ **plastic** ☐ **metal** ☐

3. The bottle is...
plastic ☐ **glass** ☐ **metal** ☐

4. The jacket is...
wool ☐ **leather** ☐ **plastic** ☐

5. The chairs are...
plastic ☐ **wooden** ☐ **metal** ☐

6. The sweater is...
wool ☐ **leather** ☐ **nylon** ☐

7. The table is...
metal ☐ **glass** ☐ **wooden** ☐

8. The bag is...
leather ☐ **plastic** ☐ **paper** ☐

9. The scarf is...
wool ☐ **leather** ☐ **silk** ☐

10. The bottle is...
glass ☐ **plastic** ☐ **metal** ☐

11. The bag is...
paper ☐ **plastic** ☐ **leather** ☐

12. The lamp is...
metal ☐ **glass** ☐ **wooden** ☐

13. The chairs are...
wooden ☐ **metal** ☐ **plastic** ☐

Aa **35.6** COMPLETA LOS ESPACIOS CON LAS PALABRAS DEL RECUADRO

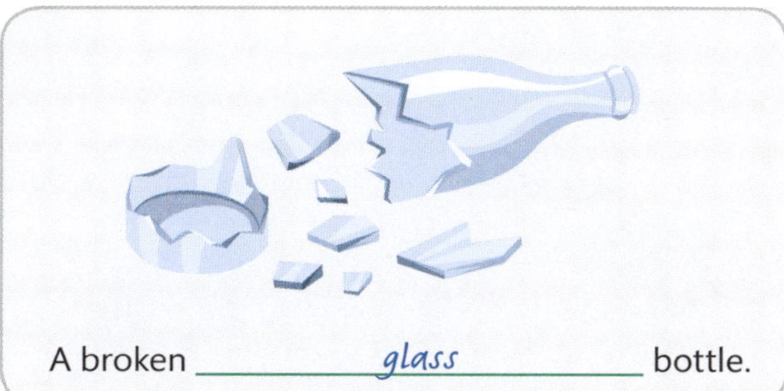

A broken ___glass___ bottle.

4 Three ______________ chairs.

1 Four ______________ cups.

5 A green ______________ sweater.

2 An ugly ______________ table.

6 A brown ______________ bag.

3 An old ______________ jacket.

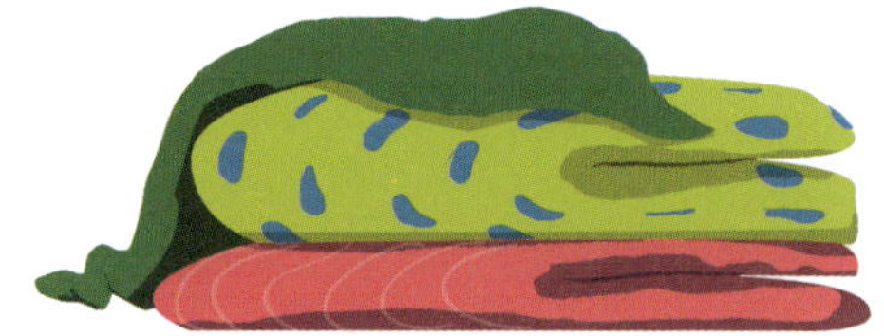

7 Beautiful ______________.

plastic	wooden	~~glass~~	paper	wool	leather	metal	fabric

36 Vocabulario

Aa 36.1 **DEPORTES** ESCRIBE LAS PALABRAS DEL RECUADRO BAJO SUS IMÁGENES

volleyball

1 ______ 2 ______ 3 ______

4 ______ 5 ______ 6 ______ 7 ______

8 ______ 9 ______ 10 ______ 11 ______

12 ______ 13 ______ 14 ______ 15 ______

skateboarding ice hockey baseball roller-skating tennis
cycling rugby snowboarding running skiing ~~volleyball~~
basketball swimming badminton golf horse riding

Aa 36.2 **EQUIPO E INSTALACIONES DEPORTIVAS** ESCRIBE LAS PALABRAS DEL RECUADRO BAJO SUS IMÁGENES

tennis racket

1 ______

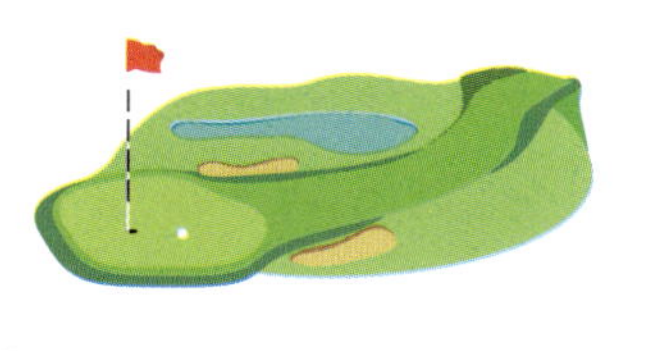
2 ______

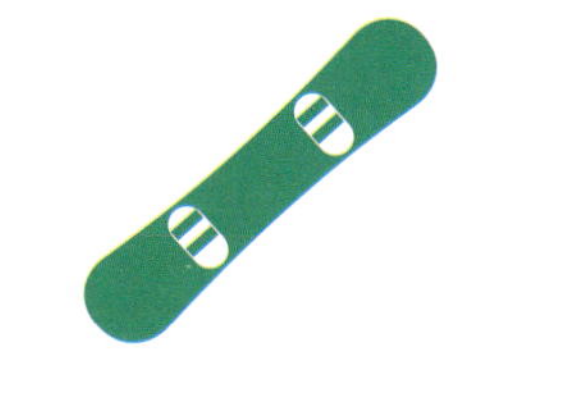
3 ______

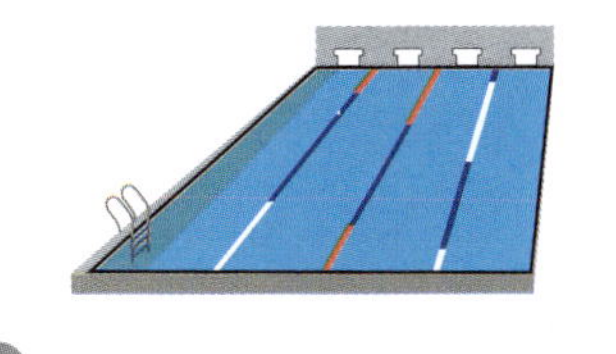
4 ______

5 ______

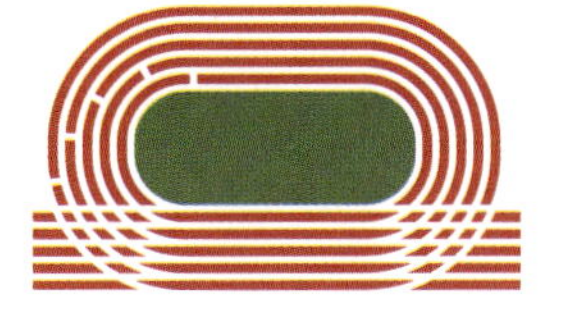
6 ______

7 ______

8 ______

9 ______

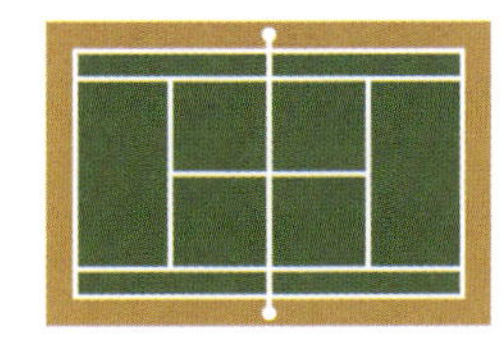
10 ______

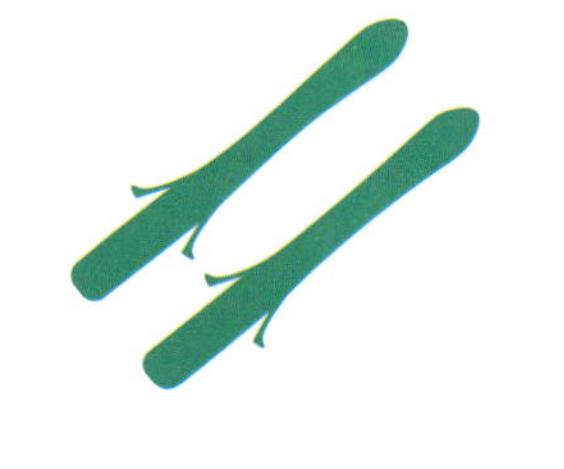
11 ______

surfboard	baseball bat	stadium	snowboard
swimming pool	~~tennis racket~~	tennis court	skateboard
golf club	running track	skis	golf course

37 Hablar sobre deportes

Para describir la práctica de algunos deportes, se utiliza el verbo "go" más el gerundio. Para otros deportes, se utiliza "play" más el sustantivo.

Lenguaje "Go" y "play"
Aa Vocabulario Deportes
Habilidad Hablar sobre deportes

37.1 COMPLETA LOS ESPACIOS PARA TERMINAR LAS FRASES

My friend Kim *goes running* (run) three times a week in the park.

1. Douglas ______________________ (cycle) with his brother on Sundays.
2. Phil and John ______________________ (skate) in the winter.
3. Mr. Henderson ______________________ (sail) in the Mediterranean in the summer.
4. Veronica ______________________ (dance) with her friends on the weekend.
5. They ______________________ (hike) in the mountains in Scotland.
6. Lawrence ______________________ (swim) on Tuesdays.
7. Ted ______________________ (skateboard) on Saturday morning.
8. I ______________________ (ride) in France each year.
9. She ______________________ (shop) in Milan at Christmas.
10. We ______________________ (fish) after work on Mondays.
11. Anne ______________________ (surf) in California.

37.2 TACHA LAS FORMAS MAL CONSTRUIDAS

We go ~~skateing~~ / skating in the park.

1. Jane goes dancing / danceing on Friday nights.
2. Our dad goes sailing / saileing in the summer.
3. I go fisheing / fishing in the evening.
4. Do you go running / runing in the morning?
5. They go cycling / cycleing in the summer.
6. Sam goes swiming / swimming on Sundays.
7. I go horseback riding / horseback ridding daily.
8. Claire goes shopping / shopeing in London.
9. Omar goes skateboarding / skateboardding daily.
10. Do you go dancing / danccing with her?
11. Rachel goes hikking / hiking in Peru.
12. I go snowboarding / snowbording in the winter.
13. Bob and Steve go surphing / surfing in Tahiti.

37.3 ESCRIBE EL GERUNDIO DE CADA VERBO

skate = *skating*

1. snowboard = ____________
2. run = ____________
3. fish = ____________
4. swim = ____________
5. skateboard = ____________
6. dance = ____________
7. surf = ____________
8. shop = ____________
9. cycle = ____________
10. sail = ____________
11. ride = ____________

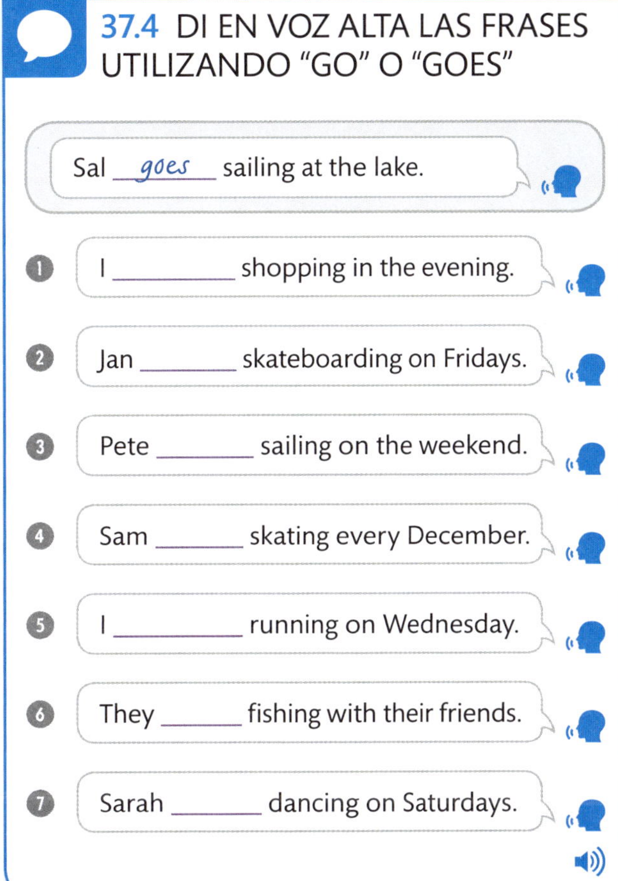

37.4 DI EN VOZ ALTA LAS FRASES UTILIZANDO "GO" O "GOES"

Sal *goes* sailing at the lake.

1. I ________ shopping in the evening.
2. Jan ________ skateboarding on Fridays.
3. Pete ________ sailing on the weekend.
4. Sam ________ skating every December.
5. I ________ running on Wednesday.
6. They ________ fishing with their friends.
7. Sarah ________ dancing on Saturdays.

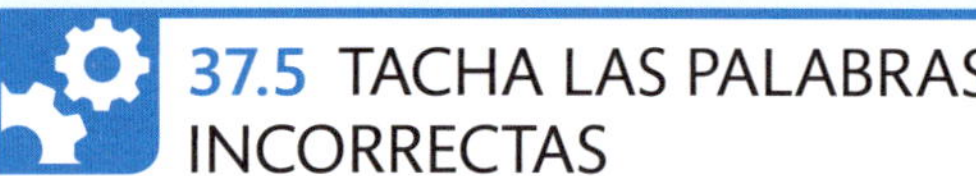

37.5 TACHA LAS PALABRAS INCORRECTAS

He ~~play~~ / plays baseball on Sundays.

1. Do you play / plays chess?
2. Paolo play / plays badminton at the weekend.
3. My father play / plays golf with his friends.
4. We don't play / doesn't play baseball anymore.
5. I play / plays tennis with my brother.
6. Greg don't play / doesn't play basketball.
7. Liz play / plays racquet ball on the weekend.
8. Your dad don't play / doesn't play soccer.
9. Our dog plays / play with its ball.
10. Mike play / plays soccer on Saturdays.
11. We don't play / doesn't play golf in the winter.
12. Pammy don't play / doesn't play tennis.

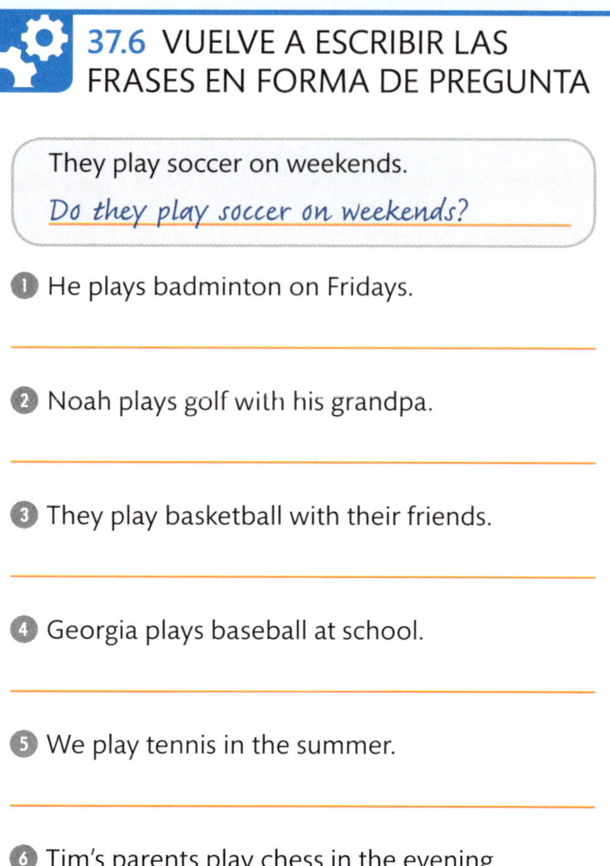

37.6 VUELVE A ESCRIBIR LAS FRASES EN FORMA DE PREGUNTA

They play soccer on weekends.
Do they play soccer on weekends?

1. He plays badminton on Fridays.

____

2. Noah plays golf with his grandpa.

____

3. They play basketball with their friends.

____

4. Georgia plays baseball at school.

____

5. We play tennis in the summer.

____

6. Tim's parents play chess in the evening.

____

37.7 ESCUCHA EL AUDIO Y RESPONDE A LAS PREGUNTAS

Mark doesn't play golf during the week.
True ☑ **False** ☐

1. Steven goes cycling in the winter.
True ☐ **False** ☐
2. Max goes running every evening.
True ☐ **False** ☐
3. Ian plays soccer four times a week.
True ☐ **False** ☐
4. Janine hates running.
True ☐ **False** ☐
5. Lila goes skating with her sister.
True ☐ **False** ☐
6. Robbie doesn't go running anymore.
True ☐ **False** ☐
7. Susan goes fishing on the weekend.
True ☐ **False** ☐

37.8 COMPLETA LOS ESPACIOS CON "GO", "GOES", "PLAY" O "PLAYS" PARA TERMINAR LAS FRASES

They ___go___ running every week.

1. John ________ badminton on Wednesday.
2. You ________ fishing with your brother.
3. My uncle ________ chess with my aunt.
4. We ________ dancing in the evening.
5. Sally's dad ________ rugby.
6. Bartou ________ cycling in the mountains.
7. Ramona ________ racquet ball with her dad.
8. Our kids ________ baseball after school.
9. Simon and Pam ________ surfing in the summer.
10. They ________ basketball every Saturday.
11. We ________ snowboarding in Austria.

37.9 OBSERVA LAS IMÁGENES Y DI LAS FRASES EN VOZ ALTA, COMPLETANDO LOS ESPACIOS

I ___play tennis___ () on Mondays, Tuesdays, and Thursdays.

1. I ________ ( ) with my friends at school.
2. Anna ________ ( ) in the afternoon on Sundays.
3. Mrs. Amir ________ ( ) with her husband in the evening.
4. Max ________ ( ) on Tuesdays and Fridays.
5. Peter ________ ( ) with his brother on Mondays and Wednesdays.

38 Vocabulario

Aa 38.1 **AFICIONES Y PASATIEMPOS** ESCRIBE LAS PALABRAS DEL RECUADRO DEBAJO DE SU IMAGEN

cook

1 ______

2 ______

3 ______

4 ______

7 ______

8 ______

9 ______

10 ______

11 ______

14 ______

15 ______

16 ______

17 ______

18 ______

21 ______

22 ______

23 ______

24 ______

25 ______

5 ______ 6 ______

12 ______ 13 ______

19 ______ 20 ______

26 ______ 27 ______

play cards paint sew

go camping write take photos

go out for a meal visit a museum

~~cook~~ watch television play chess

go shopping read do yoga

watch a movie play a musical instrument

go to the gym bake see a play

play video games walk / hike

meet friends do the gardening

draw go bird watching knit

do puzzles listen to music

39 Tiempo libre

Los adverbios de frecuencia muestran la frecuencia con que se hace algo, desde lo que se hace muy a menudo ("always") hasta lo que no se hace nunca ("never").

Lenguaje Adverbios de frecuencia
Vocabulario Pasatiempos
Habilidad Hablar sobre el tiempo libre

39.1 LEE EL CORREO Y RESPONDE A LAS PREGUNTAS

Angela wakes up at 6am.	True ☐	False ☑
1 Angela sometimes has toast for breakfast.	True ☐	False ☐
2 She always gets the bus.	True ☐	False ☐
3 She starts work at 9am.	True ☐	False ☐
4 Angela always has coffee at 11am.	True ☐	False ☐
5 She usually has lunch at 1pm.	True ☐	False ☐
6 She always finishes work at 5pm.	True ☐	False ☐
7 She always goes to bed before 11pm.	True ☐	False ☐

To: Claude
Subject: My day

Hi Claude,
Let me tell you about my typical day. Well, I wake up at about 7am. I sometimes have some toast for breakfast. I often walk to work, but sometimes I get the bus. I start work at 9:30am. I work in an office with eight other people. We sometimes have coffee at 11am and I usually have lunch at 1pm. I often work until 7pm. After that I get the bus home. I always go to bed before 11pm.
Angela

39.2 ESCRIBE DE NUEVO LAS FRASES PONIENDO LAS PALABRAS EN SU ORDEN CORRECTO

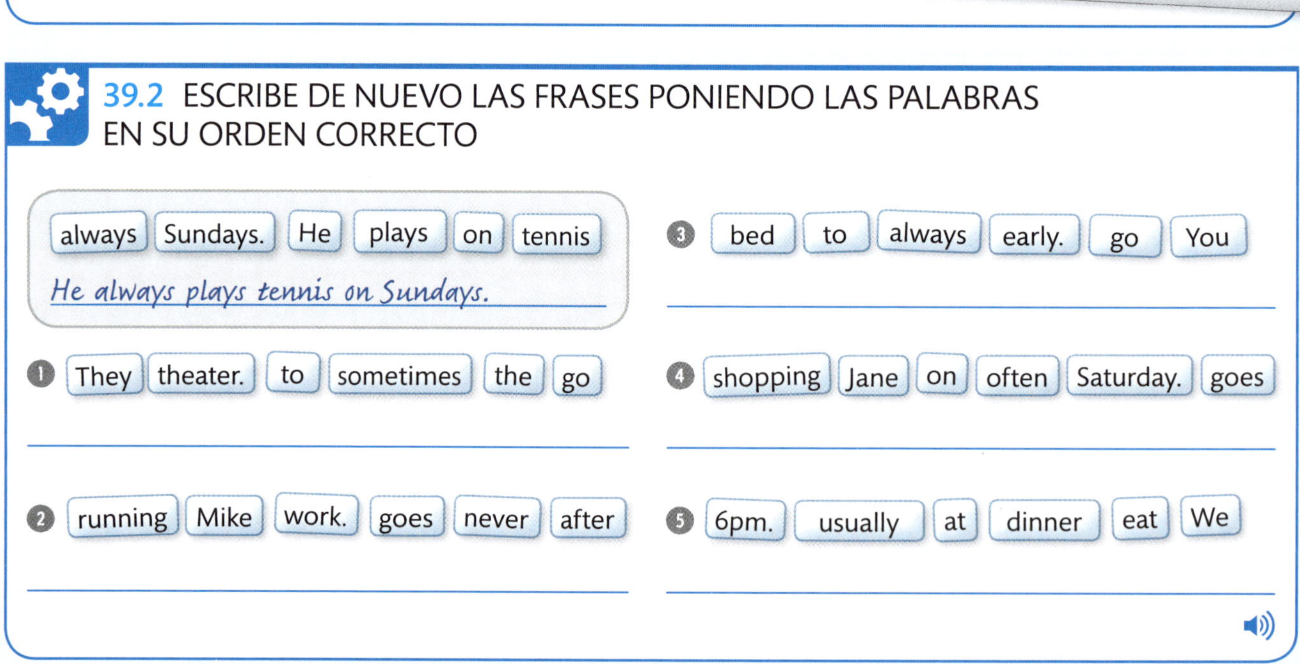

always | Sundays. | He | plays | on | tennis

He always plays tennis on Sundays.

1 They | theater. | to | sometimes | the | go

____

2 running | Mike | work. | goes | never | after

____

3 bed | to | always | early. | go | You

____

4 shopping | Jane | on | often | Saturday. | goes

____

5 6pm. | usually | at | dinner | eat | We

____

39.3 ESCUCHA EL AUDIO Y RESPONDE A LAS PREGUNTAS

How often does John go running?

- always ☐
- usually ☑
- sometimes ☐

1. How often does Chris get up early?
   - never ☐
   - sometimes ☐
   - often ☐

2. How often does Shelley go swimming?
   - never ☐
   - sometimes ☐
   - usually ☐

3. How often does Flo have tea in the morning?
   - sometimes ☐
   - often ☐
   - always ☐

4. How often does Sylvester go to bed at 10pm?
   - often ☐
   - usually ☐
   - always ☐

5. How often does Dominic play soccer?
   - never ☐
   - usually ☐
   - always ☐

6. How often does David read a newspaper?
   - sometimes ☐
   - often ☐
   - always ☐

39.4 DI LAS FRASES EN VOZ ALTA UTILIZANDO LOS ADVERBIOS

I get up early. [rarely]

I rarely get up early.

1. Clara plays chess with her grandfather. [never]
2. Enzo eats chocolate ice cream. [always]
3. Paul goes fishing in the morning. [sometimes]
4. My parents drive to work. [usually]
5. Gill goes shopping with her mom. [never]
6. You go to the gym in the town. [sometimes]
7. Shelley watches TV in the evening. [usually]
8. My dog sleeps under the table. [always]
9. We play baseball in the summer. [sometimes]
10. Tim rides his horse on the weekend. [usually]

39.5 ESCRIBE DE NUEVO LAS FRASES PONIENDO LAS PALABRAS EN SU ORDEN CORRECTO

finish | does | When | work? | Claudia

When does Claudia finish work?

1 Steph | does | TV? | watch | often | How

______

2 visit | your | dad? | often | you | do | How

______

3 play | do | soccer? | they | When

______

4 you | to | When | do | go | usually | bed?

______

5 May | often | How | does | running? | go

______

6 play | do | How | you | tennis? | often

______

7 does | Jo | How | read | a | book? | often

______

39.6 ESCRIBE RESPUESTAS A LAS PREGUNTAS COMPLETANDO LOS ESPACIOS

When does he go running?

He goes running on Sundays.

1 When does Kelly go to the gym?

______ on Wednesdays.

2 When does Pete play soccer?

______ in the evening.

3 How often does Angie go to the theater?

She never ______ .

4 How often does Jake read a newspaper?

He sometimes ______ .

5 How often does she visit her family?

______ four times a year.

6 When does Ben play baseball?

______ every afternoon.

7 How often does Marion go shopping?

______ twice a week.

8 When do you read a book?

______ every evening.

9 How often does Pam make a cake?

She sometimes ______ .

39.7 REESCRIBE LAS AFIRMACIONES COMO PREGUNTAS UTILIZANDO "HOW OFTEN"

She goes dancing every Friday.
How often does she go dancing?

1 Jimmy plays soccer once a week.

2 I phone my grandma twice a day.

3 Sheila gets up at 7am every day.

4 I read a book every evening in bed.

5 Sally goes to work every day.

6 I play badminton once a week.

7 My daughter goes running every evening.

8 Megan goes fishing twice a month.

9 I watch TV every evening.

39.8 DI LAS FRASES EN VOZ ALTA, COMPLETANDO LOS ESPACIOS CON LAS EXPRESIONES DEL RECUADRO

Helen sometimes *goes* to the gym.

1 She always ______ dancing on the weekend.

2 I often ______ fishing.

3 My mom never ______ early.

4 Seb usually ______ soccer on weekends.

5 Tracy never ______ TV in the evening.

6 We sometimes ______ the bus to work.

7 Doug often ______ tennis on Fridays.

plays · take · go · gets up · goes · watches · plays · ~~goes~~

40 Qué nos gusta y qué no

Verbos como "love", "like" y "hate" expresan tus sentimientos hacia algo. Puedes utilizarlos con sustantivos o gerundios.

Lenguaje "Love", "like" y "hate"
Vocabulario Comida, deportes y pasatiempos
Habilidad Hablar sobre tus gustos

40.1 CONECTA LAS IMÁGENES CON LAS FRASES CORRECTAS

We love basketball.

Bill doesn't like cats.

1

We like cake.

2

I hate tennis.

3

Samantha likes chocolate.

4

I don't like pasta.

5

They hate board games.

6

Shelley loves pizza.

7

40.2 ESCUCHA EL AUDIO Y ELIGE LA OPCIÓN CORRECTA

What does Doug like?
fruits ☐ **fast food** ☑

1. What does Doug hate?
salad ☐ **fries** ☐

2. What does Shelley love?
sports ☐ **painting** ☐

3. What does she like doing on the weekend?
playing tennis ☐ **reading books** ☐

4. What does she not like?
tennis ☐ **golf** ☐

5. What does Doug love doing?
watching TV ☐ **listening to music** ☐

6. What music does Doug like?
pop music ☐ **classical music** ☐

7. What does he dislike doing?
going shopping ☐ **reading newspapers** ☐

8. What does Shelley like doing in her free time?
cooking ☐ **going to the cinema** ☐

9. What does Shelley dislike?
cooking ☐ **scary films** ☐

10. What does she like doing?
taking photos ☐ **visiting museums** ☐

40.3 ESCRIBE LO OPUESTO DE CADA AFIRMACIÓN

	Jack likes London.	*Jack doesn't like London.*
1	Chris likes spiders.	
2	They love Paris.	
3	Mrs. McGregor likes cats.	
4	We love soccer.	
5	We like wine.	
6	Simone loves her horse.	
7	He likes your necklace.	
8	Jean-Marie loves sports.	
9	Colin likes pizza.	
10	Douglas likes Anne.	
11	Cynthia hates dogs.	
12	We love chocolate.	
13	You like cheese.	
14	Susan likes pizza.	

40.4 UTILIZA EL DIAGRAMA PARA CREAR 12 FRASES CORRECTAS Y DILAS EN VOZ ALTA

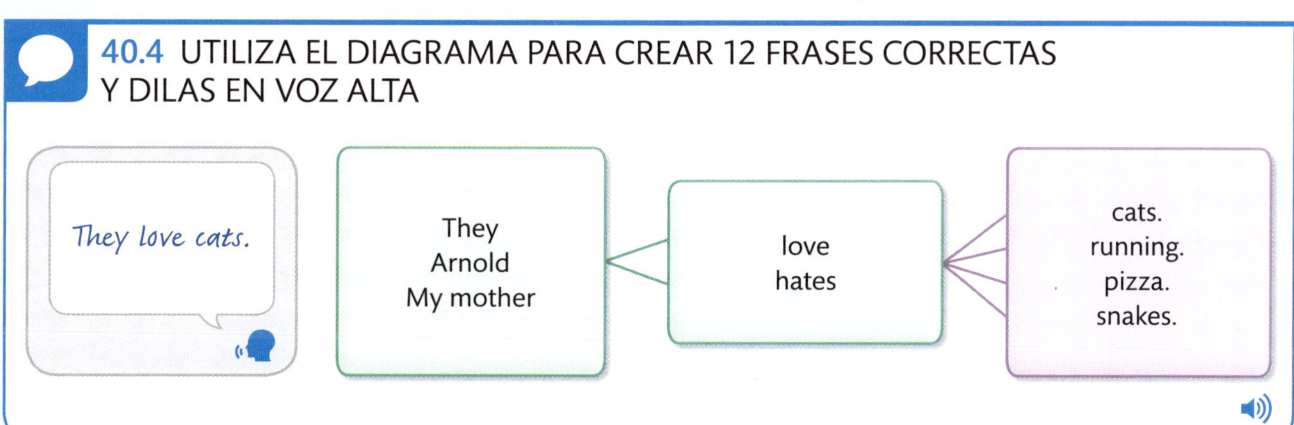

40.5 LEE EL BLOG Y RESPONDE A LAS PREGUNTAS CON FRASES COMPLETAS

What is Jane's job?
She's a doctor.

1. What does she like doing in her free time?
2. What is her favorite food?
3. What does Jane not like cooking?
4. What does she do on the weekend?
5. What food does she not like?
6. What does Jane hate?

POSTED WEDNESDAY, MARCH 23

Jane's world

I'm Jane Petersen and I write this blog. So, what about me? Well, I'm 29 years old and come from New York. I'm a doctor, but I love cooking in my free time...

My grandmother is from Italy, so I like cooking Italian food. It's my favorite. I'm a vegetarian, so I don't like cooking meat. But I love cooking fish. On weekends I love cooking for my friends and family. What else? In my free time I like jogging, and going to the gym with my friends. What do I not like? Well, I don't like fast food. Oh, and I hate candy!

I hope you enjoy my blog!

40.6 COMPLETA LOS ESPACIOS CON LA FORMA CORRECTA DE LA PALABRA ENTRE PARÉNTESIS

Claire *does not like* **(not like)** swimming, but she *loves* **(love)** playing tennis.

1. I ______ **(hate)** cities, but I ______ **(love)** the country.
2. Archie ______ **(like)** ice cream, and he ______ **(love)** pizza.
3. He ______ **(love)** meat, but he ______ **(hate)** fish.
4. Francis ______ **(not like)** coffee, but he ______ **(like)** tea.
5. We ______ **(hate)** Mondays, but we ______ **(love)** Fridays.
6. My dad ______ **(dislike)** classical music, but he ______ **(love)** rock.

40.7 CONECTA EL INICIO CON EL FINAL DE LAS FRASES

I hate cheese. → I think it's disgusting.

1. Sam likes watching soccer
2. Marie loves pizza.
3. I love reading history books
4. Sally doesn't like running
5. Peggy does not like eating meat
6. Paolo does not eat chocolate
7. Jemma hates snakes.

- She thinks it's delicious.
- because she is a vegetarian.
- because it is tiring.
- I think it's disgusting.
- because he doesn't have a sweet tooth.
- because they're really interesting.
- She thinks they are scary.
- because it's exciting.

40.8 LEE EL CORREO Y RESPONDE A LAS PREGUNTAS

The cafés and bars by the sea are...
boring ☐ **exciting** ☑ **interesting.** ☐

1. The weather in Sardinia is...
hot ☐ **cold** ☐ **rainy.** ☐

2. The museum in the town is really...
exciting ☐ **interesting** ☐ **tiring.** ☐

3. Si loves pizza because it is...
disgusting ☐ **tiring** ☐ **delicious.** ☐

4. Samantha hates pasta because it is...
interesting ☐ **boring** ☐ **delicious.** ☐

5. Si doesn't like walking because it's...
exciting ☐ **tiring** ☐ **boring.** ☐

To: Charles

Subject: Italy trip

Hi Charles,

We're in Sardinia on holiday. It's very hot here. There are some great cafés and bars by the ocean. They're really exciting in the evening. There's also an interesting museum in the town. I like it a lot, and there are lots of exhibits.

The food here is amazing. I love the pizza here. It's delicious. Samantha hates the pasta, though. She thinks it's really boring!

In the afternoons we go walking. Samantha loves it, but I don't! I really hate it because it's so tiring.

Hope you're all well,

Si

41 Vocabulario

Aa 41.1 **MÚSICA** ESCRIBE LAS PALABRAS DEL RECUADRO BAJO SUS IMÁGENES

band

1 ______

2 ______

3 ______

7 ______

8 ______

9 ______

10 ______

14 ______

15 ______

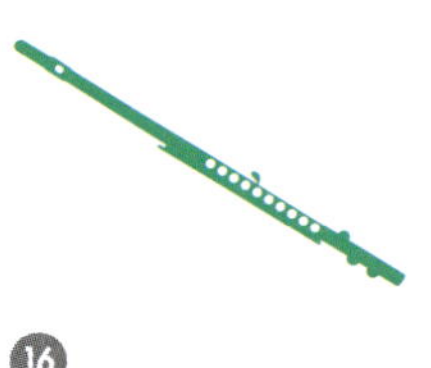
16 ______

17 ______

21 ______

22 ______

23 ______

24 ______

4 ______

5 ______

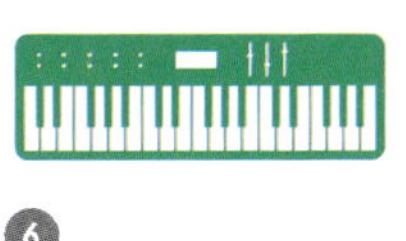

6 ______

11 ______

12 ______

13 ______

18 ______

19 ______

20 ______

25 ______

26 ______

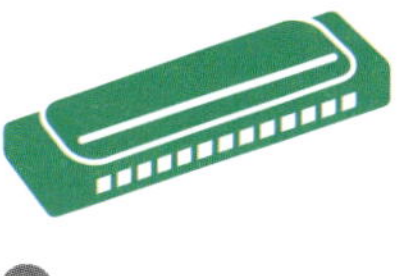

27 ______

guitar player		orchestra
headphones		Latin
flute		sing a song
~~band~~	rap	drum
rock	saxophone	trumpet
play the trumpet		violin
dance		piano
concert		microphone
conductor		keyboard
harmonica		jazz
audience		country
album		electric guitar
opera		guitar

42 Expresar preferencias

Utiliza "like" y "love" para indicar cuánto te diviertes con algo. "Favorite" se utiliza para identificar las cosas que más te gustan.

Lenguaje Utilizar "favorite"
Aa Vocabulario Comida y música
Habilidad Hablar sobre tus cosas favoritas

42.1 MARCA LA FRASE QUE CORRESPONDE A CADA DIBUJO

Ellie's favorite color is purple. ☑
Ellie's favorite color is green. ☐

1 Nick's favorite uncle is an actor. ☐
Nick's favorite uncle is a painter. ☐

2 Jo's favorite movie is *Puzzling People*. ☐
Jo's favorite book is *Puzzling People*. ☐

3 Jay's favorite instrument is the piano. ☐
Jay's favorite instrument is the violin. ☐

4 Paul's favorite drink is orange juice. ☐
Paul's favorite drink is milk. ☐

5 Blake's favorite animal is the tiger. ☐
Blake's favorite animal is the snake. ☐

6 Dan's favorite place is the beach. ☐
Dan's favorite place is his garden. ☐

7 Sanjay's favorite season is winter. ☐
Sanjay's favorite season is spring. ☐

8 Max's favorite hobby is painting. ☐
Max's favorite hobby is reading. ☐

9 Greg's favorite food is rice. ☐
Greg's favorite food is cake. ☐

10 Levi's favorite sport is soccer. ☐
Levi's favorite sport is baseball. ☐

11 Martha's favorite country is France. ☐
Martha's favorite country is India. ☐

12 Simone's favorite lesson is English. ☐
Simone's favorite lesson is science. ☐

13 Maya's favorite dessert is ice cream. ☐
Maya's favorite dessert is cake. ☐

14 Karina's favorite fruit is pineapple. ☐
Karina's favorite fruit is grapes. ☐

15 Their favorite city is London. ☐
Their favorite city is New York. ☐

16 Kate's favorite pet is her parrot. ☐
Kate's favorite pet is her kitten. ☐

17 Zoe's favorite pastime is singing. ☐
Zoe's favorite pastime is dancing. ☐

42.2 ESCUCHA EL AUDIO Y COMPLETA LAS FRASES

Un grupo de personas hablan sobre sus cosas favoritas.

Dave's favorite type of music in the morning is...	**soul**	☑	**jazz**	☐	**rock.**	☐
1 Jenny's favorite subject at school is...	**physics**	☐	**math**	☐	**biology.**	☐
2 Mike's favorite day of the week is...	**Monday**	☐	**Wednesday**	☐	**Friday.**	☐
3 Colin's favorite color is...	**red**	☐	**yellow**	☐	**purple.**	☐
4 Sally's favorite dessert is...	**ice cream**	☐	**chocolate cake**	☐	**apple pie.**	☐
5 Danny's favorite sport is...	**soccer**	☐	**basketball**	☐	**baseball.**	☐
6 Clarice's favorite season is...	**summer**	☐	**fall**	☐	**winter.**	☐

42.3 ESCRIBE DE NUEVO LAS FRASES CORRIGIENDO LOS ERRORES

Her love type of music is rock.
Her favorite type of music is rock.

1 Barbara likes listen to music in the evening.

2 Arnold favorite food is ice cream and pizza.

3 Craig don't like getting up in the morning.

4 Seb's favorite type music is hip-hop.

5 Ruth like orange juice.

6 Daniel favorite animal is the lion.

7 I likes bacon and eggs for breakfast.

8 Aziz don't like lasagna or spaghetti.

9 Miguel love going to the movie theater.

42.4 LEE EL CORREO Y RESPONDE A LAS PREGUNTAS

To: Ben

Subject: My town

Hi Ben,

Netherton is small, very small. Only 800 people live here, but there's lots to do. In the morning, a lot of people take their dogs for a walk. Some people like to go to the park, but the favorite place is by the river. It's beautiful.

Drinking coffee is popular here. Some people go to Dino's café, and there's a café in the supermarket. But the favorite place is Alfredo's. It's always very busy in the morning.

Dino's café is very popular at lunchtime, though, because they serve delicious pizzas there. It's the favorite place for lunch. There's a French restaurant called Chez Jean-Claude, but it's very expensive.

There's a swimming pool and a tennis court. The tennis court is the favorite place for young people to go in the summer. In the winter everyone likes to go to the swimming pool.

In the evening, there isn't much to do. There is one bar and a nightclub, but people don't like to go there. A lot of people go to the nearest city of Silchester on weekends. There are lots of nightclubs there.

Norah

Netherton is a small town. True ☑ False ☐

1. A lot of people walk their dogs in Netherton. True ☐ False ☐
2. The park is people's favorite place to walk their dogs. True ☐ False ☐
3. Alfredo's is always empty in the mornings. True ☐ False ☐
4. Dino's café is people's favorite place to drink coffee. True ☐ False ☐
5. Dino's is the favorite place to eat lunch. True ☐ False ☐
6. Chez Jean-Claude is a cheap restaurant. True ☐ False ☐
7. People go to the tennis court in the winter. True ☐ False ☐
8. The bar and disco are not very popular. True ☐ False ☐
9. People go to the city on weekends. True ☐ False ☐
10. There are lots of nightclubs in Silchester. True ☐ False ☐

42.5 COMPLETA LOS ESPACIOS CON LAS PALABRAS DEL RECUADRO

Liz's favorite fruit is an *apple*.

1  Arnie's favorite sport is ______________________.

2  Joan's favorite animal is a ______________________.

3  Hassan's favorite actor is ______________________.

4  Pam's favorite number is ______________________.

5  Jane's favorite sport is ______________________.

6  Dora's favorite ice cream is ______________________.

7  Jim's favorite food is ______________________.

spaghetti
Chris Minota
tennis
~~apple~~
strawberry
dolphin
21
badminton

42.6 UTILIZA EL DIAGRAMA PARA CREAR 14 FRASES CORRECTAS Y DILAS EN VOZ ALTA

She Simon Her	loves likes favorite	food is sport is	salsa dancing. sailing. chocolate ice cream.

43 Vocabulario

Aa 43.1 **HABILIDADES** ESCRIBE LAS PALABRAS DEL RECUADRO DEBAJO DE SU IMAGEN

1 ______

2 ______

3 ______

7 ______

8 ______

9 ______

10 ______

14 ______

15 ______

16 ______

17 ______

21 ______

22 ______

23 ______

24 ______

4 ______

5 ______

6 ______

11 ______

12 ______

13 ______

18 ______

19 ______

20 ______

25 ______

26 ______

27 ______

act	lift
drive	catch
work	jump
~~whisper~~	listen
sit	understand
subtract	fly
kick	climb
shout	spell
make (a snowman)	
add	throw
move	hit
carry	see
stand up	walk
talk	ride
do (homework)	

44 Qué sabes hacer y qué no

Utiliza "can" para hablar de las cosas que sabes hacer, como por ejemplo ir en bicicleta o tocar la guitarra. Utiliza "cannot" o "can't" para cosas que no sabes hacer.

Lenguaje "Can", "can't" y "cannot"
Vocabulario Talentos y habilidades
Habilidad Expresar qué sabes hacer y qué no

44.1 COMPLETA LOS ESPACIOS Y ESCRIBE CADA FRASE DE TRES MANERAS DISTINTAS

	I can read Russian.	*I cannot read Russian.*	*I can't read Russian.*
1		I cannot ride a horse.	
2	I can climb a tree.		
3			I can't speak French.
4		I cannot sing.	
5			I can't lift a box.
6		I cannot fly a kite.	
7	I can catch a fish.		
8		I cannot swim.	

44.2 ESCRIBE DE NUEVO LAS FRASES CORRIGIENDO LOS ERRORES

Ben **can't to cook** paella.
Ben can't cook paella.

1. Kate **can hitting** the ball.
2. Paul **can't to do** math.
3. Helen **can to spell** very well.
4. Ivan **can't running** very fast.
5. Sara **can to move** the chair.
6. Alex **can't to play** badminton.
7. Lynn **can riding** a bicycle.

44.3 ESCRIBE DE NUEVO LAS FRASES PONIENDO LAS PALABRAS EN SU ORDEN CORRECTO

that | chair. | can | Sylvia | carry

Sylvia can carry that chair.

1. drive | car. | Eliza | cannot | a
2. piano. | Jonathan | play | can | the
3. jump | very | can't | high. | Cathy
4. stick. | can | a | Mick | throw
5. math. | can't | Laura | do
6. lift | can | the | Alan | box.
7. far. | very | can't | Julia | swim

44.4 ESCUCHA EL AUDIO Y MARCA SI INA SABE O NO SABE HACER LA ACTIVIDAD DE CADA UNA DE LAS IMÁGENES

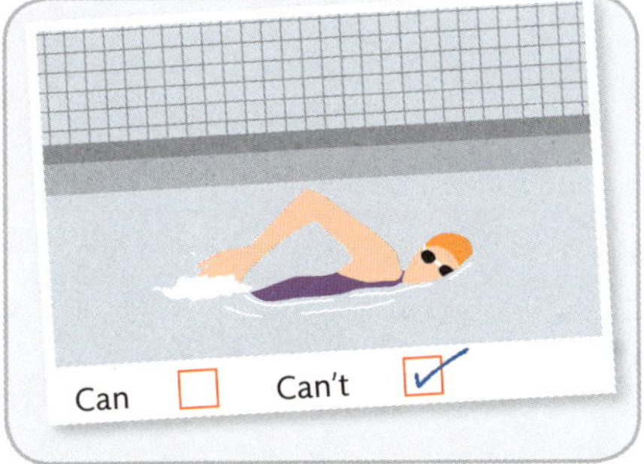

44.5 REESCRIBE LAS AFIRMACIONES EN FORMA DE PREGUNTAS

Paul and Mary can speak Russian.
Can Paul and Mary speak Russian?

1. Maria and Juan can spell English words.
   ______
2. The children can't do their math homework.
   ______
3. I can't sing difficult jazz songs.
   ______
4. Mark can't ride a horse.
   ______
5. Jack can climb a tree.
   ______
6. He can't carry that box. It's too heavy.
   ______
7. Carlos can kick a football.
   ______
8. Adam and Ella can dance the tango.
   ______
9. Peter and John can't swim.
   ______

44.6 COMPLETA LOS ESPACIOS CON LAS PALABRAS DEL RECUADRO

Janet is a chef at a five star restaurant. She can *cook very well*.

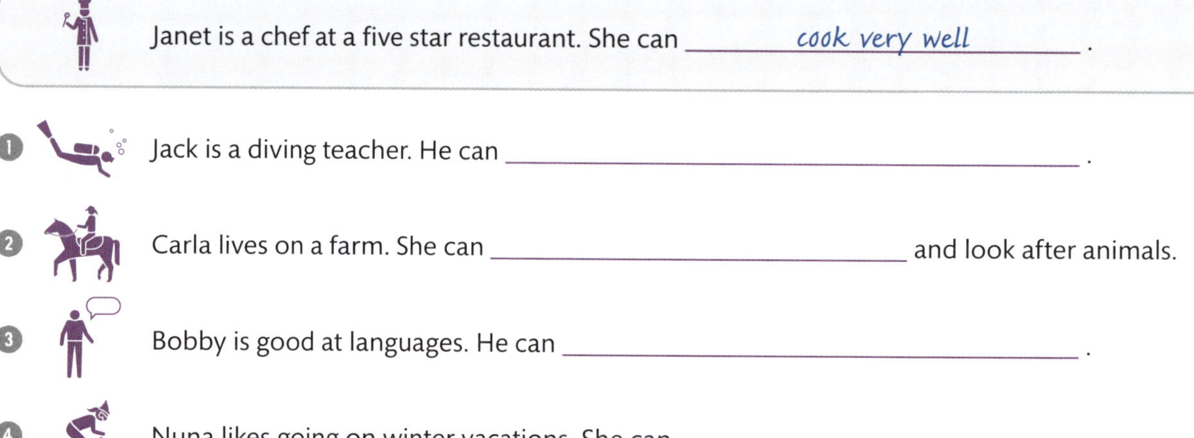

1. Jack is a diving teacher. He can ______.
2. Carla lives on a farm. She can ______ and look after animals.
3. Bobby is good at languages. He can ______.
4. Nuna likes going on winter vacations. She can ______.
5. Jim is a great children's teacher. He can ______ well.

speak Russian | ~~cook very well~~ | ski well | tell stories | swim very well | ride a horse

44.7 RESPONDE AL AUDIO EN VOZ ALTA COMPLETANDO LOS ESPACIOS

Can you lift a heavy box?
Yes, *I can.*

1. Can you jump over the wall?
Yes, ______________________

2. Can you catch that big fish?
No, ______________________

3. Can you throw a stick for the dog?
Yes, ______________________

4. Can you speak Italian?
No, ______________________

5. Can you play the violin?
No, ______________________

6. Can you climb that tree?
Yes, ______________________

7. Can you do Sudoku puzzles?
No, ______________________

8. Can you sing?
No, ______________________

9. Can you ride a bicycle?
No, ______________________

10. Can you move the kitchen table?
Yes, ______________________

11. Can you cook roast chicken?
Yes, ______________________

44.8 UTILIZA EL DIAGRAMA PARA CREAR 18 FRASES CORRECTAS Y DILAS EN VOZ ALTA

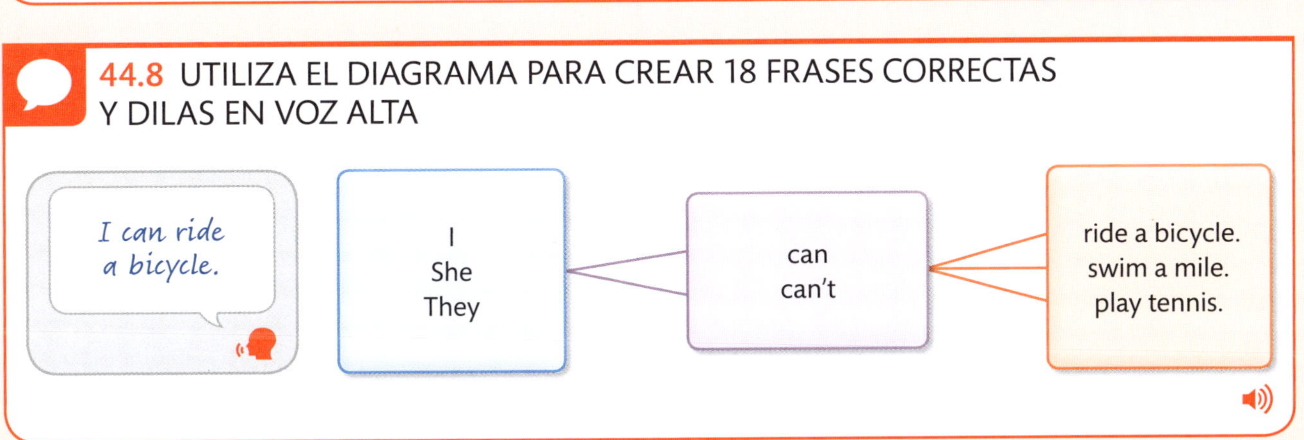

45 Describir acciones

Las palabras como "quietly" y "loudly" se llaman adverbios. Proporcionan más información sobre los verbos. Se utilizan para describir cómo se hace algo.

Lenguaje Adverbios regulares e irregulares
Aa Vocabulario Aficiones y actividades
Habilidad Describir actividades

45.1 COMPLETA LOS ESPACIOS CON LAS PALABRAS DEL RECUADRO

Sanjay plays the guitar *badly*.

1. My friend speaks too ______.
2. A turtle walks very ______.
3. Alan can speak German ______.
4. My dog can run very ______.
5. I get up very ______.

early | well | quietly | slowly | fast | ~~badly~~

45.2 VUELVE A ESCRIBIR LAS FRASES EN SU OTRA FORMA

	Sally speaks Japanese well.	*Sally's good at speaking Japanese.*
1	Patrick dances well.	
2		Caitlin is good at baking.
3	My mother writes well.	
4		Ethan is good at playing the guitar.
5	Aimee skis well.	
6		They are good at swimming.
7	We speak English well.	
8		Lara is good at climbing trees.

45.3 ESCRIBE DE NUEVO LAS FRASES CORRIGIENDO LOS ERRORES

My sister dances very **good**.
My sister dances very well.

1. Haruda sometimes arrives **lately** for school.
2. My cousin Paul runs **quick**.
3. Shelley sings **beautiful**.
4. Our neighbors talk so **noisy** at night.
5. Rosa reads very **slow**.
6. I can pass this exam **easy**.
7. My aunt drives very **careful**.
8. Anita works very **hardly**.
9. We **usual** go to bed at 11pm.
10. Angela speaks English **bad**.
11. A cheetah runs very **fastly**.
12. Sarah eats her food very **quick**.
13. Andrew does his homework **good**.

45.4 UTILIZA EL DIAGRAMA PARA CREAR 18 FRASES CORRECTAS Y DILAS EN VOZ ALTA

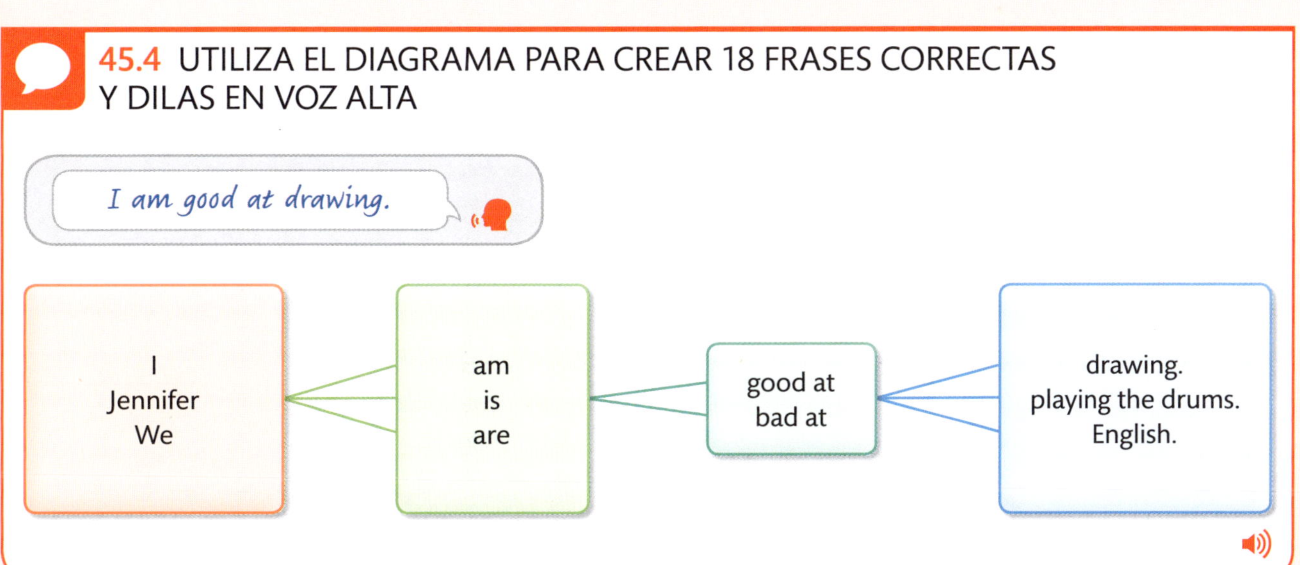

46 Describir habilidades

Palabras como "quite" y "very" son adverbios modificadores. Puedes utilizarlos antes de otros adverbios para dar más información sobre cómo haces algo.

Lenguaje Adverbios modificadores
Aa Vocabulario Aptitudes y habilidades
Habilidad Decir lo bien que haces algo

46.1 MARCA LAS FRASES QUE SON CORRECTAS

Your cousin at skiing is very good. ☐
Your cousin is very good at skiing. ☑

1. Pedro is really good at history. ☐
   Pedro really good is at history. ☐

2. You speak really well French. ☐
   You speak French really well. ☐

3. Sandra is very good at singing. ☐
   Sandra very good is at singing. ☐

4. Sal is at skiing quite good. ☐
   Sal is quite good at skiing. ☐

5. Very well your uncle can swim. ☐
   Your uncle can swim very well. ☐

6. They quite fast can run. ☐
   They can run quite fast. ☐

7. Mr. Henderson is really good at golf. ☐
   At golf Mr. Henderson is really good. ☐

46.2 ESCRIBE DE NUEVO LAS FRASES PONIENDO LAS PALABRAS EN SU ORDEN CORRECTO

quite | soccer. | good at | is | playing | Tim

Tim is quite good at playing soccer.

1. isn't | at | very | art and design. | good | Arnold

____

2. is | English. | speaking | really | cousin | good | at | My

____

3. is | at | climbing | Jean | quite | mountains. | good

____

46.3 COMPLETA LOS ESPACIOS PARA ESCRIBIR LAS FRASES UTILIZANDO "WELL" O "GOOD AT"

	Sam and Pauline are very good at singing.	*Sam and Pauline sing very well.*
1		My aunt speaks Polish quite well.
2	Your brother is really good at surfing.	
3	Katie is very good at painting.	
4		Silvia sings really well.
5		Martina dances very well.
6	Serge is quite good at cooking.	
7		Sonia plays chess really well.
8	Ricky is very good at running.	
9		Peter draws quite well.
10	My mom is really good at speaking Greek.	
11		David plays the drums very well.

46.4 DI LAS FRASES EN VOZ ALTA, PONIENDO LOS ADVERBIOS MODIFICADORES EN EL LUGAR CORRECTO

My brother can run fast. [very]

My brother can run very fast.

1. Charlotte can ski well. [quite]
2. Harry sings quietly. [really]
3. My aunt walks slowly. [very]
4. Elizabeth speaks Russian well. [very]
5. My dog can jump high. [quite]
6. William speaks Japanese badly. [really]
7. Philip eats noisily. [quite]

47 Deseos y ambiciones

Puedes utilizar "I want" y "I would like" para hablar de lo que quieres hacer. También puedes usar la forma negativa de estas frases para indicar lo que no te gustaría hacer.

Lenguaje "Would" y "want"
Aa Vocabulario Actividades de ocio
Habilidad Hablar de tus ambiciones

47.1 COMPLETA LOS ESPACIOS ESCRIBIENDO CADA FRASE DE TRES MANERAS DISTINTAS

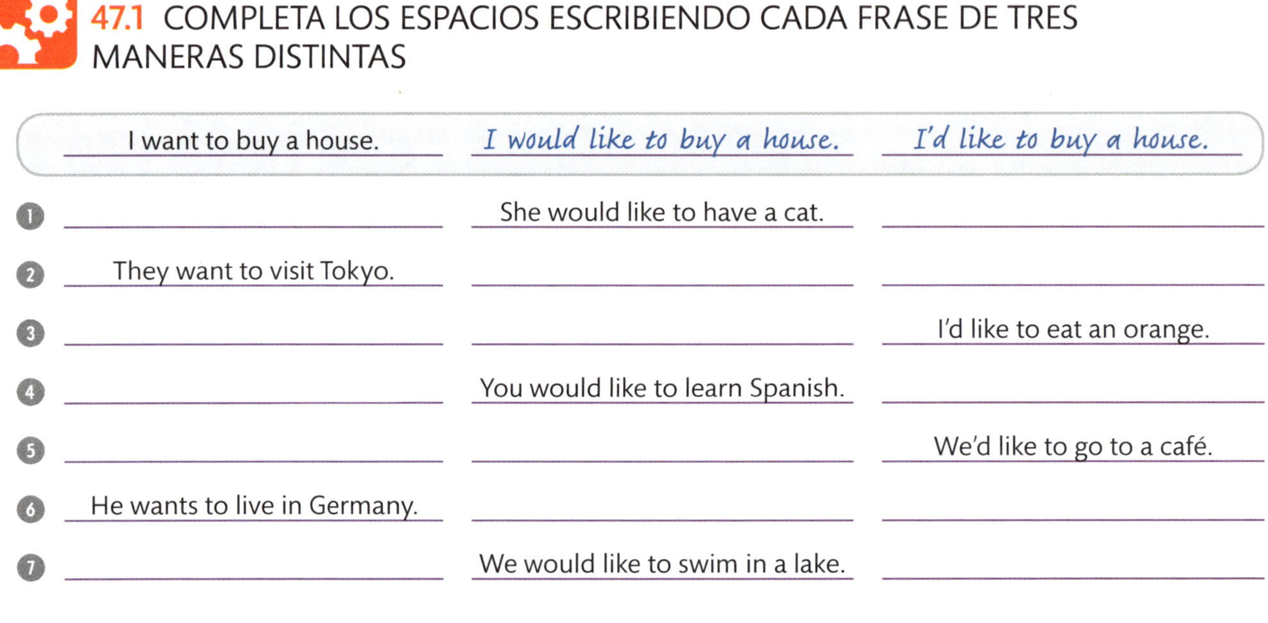

	I want to buy a house.	*I would like to buy a house.*	*I'd like to buy a house.*
1		She would like to have a cat.	
2	They want to visit Tokyo.		
3			I'd like to eat an orange.
4		You would like to learn Spanish.	
5			We'd like to go to a café.
6	He wants to live in Germany.		
7		We would like to swim in a lake.	

Aa 47.2 CONECTA LOS DIBUJOS CON LAS FRASES CORRECTAS

1  2  3  4  5

- Dan would like to travel to New York.
- He wants to learn to play the saxophone.
- They'd like to go sailing on a sailboat.
- We want to go on vacation to Tahiti.
- Sharon wants to read her book.
- Doug would like to climb a mountain.

47.3 VUELVE A ESCRIBIR LAS FRASES CON LAS PALABRAS QUE FALTAN EN SU LUGAR CORRECTO

She would like go to Paris. [to]
She would like to go to Paris.

1. Douglas to have pasta. [wants]

2. They'd to go home tomorrow. [like]

3. Does Chris want go swimming later? [to]

4. Sheila doesn't to see Paul. [want]

5. Would you to visit us tomorrow? [like]

6. Our children want go to college. [to]

7. She'd to buy a new cell phone. [like]

8. Jenny to go shopping on Friday. [wants]

9. Simon like to be a doctor. [would]

10. I like to have a hamburger. [would]

11. Would like to be a vet? [you]

12. Chloe want to eat that pizza. [doesn't]

13. You want to read this book? [Do]

14. They like to watch TV. [would]

15. She wants go to the party. [to]

47.4 UTILIZA EL DIAGRAMA PARA CREAR 12 FRASES CORRECTAS Y DILAS EN VOZ ALTA

I'd like We want Greg wants	to drive to travel	to Miami. around America.

47.5 ESCUCHA EL AUDIO Y RESPONDE A LAS PREGUNTAS

Dos amigos hablan sobre lo que quieren hacer.

Does Pete want to play basketball later?
Yes, he does. ☐ **No, he doesn't.** ☑

1 Would Pete like to read his book?
Yes, he would. ☐ **No, he wouldn't.** ☐

2 Does Pete want to stay at home tomorrow?
Yes, he does. ☐ **No, he doesn't.** ☐

3 Would Pete like to go shopping?
Yes, he would. ☐ **No, he wouldn't.** ☐

4 Does Kat want to buy a new dress?
Yes, she does. ☐ **No, she doesn't.** ☐

5 Does Kat want to go to see a movie?
Yes, she does. ☐ **No, she doesn't.** ☐

6 Does Pete want to go to a French restaurant?
Yes, he does. ☐ **No, he doesn't.** ☐

7 Does Kat want to order spaghetti at the restaurant?
Yes, she does. ☐ **No, she doesn't.** ☐

47.6 ESCRIBE DE NUEVO LAS FRASES PONIENDO LAS PALABRAS EN SU ORDEN CORRECTO

like | go | you | to | Would | to | year? | New York | next

Would you like to go to New York next year?

1 Austria. | to | Marie | go | snowboarding | wants | in

2 doesn't | go | school | to | Mario | today. | want | to

3 climb | mountain. | wants | to | that | She

4 in | Tony | play | to | would | Scotland. | like | golf

47.7 ESCRIBE DE NUEVO LAS FRASES CORRIGIENDO LOS ERRORES

Would you want to go home?
Would you like to go home?

1. Do you want go home now?
2. Claude would likes to learn French.
3. He would likes to go swimming.
4. Paolo wants get a new cat.
5. Would you like visit China?
6. He's like to go to work later today.
7. Peter want to go to college next year.
8. They doesn't want to go to school today.
9. My sister want to go to Greece this summer.

47.8 DI LAS FRASES EN VOZ ALTA EN FORMA DE PREGUNTA

She wants to play chess.
Does she want to play chess?

1. Peter would like to go fishing.
2. Marion wants to play tennis on Saturday.
3. He'd like to visit India.
4. Mr. Evans would like to play chess tonight.
5. We'd like to play squash this evening.
6. Sam wants to go to the park again.
7. They'd like to travel around China.

48 Estudiar

Cuando hablamos de nuestros estudios, podemos utilizar "I would" y "I want" para decir qué materias te gustaría estudiar. Utiliza adverbios para decir cuánto te gustaría estudiarlas.

Lenguaje Adverbios y artículos
Aa Vocabulario Asignaturas
Habilidad Hablar sobre tus estudios

48.1 ESCRIBE DE NUEVO LAS FRASES PONIENDO LAS PALABRAS EN SU ORDEN CORRECTO

his | Peter | really | would | to pass | driving test. | like

Peter would really like to pass his driving test.

1. to travel | mother | like | to Spain. | really | My | would

2. like | French. | would | to learn | Doug | quite

3. an | would | art degree. | quite | Sally | like | to do

4. would | the piano. | Don's brother | to practice | like

5. tonight. | really | to a | I'd | rock concert | to go | like

6. would | in college. | like | chemistry | to study | Martha

7. quite | German | would | to study | at school. | My kids | like

48.2 DI LAS FRASES EN VOZ ALTA, AÑADIENDO EL MODIFICADOR

She'd like to do a French degree. [quite]

She'd quite like to do a French degree.

1. Edith would like to read her new book. [really]

2. They'd like to go to a concert. [really]

3. I'd like to go to France on vacation. [really]

4. Jean-Paul would like to speak to you. [quite]

5. We'd like to eat pizza tonight. [quite]

6. Jeremy would like to play his piano. [really]

7. They'd like to pass their chemistry exam. [really]

8. Sophie would like to speak Mandarin. [quite]

9. David would like to visit his son. [really]

48.3 UTILIZA EL DIAGRAMA PARA CREAR 14 FRASES CORRECTAS Y DILAS EN VOZ ALTA

I'd really like to improve my English.

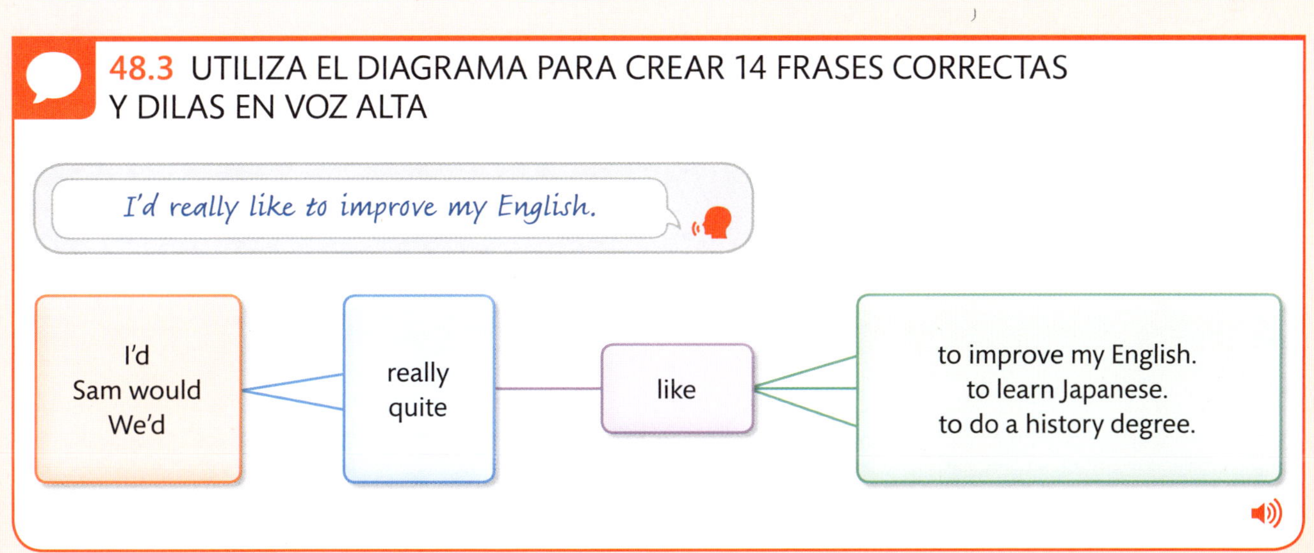

Aa 48.4 BUSCA LOS OCHO TÉRMINOS ESCOLARES DEL RECUADRO

review music study drama
~~history~~ math degree exams

48.5 TACHA LAS PALABRAS INCORRECTAS DE CADA FRASE

Jim went to **bed** / ~~**the bed**~~ hours ago.

1. Phillipa goes to **college** / **the college.**
2. Rome is **beautiful city** / **a beautiful city.**
3. We are at **home** / **the home** at the moment.
4. Sharon goes to **the school** / **school** at 9am.
5. **College** / **The college** is far away.
6. Peter goes to **bed** / **the bed** at 10pm.
7. My uncle is at **mosque** / **the mosque** today.
8. Jim goes to **church** / **the church** on Sundays.
9. Sean leaves **home** / **a home** at 7:30am.
10. Seb lives next to **hospital** / **the hospital.**

48.6 MARCA LAS FRASES QUE SON CORRECTAS

Shirley works in the hospital in Bigton. ☑
Shirley works in hospital in Bigton. ☐

1. Carol leaves work at 6pm every day. ☐
   Carol leaves a work at 6pm every day. ☐
2. Jane can drive you to school tomorrow. ☐
   Jane can drive you to a school tomorrow. ☐
3. Chris lives across from hospital. ☐
   Chris lives across from the hospital. ☐
4. Carl is at a home at the moment. ☐
   Carl is at home at the moment. ☐
5. Julia has beautiful horse. ☐
   Julia has a beautiful horse. ☐
6. The hospital isn't very far. ☐
   Hospital isn't very far. ☐
7. We go to bed at 11pm usually. ☐
   We go to the bed at 11pm usually. ☐
8. Ottersley is a beautiful town. ☐
   Ottersley is beautiful town. ☐

9. Your shoes are under bed. ☐
   Your shoes are under the bed. ☐

48.7 ESCRIBE DE NUEVO LAS FRASES CORRIGIENDO LOS ERRORES

Does your sister work in school?
Does your sister work in a school?

1. Sally is in the hospital. She is ill.

2. York is the pretty town.

3. She is at a home now.

4. Lizzie goes to the church on Sundays.

5. Bob is at the work at the moment.

6. Christopher has new car.

7. Jim goes to the bed early on Sundays.

8. Carlos is the very talented boy.

9. Sarah and John are great team.

10. Mary bought the three new pens.

11. He jumped into a water and started swimming.

12. New York is the beautiful city.

13. A children were playing in the sun.

14. I can't play the soccer on Monday.

15. Can you play a classical guitar?

48.8 ESCUCHA EL AUDIO Y CONECTA LOS DIBUJOS CON LOS NOMBRES

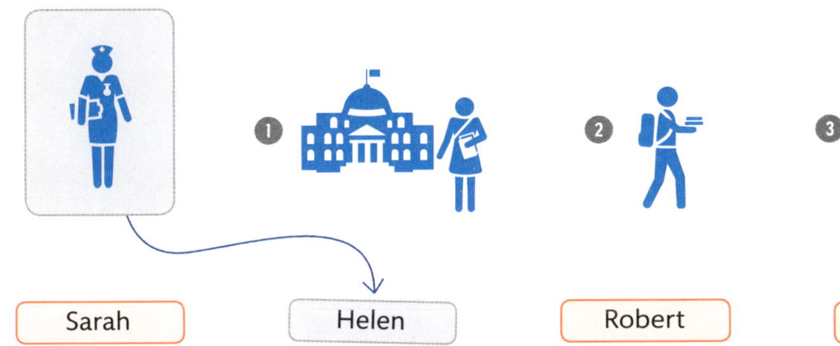

Sarah | Helen | Robert | Oliver | Eddie

Transcripciones de los ejercicios de escucha

UNIDAD 1

1.2.1 Hi! My name's Peter.
1.2.2 Hello! I'm Jo.
1.2.3 Hi! My name's Rachel.
1.2.4 Hello there! I'm Terry.
1.2.5 Hello! My name's Simone.
1.2.6 Hi! I'm Carl.

1.4 ej.: R-A-C-H-E-L H-A-R-P-E-R
1.4.1 N-O-A-H A-N-D-E-R-S-O-N
1.4.2 M-A-S-O-N H-U-G-H-E-S
1.4.3 E-L-I S-A-N-D-E-R-S
1.4.4 A-L-I-C-I-A
1.4.5 Z-O-E S-P-I-E-G-E-L-M-A-N
1.4.6 B-E-N
1.4.7 N-O-R-A J-A-M-E-S
1.4.8 A-M-I-R A-N-S-A-R-I
1.4.9 N-I-N-A E-D-W-A-R-D-S
1.4.10 L-U-C-Y
1.4.11 A-M-A-N S-H-A-R-M-A
1.4.12 A-I-D-E-N
1.4.13 K-E-I-T-H
1.4.14 F-I-O-N-A
1.4.15 J-A-M-E-S T-H-O-M-A-S

UNIDAD 6

6.2

Rachel: Hi, Mom. Let me show you some of my boyfriend Sam's family.
Mom: Oh! That sounds interesting, Rachel!
Rachel: Well, this is Angela. She's Sam's grandmother. She's 80. And next to her is Arthur, Sam's grandfather. He's French.
Mom: And this man?
Rachel: That's Frank, Sam's father.
Mom: Oooh! He looks nice.
Rachel: Here's Charlotte. She's Sam's mother.
Mom: She's very tall, isn't she?
Rachel: And this is Micky, Sam's little brother. He's only seven.
Mom: Aww!
Rachel: And this is a photo of Sally. She's Sam's big sister. She is 19.
Mom: Oh, she looks smart!
Rachel: This photo is of Ronaldo. He's Sam's friend from school.
Mom: And this girl? Who is she?
Rachel: That's Rebecca. Sam's cousin. She's from America.
Mom: They're lovely photos, Rachel.

UNIDAD 8

8.8 ej.: Those books are mine.
8.8.1 That dog is yours.
8.8.2 These sandwiches are Dan's.
8.8.3 That bag is hers.
8.8.4 Those sandwiches are ours.
8.8.5 That purse is Stacey's.
8.8.6 This key is his.
8.8.7 This newspaper is theirs.
8.8.8 That necklace is Linda's.
8.8.9 Those children are ours.

UNIDAD 10

10.8 ej.: Hi. My name's Pete. I work on a farm with lots of animals. I'm a farmer.

10.8.1 Hi, I'm Simon and I work outside. I'm a gardener and I work with plants.

10.8.2 Hello. My name's Sue. I'm a teach I work with children and I teach French and Spanish.

10.8.3 I'm John. I'm a doctor and I work with patients in a hospital.

10.8.4 My name is Alberto. I work in an Italian restaurant and I am a waiter.

10.8.5 I'm Susan. And this is Pam. We wor together in a beauty salon. We're hairdress

10.8.6 Hello! My name is Douglas. I'm an actor and I work in the theater.

10.8.7 Hello. I'm Danny. I work outside on a construction site. I'm a contractor. It gets very cold here sometimes!

UNIDAD 11

11.2 ej.:

A: Hi. Have you got the time?
B: Yes. It's a quarter to six.

11.2.1

A: Excuse me, sir. Do you have the time?
B: Sure. It's a quarter after eight.

11.2.2

A: Hello. Do you know what time it is?
B: Erm. Yep. It's half past eight.

.2.3

Excuse me. Do you know what time it is?

It's quarter past eleven.

.2.4

Hello. Have you got the time?

It's nine twenty.

.2.5

When do you go to bed?

I go to bed at eleven o'clock.

.2.6

iend: Hi, Sarah! Do you know what ne it is?

rah: It's a quarter after seven.

.2.7

Excuse me. Do you have the time?

Yes. It's three twenty-five.

.2.8

When did you have breakfast today?

I had breakfast at quarter to ten.

.2.9

iend: Hi, Jake! Do you know what time s?

ke: Sure. It's six twenty-eight.

.2.10 Ali wakes up at half past five.

.2.11 Ali goes to bed at ten o'clock.

.2.12

Hello! Have you got the time?

Ah, yes. It's almost two thirty.

11.2.13

A: Excuse me. Do you know what time it is?

B: It's a quarter after eight.

UNIDAD 14

14.7.1 Hi. I'm Kate. I'm a teacher and I work every day from 9am to 5pm. It's hard work, but I go to the gym on Friday. It helps me to relax.

14.7.2 Hello. My name's Paul. I'm a farmer and I work with animals. I work every day from 6am to 9pm. I'm very busy. But I play soccer most weekends with my friends.

14.7.3 I'm Jane. I'm a nurse. I work three days a week, from Wednesday to Friday. On the weekend, I go to a restaurant with my boyfriend, Dan.

14.7.4 Hi there! I'm Sally. I'm a student. I get up at 8am from Monday to Thursday to go to college. On Saturdays, I go swimming with my friends.

14.7.5 My name is Eric. I'm an actor and I work at the theater three times a week. I work on Thursdays, Fridays, and Saturdays. On Sundays, I relax and read the newspaper.

14.7.6 I'm Claire and I'm a waitress. I work in a restaurant from Tuesday to Sunday, and I work late from 6pm to 11pm. On Mondays, I play tennis with my friend, Paul.

UNIDAD 15

15.3.1 My name's Cath and I'm 26 years old. I work in a hospital, but I'm not a doctor. I'm a nurse and I work with sick children every day.

15.3.2 I'm Joe and I'm an actor. I work in a theater. I'm 50 years old. I live with my wife, Anne and our three cats in our small house in the country.

15.3.3 My name's Miguel and I'm a mailman. I live in New York. It's a really big city! Some people think I'm from Spain, but I'm not Spanish. I come from Argentina.

15.3.4 My name's Pete and I'm 24 years old. I work in a restaurant, but I'm not a waiter. I'm a chef and I cook Italian food from Monday to Friday.

UNIDAD 16

16.6

Julie: Hi, I'm Julie. I work in the museum in the town center. It's an interesting job and I meet lots of people. My work starts at 10am, so I don't get up early. I usually get up at 8am. I work from Tuesday to Friday. I don't work on Mondays, because the museum is closed. Most days I have lunch with my friends. I work with nice people, and I play tennis with my best friend Sally on Thursday evenings. I get home at 8pm. I eat my dinner and then I watch TV before I go to bed.

UNIDAD 18

18.4

Jane: Hi there.

Bob: Hello! Are you Jane, the new teacher?

Jane: Yes, I am. Nice to meet you!

Bob: I'm Bob. Nice to meet you.

Jane: What do you teach, Bob?

Bob: I'm an English teacher. What about you?

Jane: I teach biology.

Bob: You sound Irish, Jane. Are you from Dublin?

Jane: No, I'm not. I'm from Belfast. But my husband Paul is from Dublin.

Bob: And is your husband a teacher here, too?

Jane: No, he isn't. He's a doctor.

Bob: Oh, does he work at the hospital?

Jane: No, he doesn't. He works in a clinic near our house.

Bob: Oh, great! Does he start work early, too?

Jane: No, he doesn't. He starts work at 8:30am.

Bob: My wife works in a bank, so we both have the weekend free. We play a lot of tennis. Do you play tennis, Jane?

Jane: No, I don't. I go to the movies a lot, though.

UNIDAD 19

19.3

Greg: Let me tell you a bit about my family. Well, there's my grandmother. Her name is Ellie and she's the oldest member of our family. She's 84 years old. She lives in my town near the supermarket.

My mom and dad are called Sharon and Phil. Sharon works in the school on Elm Road and she's a receptionist. My dad, Phil, works in a factory. They make vacuum cleaners there.

I have two sisters. Claire is 21 and Samantha is 19. Claire's a student at the local college, and Samantha works in a beauty salon. And me? I'm a student, too. I study history. I love it, and I want to be a teacher one day.

UNIDAD 21

21.4.1 I live in a big town called Brookfield. There's a hospital and a hotel. There are three schools and a supermarket near my house. There is a good restaurant, but there isn't a movie theater.

21.4.2 My town's called Alderson. There's a bus station, but there isn't an airport. There are two hotels and a library. There is an old castle, but there aren't any bars or cafés, so it's a little boring.

21.4.3 I live in Barnwell. It's a beautiful town. There's a castle and a church. There is one café, but there aren't any restaurants. There is a museum. My sister works there on the weekend.

21.4.4 I live in Allerton. There is an airport and a train station here. There are two factories and there is a big supermarket. There are no restaurants, but there is a nice café. I go there in the evening.

21.4.5 I live in Weldon. There is a big factory. I work there. There are two cafés near the post office and there is a movie theater, too. There isn't a museum or a church but there is a swimming pool.

21.6

Gordon: Hi, I'm Gordon. I live in Melcome Canada. There's a town hall and two churches in my town, and there are three schools, too. I'm a teacher and work in a primary school. There is a beautiful park in the center and a small café. I go there in the evening. Melcome is an exciting town: ther are two cinemas and a theater. I love the theater! My wife is a doctor and works in th hospital near my house. My son is a police officer and works at the police station.

There aren't any castles in Melcome. It' a very modern city. But there are three ne hotels near the airport.

UNIDAD 22

22.8

James: My name's James. I live on a farm There are two towns near my home: Stonehill and Eastford. I visit them in the evening with my friends.

Stonehill is a new town, but it has an interesting museum. I go there on the weekend. There are lots of stores and there a wonderful French restaurant in the cente and I often go there with my girlfriend. There are some great bars, too, but there aren't any theaters.

Eastford is really small and is very old. There's a castle and two churches in the center. There aren't any restaurants in Eastford, but there's a nice café. It's very quiet. There are some nice stores. I sometimes buy a present for my girlfrienc

ere. In the evening you can go to the eater. It's tiny, but it's a lot of fun.

NIDAD 23

3.7 ej.:

: Is there a theater in Greendale?

: Yes. Turn left and the theater is on your ght across from the church.

3.7.1

: Excuse me. Where's Franco's restaurant?

: OK, take the third road on the left. The staurant is on the right next to the bank.

3.7.2

: Excuse me. Could you tell where the niversity is?

: Sure. Go straight ahead and it's the urth road on the right. The university is n the left.

3.7.3

: Excuse me. Where's the supermarket?

: Turn right, then take the first left. The ıpermarket is on the left next to the castle.

3.7.4

: Excuse me. How do I get to an-Paul's café?

: Go straight ahead. The café is on the orner next to the church.

3.7.5

: Could you tell me where the hotel is?

: Sure. Go straight ahead and take the econd road on your right. It's across from e park.

23.7.6

A: Do you know where the museum is?

B: Yeah, it's next to the town hall. Go straight ahead and take the third left.

23.7.7

A: Excuse me. Is the hospital near here?

B: Yes it is. It's behind the park. Turn right, then take the second left. The hospital is on the corner on the left.

23.7.8

A: Excuse me. How do I get to the café?

B: Turn right. Go past the hotel and the café is on the left.

UNIDAD 24

24.2 ej.: There is a castle and a mosque in my town. They're beautiful.

24.2.1 Newtown has a library and a restaurant.

24.2.2 There's a school and a hospital in Fulchester.

24.2.3 My mom goes to the bank and the supermarket once a week.

24.2.4 I work in two places: a restaurant on Monday evenings and a movie theater on Wednesdays.

24.2.5 There's a museum and a church in my town.

UNIDAD 25

25.5

Kirsty: My name's Kirsty. I live and work in Braemore. It's a small town in the mountains in Scotland. There are lots of trees and a few lakes near my town. It's beautiful here.
In the center of my town, there are a few old buildings. There's a beautiful church and an old castle. There are lots of hotels and cafes, too. Braemore is very popular with tourists. Lots of people come for a weekend break.

I work in a bar in a large hotel. It's horrible. It's very crowded every weekend and I'm very busy. But when I have some free time, I go to a café with my friends.

UNIDAD 26

26.2 ej.: My name is Leo. I work in an office, so I use a computer every day.

26.2.1 I'm Rick. I live in Cornwall and I work outside. That's because I'm a farmer. I have more than 200 cows.

26.2.2 My name's Mary Lou. I live in Tennessee and I work with children every day, because I'm a teacher.

26.2.3 My name's Carl. I go to the library every day because I'm a student. I'm studying chemistry.

26.2.4 I'm Sally. I get up at 6am because I go to the gym in the morning, before I go to work at the gallery.

26.2.5 My name is Pete and I work in the theater on Park Road. I'm an actor and I have been in many plays.

26.2.6 I'm Michael. I can't go to work today because I have the flu.

26.2.7 I'm Sana. I work in a restaurant in New York because I'm a chef.

UNIDAD 28

28.7 ej.: John's sister has got a cat.
28.7.1 Our town has an old church.
28.7.2 Adam and I have got two daughters.
28.7.3 Sally and Jonathan have a new car.
28.7.4 My friend Sam's got a computer.
28.7.5 Our house has got three rooms.

UNIDAD 29

29.3 ej.: John has a new kitchen. It's quite large and it's in the basement of his house. He has a big refrigerator. You know, John loves cooking.

29.3.1 Claudia has a really good oven. She loves baking cakes.

29.3.2 Paul has a toaster. He makes a lot of toast!

29.3.3 Jenny has a kettle in her office. She can make a cup of tea when she wants one.

29.3.4 Colin has a new washing machine. His mom's very happy, because he doesn't use hers any more.

29.3.5 Roberto has lots of plates and bowls in the cupboards in his kitchen.

UNIDAD 31

31.5

Kate: Hey, Steve. I'm just doing the shopping list. What do we need this week?
Steve: Good idea, Kate. Let me see. I want to make a cake. We've got three bags of flour in the cupboard! But one bag of sugar. Get me another bag of sugar, please.
Kate: OK. I thought we could make a pizza for dinner tonight.
Steve: We don't have any tomatoes. Can you buy two tins of tomatoes? And we've only got one block of cheese, so please buy some more. Oh, and we've got one carton of juice. Can you get some orange juice?
Kate: Juice, OK. Anything else?
Steve: Well, we need some more fruit. We've only got two oranges. So let's get five more oranges, and six bananas.
Kate: And some apples?
Steve: No, we've got lots of apples.
Kate: OK. We need some coffee, so I'll get two packets. Oh, I don't have any chocolate, so I'll buy two bars of milk chocolate.
Steve: Can you think of anything else?
Kate: Yes, we need some vegetables. We have a lot of onions, but we don't have any other vegetables. I'll buy 500 grams of carrots and some tomatoes.
Steve: Do we have any rice?
Kate: Ooh, no, we haven't. I'll get a bag of rice as well.

UNIDAD 32

32.4

Bruce: I'm hungry. Let's make a sandwich. Do we have any bread?
Shelley: Let me see. Yes, we do.
Bruce: And some butter?
Shelley: I'm sorry. We don't have enough butter.
Bruce: So, shall we make a pizza, then? You've got a recipe, haven't you?
Shelley: Yes, I have.
Bruce: Right. So, we need some flour. How much flour have we got?
Shelley: Let me see. We've got four bags.
Bruce: That's too many. We only need two.
Shelley: Great. So, here are two bags.
Bruce: What else? Some salt. Do we have any salt?
Shelley: We've got seven ounces of salt.
Bruce: That's too much! We only need one ounce.
Shelley: Brilliant. Now we need some tomatoes, so let's have a look.... 10 ounces. Is that enough?
Bruce: That's not enough. We need 20 ounces.
Shelley: Oh, dear! And what about the cheese?
Bruce: We need six ounces.
Shelley: We've got about seven.
Bruce: OK, that's enough.
Shelley: What else do we need?
Bruce: Well, we've got lots of ham, so let's make a ham pizza.
Shelley: Great!

NIDAD 34

.5 ej.:

ıth: Jane, look at those cardigans there.

ne: Oh, I don't want a red one, Ruth.

ıth: There is a black one here.

ne: But they're all quite short. I need ong black cardigan for work.

ıth: How about this one here? It's long d black.

ne: Perfect! Now, do they have n my size?

.5.1

ıth: These T-shirts are nice, aren't ey, Jane?

ne: Yes, they're pretty. But I've got lots T-shirts already.

ıth: And they have some nice tton shirts.

ne: I don't need a shirt. Do they have y skirts?

ıth: Yes. There are red ones and ue ones.

ne: I want a red skirt. Can I find ne that fits?

.5.2

ıth: I want to buy a present my mother.

ne: What about these yellow gloves, Ruth?

ıth: No. They're too expensive.

ne: How about a hat?

ıth: She has so many hats already. Those arves are nice.

ne: Yes. And not too expensive.

ıth: I think I'll get her a red scarf.

34.5.3

Jane: Do you like these boots, Ruth?

Ruth: No, they're not my style. I love these shoes though.

Jane: Yes, they're great. Do you want to get the black ones?

Ruth: No, I have some black shoes already. I prefer the brown ones. Do they have them in size 5?

Jane: Let's see.

34.5.4

Ruth: What do you want to get next, Jane?

Jane: Some jeans.

Ruth: What about these?

Jane: They're great, but I want to get some blue ones. I've already got a pair of black jeans.

Ruth: Right. How about these?

Jane: Yes, they look nice.

34.5.5

Ruth: Hey, Jane. There are some gorgeous coats over here.

Jane: Oh, I don't know. They're black. I want something more colorful.

Ruth: How about these here? They have some lovely red ones here.

Jane: They're very cheap. I want something more expensive.

Ruth: OK then, what about that green one there?

Jane: Yes, I'll try it on.

UNIDAD 35

35.5 ej.:

A: I love your shoes! What are they made of?

B: They're leather. From Spain.

35.5.1

A: Do you want to come to our party tonight?

B: Sure, I'll bring some wine and some plastic cups.

35.5.2

A: What a beautiful wooden table you have! Is it old?

B: Yes. It's an antique.

35.5.3

A: That's a nice green glass bottle.

B: Thanks. It's a present for my mom.

35.5.4

A: You've got a new leather jacket, haven't you?

B: No. It's quite old, actually.

35.5.5

A: Are those plastic chairs you have?

B: Yes, they're for the yard.

35.5.6

A: What a nice wool sweater you have!

B: Thanks. My sister made it.

35.5.7 My sister has a wooden table, but she doesn't have any chairs.

35.5.8 When I go shopping, I put my fruit in a paper bag.

35.5.9
A: It's my girlfriend's birthday.
What should I buy her?
B: Why don't you get her a wool scarf?
She'd like that.

35.5.10 I always carry a plastic bottle with me. I put water in it.

35.5.11
Friend: Claire, do you like my new bag?
Claire: Yes, it's gorgeous. Is it leather?
Friend: Of course! It's a present from Tim.

35.5.12
A: That's a beautiful lamp. Is it made of glass?
B: No, it's metal.

35.5.13
A: We have some new chairs for the kitchen.
B: Are they wooden?
A: No. They're metal.

UNIDAD 37

37.7 ej.: I'm Mark and I work in a bank in London. I often play golf on the weekend. I don't have much time during the week, because I work a lot.

37.7.1 I'm Steven and I love cycling. I often go cycling in France in the summer with my wife.

37.7.2 My name's Max. I do a lot of sports because I like to stay fit. I go running every evening after I get home from work. It helps me relax.

37.7.3 Hi, I'm Ian, and I play soccer twice a week, when I meet up with my old school friends.

37.7.4 I'm Janine. I'm not very sporty. I don't like tennis and I hate running.

37.7.5 My name is Lila. What sports do I like? Well, I go skating with my brother in the winter.

37.7.6 My name's Robbie. I don't do much sport. I'm so busy at work that I don't even go running any more.

37.7.7 I'm Susan. I love fishing. I usually go with my grandson Pete on the weekend.

UNIDAD 39

39.3 ej.: John usually goes running.

39.3.1 Chris never gets up early.

39.3.2 Shelley sometimes goes swimming.

39.3.3 Flo often has tea in the morning.

39.3.4 Sylvester usually goes to bed at 10pm.

39.3.5 Dominic always plays soccer on Fridays.

39.3.6 David often reads a newspaper on Sundays.

UNIDAD 40

40.2
Shelley: So, tell me a bit about yourself, Doug. What kinds of things do you like?
Doug: Well, Shelley, I love my food. I really like fast food. You know, pizza, hamburgers, and fries. What don't I like? Well, to be honest, I don't like fruit and I hate salad. How about you?
Shelley: I just love sport. I go running every day, and on the weekend I like playing tenn I don't like golf, though. I think it's boring.
Doug: Me, too! I'm not great at sport, to be honest. But I love reading history books an listening to classical music. I dislike pop music. Oh, and I hate shopping. What else do you do in your free time?
Shelley: I like going to the cinema, but I don't like scary films. I also love taking photos of my friends and family.

UNIDAD 42

42.2 ej.: Hi, I'm Dave. My favorite type of music is jazz. I listen to it in the morning while I drive to work.

42.2.1 Hello! My name is Jenny. I'm still at school and my favorite subject is math. I want to be an engineer when I grow up.

42.2.2 Hi, I'm Mike and I'm a policeman. My favorite day is Friday. Why? Because I'm free on Saturday and don't go to work.

42.2.3 My name's Colin and my favorite color is red. The same color as my favorite football team.

2.2.4 I'm Sally and I love desserts. I like e cream, but my favorite is, of course, ocolate cake.

2.2.5 Hello, I'm Danny. I like soccer and eally like basketball. But my favorite sport baseball.

2.2.6 Hi, my name is Clarice. I'm a forest nger and I work outside. I like summer, ut my favorite season is fall, when all the aves are red and gold.

NIDAD 44

4.4 ej.: Friend: Hi, Ina. Are you going James's beach party tomorrow?

a: I'm not sure. I can't swim so I won't ave much fun.

iend: Well, you can play beach olleyball instead.

4.4.1

iend: And where are you going n vacation this summer, Ina?

a: I'm going on a horseback riding acation in Scotland.

iend: Is that difficult?

a: No, it's quite easy. I can ride well.

4.4.2

riend: Can you speak Mandarin?

a: Yes, I can but only a little.

riend: It's a difficult language to learn. an you write in Mandarin?

a: Oh, no. I can only speak it.

44.4.3

Friend: Can you play tennis?

Ina: No, I'm terrible at it. I can't even hit the ball.

Friend: That's a shame. I'd like to play a game this afternoon.

44.4.4

Friend: Are you musical, Ina?

Ina: Yes, I suppose I am. I can play the piano and the guitar.

Friend: Wow. I can't play any musical instruments.

44.4.5

Ina: How did the kite flying go with your daughter this weekend?

Friend: It didn't go very well. We couldn't get the kite to fly.

Ina: Do you want me to help you next weekend?

Friend: Can you fly a kite?

Ina: Sure I can. I'm really good at that.

UNIDAD 47

47.5

Kat: What do you want to do later, Pete? Play basketball?

Pete: No thanks, Kat. I'd really like to finish my book.

Kat: No problem. What would you like to do tomorrow?

Pete: Well, I'd really like to go to the park. Do you want to come with me?

Kat: I'd like that. Would you like to go shopping afterwards?

Pete: Yes, I would.

Kat: Great! I want to buy a new dress.

Pete: Do you want to go to see a movie in the evening?

Kat: Actually, I would like to go to a restaurant.

Pete: Oh, good idea. I really want to go to the new Italian restaurant in town.

Kat: I'd like to go there, too. I want to try their spaghetti.

UNIDAD 48

48.8

A: That's enough about me! Tell me a bit about your grandchildren. How are they?

B: Well, Helen is studying to be a nurse. She'd really like to work in the hospital in the center. She really enjoys the course.

A: And your other granddaughter, Sarah?

B: Sarah is in college in Scotland. She's not sure what she wants to do later, but she thinks she'd really like to be a teacher.

A: And the boys? What are your grandsons doing?

B: Eddie is still at school. He finishes next year, and he wants to get a degree in mathematics. He's a clever one! And then there's Robert. Robert loves music and he'd really like to study it. At the moment he works at a local restaurant where he plays the piano.

A: And Oliver?

B: Oh, Oliver works in the bank on Park Lane. He'd really like to buy a house with his girlfriend, Jane. But it's so expensive. And what about your grandchildren?

Respuestas

01

1.1
1. I'm Natalie.
2. My name's Sue.
3. I'm Ryan.
4. My name's Mia.
5. My name's Amelia.

1.2
A 3 B 1 C 2 D 6 E 4 F 5

1.3
1. Hi! I am Charlotte.
2. Hi! My name is Charlotte.
3. Hello! I am Charlotte.
4. Hello! My name is Charlotte.
5. Hi! I am Carla.
6. Hi! My name is Carla.
7. Hello! I am Carla.
8. Hello! My name is Carla.
9. Hi! I am Fatima.
10. Hi! My name is Fatima.
11. Hello! I am Fatima.
12. Hello! My name is Fatima.

1.4
1. N-o-a-h A-n-d-e-r-s-o-n
2. M-a-s-o-n H-u-g-h-e-s
3. E-l-i S-a-n-d-e-r-s
4. A-l-i-c-i-a
5. Z-o-e S-p-i-e-g-e-l-m-a-n
6. B-e-n
7. N-o-r-a J-a-m-e-s
8. A-m-i-r A-n-s-a-r-i
9. N-i-n-a E-d-w-a-r-d-s
10. L-u-c-y
11. A-m-a-n S-h-a-r-m-a
12. A-i-d-e-n
13. K-e-i-t-h
14. F-i-o-n-a
15. J-a-m-e-s T-h-o-m-a-s

1.5
1. My name is Terry, T-e-r-r-y.
2. My last name is Singh, S-i-n-g-h.
3. I'm Mario, M-a-r-i-o.
4. My name is Yasmin Khan, Y-a-s-m-i-n K-h-a-n.
5. I am Jacob, J-a-c-o-b.

02

2.1
1. South Korea
2. Thailand
3. Greece
4. Poland
5. Argentina
6. Russia
7. Australia
8. Canada
9. Philippines
10. Pakistan
11. Slovakia
12. Republic of Ireland
13. China
14. Portugal
15. South Africa
16. Brazil
17. Netherlands
18. Spain
19. Czech Republic
20. Singapore
21. Egypt
22. Mongolia
23. United Kingdom
24. France
25. Mexico
26. India
27. United States of America
28. Japan
29. Indonesia
30. United Arab Emirates
31. New Zealand
32. Germany
33. Austria
34. Switzerland

03

3.1
1 85 2 21 3 90 4 17 5 84 6 62
7 47 8 50 9 71 10 12 11 33

3.2
1. Chloe is thirty-one years old.
2. Heidi is fifty-two years old.
3. Zach is sixteen years old.
4. Charlie is ten years old.
5. Marcel is eighty years old.
6. Claire is twenty-one years old.
7. Dan is thirty-six years old.
8. Eleanor is twenty-eight years old.
9. Rebecca is forty-three years old.

3.3
1. I am twenty-three years old.
2. I am thirty-two years old.
3. I am sixty-eight years old.
4. Dan is twenty-three years old.
5. Dan is thirty-two years old.
6. Dan is sixty-eight years old.
7. You are twenty-three years old.
8. You are thirty-two years old.
9. You are sixty-eight years old.

3.4
1. Abe **is** 72 years old. She **is** Japanese.
2. Mia and Leo **are** 12. They **are** from Italy.
3. Chantal **is** 66 years old. She **is** French.
4. Amir and Aamna **are** 90 years old. They **are** from Pakistan.
5. I **am** 24 years old. I **am** Irish.
6. Max **is** 47 years old. He **is** German.
7. We **are** 38 years old. We **are** from New Zealand.
8. My sister **is** 4 years old. She **is** from Canada.

04

4.1
1. grandfather
2. father
3. uncle
4. sister
5. son
6. daughter
7. grandson
8. granddaughter

4.2
1. cat
2. chicken

3 rabbit
4 tortoise
5 parrot
6 dog
7 fish
8 snake
9 pig
10 horse
11 guinea pig

05

5.1

1 **Their** dog is called Beth.
2 **His** tortoise is 50 years old.
3 **My** cat is called Sam.
4 **Our** lion is from Kenya.
5 **Your** rabbit eats grass.
6 Here is **its** bed.
7 **Their** snake is called Sid.
8 Buster is **my** monkey.
9 **Your** parrot is from Venezuela.
10 **Her** cat is called Tabatha.
11 **Their** monkey is from Morocco.
12 **Her** pig lives on a farm.
13 **His** horse is called Prancer.
14 **Our** chicken lives in the garden.

5.2

1 Fido is **my** dog.
2 Cookie is **his** cat.
3 It is **our** chicken.
4 Ziggy is **your** parrot.
5 Hiss is **their** snake.
6 Max is **our** monkey.
7 It is **her** rabbit.
8 Ed is **my** horse.
9 Rex is **your** dog.
10 Nemo is **her** fish.
11 It is **our** sheep.

5.3

1 **This** is her rabbit.
2 **This** is its ball.
3 **That** is our dog.
4 **This** is his snake.
5 **That** is my horse.

5.4

1 Their fish is called Bob.
2 This is their cow.
3 His snake is called Harold.
4 Her cat is 12 years old.
5 Barney is our rabbit.

5.5

1. This is her cat.
2. This is her parrot.
3. This is their cat.
4. This is their parrot.
5. This is my cat.
6. This is my parrot.
7. That is her cat.
8. That is her parrot.
9. That is their cat.
10. That is their parrot.
11. That is my cat.
12. That is my parrot.

06

6.1

1 Joe and Greg's dog
2 Dolly's granddaughters
3 Sue's house
4 Pete and Aziz's snake

6.2

1 Arthur is **Sam's grandfather.**
2 Frank is **Sam's father.**
3 Charlotte is **Sam's mother.**
4 Micky is **Sam's brother.**
5 Sally is **Sam's sister.**
6 Ronaldo is **Sam's friend.**
7 Rebecca is **Sam's cousin.**

6.3

1 True 2 False 3 False
4 True 5 False

6.4

1 That's my grandparents' car.
2 These are Pete and Omar's cats.
3 I am Sally's granddaughter.
4 Where is your parents' house?
5 Samantha is Barry's new wife.

6.5

1 Sooty is **my brothers'** cat.
2 They are **Tammy's** parents.
3 This is our **children's** snake.
4 My **parents'** house is small.

07

7.1

1 notebook
2 sunglasses
3 keys
4 pen
5 necklace
6 newspaper
7 ID card
8 letter
9 toothbrush
10 hairbrush
11 bottle of water
12 laptop
13 earphones
14 pencil
15 dictionary
16 apple
17 book
18 tablet
19 mirror
20 coins
21 passport
22 magazine
23 camera
24 glasses
25 map
26 umbrella
27 sandwich

08

8.1

1 **These** are my mom's glasses.
2 **Those** are Samantha's keys.
3 **This** is Tom's umbrella.
4 **This** is my dog.
5 **Those** are Pete's books.
6 **That** is your newspaper.
7 **These** are my tickets.
8 **These** are Marge's earrings.
9 **These** are his daughters.
10 **That** is my teacher.
11 **That** is your watch.

8.2

1 This is my letter.
2 These are my purses.

3. That is Greg's key.
4. Those are my cats.
5. This is my sister's pencil.
6. Those are your dictionaries.
7. These are Dan's houses.
8. That is Stan's book.
9. That is my brother.

8.3

1. pencils
2. fishes / fish
3. brothers
4. diaries
5. necklaces
6. brushes
7. watches
8. boxes
9. dictionaries
10. sisters
11. umbrellas
12. laptops

8.4

1. brushes
2. boxes
3. dictionaries
4. dogs
5. notebooks
6. toothbrushes
7. books
8. pencils
9. letters
10. newspapers
11. glasses
12. passports
13. magazines

8.5

1. three sandwiches
2. two necklaces
3. four bags
4. three toothbrushes
5. two diaries / planners
6. two cats
7. one apple

8.6

1. his
2. its
3. hers
4. yours
5. theirs
6. ours

8.7

1. This dog is his.
2. Those books are mine.
3. That fish is yours.
4. These bags are theirs.
5. These boxes are ours.

8.8

1. That dog is yours.
2. These sandwiches are Dan's.
3. That bag is hers.
4. Those sandwiches are ours.
5. That purse is Stacey's.
6. This key is his.
7. This newspaper is theirs.
8. That necklace is Linda's.
9. Those children are ours.

8.9

1. **These** are my books.
2. **This** is your dog.
3. **These** are her bags.
4. **These** are their boxes.
5. **This** is my toothbrush.
6. **This** is his diary.
7. **This** is your apple.
8. **These** are my apples.
9. **These** are your glasses.
10. **These** are Kevin's keys.
11. **This** is my dad's car.

8.10

DETERMINANTES: **your**, **his**, **my**
PRONOMBRES: **hers**, **mine**

09

9.1

1. pilot
2. fire fighter
3. gardener
4. driver
5. electrician
6. actor
7. nurse
8. farmer
9. chef
10. receptionist
11. businesswoman
12. police officer
13. dentist
14. vet
15. teacher
16. businessman
17. mechanic
18. waiter
19. engineer
20. cleaner
21. artist
22. hairdresser
23. waitress
24. construction worker
25. doctor
26. sales assistant
27. judge

10

10.1

1. He / She is a doctor.
2. You are teachers.
3. I am a hairdresser.
4. We are mechanics.
5. You are a cleaner.
6. They are chefs.
7. He / She is an actor.
8. They are vets.
9. I am a police officer.
10. You are farmers.
11. You are a waitress.
12. We are gardeners.
13. I am an artist.

10.2

1. I **am an** actor.
2. He **is a** teacher.
3. He **is a** chef.
4. You **are an** engineer.
5. We **are** hairdressers.
6. They **are** farmers.
7. You **are a** vet.
8. I **am a** waiter.
9. She **is a** nurse.

10.3

1. I **am** a vet.
2. She **is** a businesswoman.
3. We **are** doctors.
4. They **are** teachers.
5. He **is** a mechanic.
6. I **am** a driver.
7. We **are** receptionists.

8. They **are** waitresses.
9. She **is** a police officer.
10. I **am** a judge.
11. You **are** a nurse.
12. We **are** farmers.
13. She **is** a sales assistant.
14. I **am** a chef.

10.4

1. laboratory
2. restaurant
3. garden
4. hospital
5. school

10.5

1. He works **in** a doctor's office.
2. We work **on** a farm.
3. My dad works **on** a building site.
4. My sister works **in** a café.
5. We work **in** people's gardens.
6. Dan works **in** a hospital.
7. I work **in** a restaurant.
8. We work **in** a school.
9. Chris works **in** a supermarket.

10.6

1. Abby **is a nurse**. She **works in a hospital**.
2. Julie **is an engineer**. She **works on a construction site**.
3. Simon **is a gardener**. He **works in a park**.
4. Adam **is a police officer**. He **works in a police station**.
5. Max **is a farmer**. He **works on a farm**.
6. Carol **is a hairdresser**. She **works in a beauty salon**.

10.7

1. Sam is a **doctor** and she works with **patients**.
2. Gabriella is a **chef** and she works with **food**.
3. Dan is a **vet** and he works with **animals**.
4. John is a **farmer** and he works with **crops**.
5. Tom is an **actor** and he works in a **theater**.

10.8

1. gardener
2. teacher
3. doctor
4. waiter
5. hairdressers
6. actor
7. contractor

11

11.1

1. It's four thirty.
2. It's seven fifty.
3. It's midnight.
4. It's a quarter after six.
5. It's half past eight.
6. It's three thirty.
7. It's a quarter to nine.
8. It's five forty-five.

11.2

1. 08:15
2. 08:30
3. 11:15
4. 09:20
5. 11:00
6. 07:15
7. 03:25
8. 09:45
9. 06:28
10. 05:30
11. 10:00
12. 02:30
13. 08:15

11.3

1. 11:15
2. 11:00
3. 8:24
4. 3:30
5. 2:45
6. 5:25
7. 3:49
8. 2:15
9. 9:00
10. 7:45
11. 11:30
12. 9:25
13. 10:15
14. 11:20
15. 1:55
16. 6:45
17. 6:45

11.4

1. It's a quarter to ten. / It's nine forty-five.
2. It's four o'clock.
3. It's ten twenty.
4. It's half past eleven. / It's eleven thirty.
5. It's three forty-seven.
6. It's a quarter past three. / It's three fifteen.
7. It's half past six. / It's six thirty.
8. It's eight twenty-two.
9. It's one twenty-five.

12

12.1

1. buy groceries
2. take a bath
3. have lunch
4. clear the table
5. start work
6. wash your face
7. get up
8. cook dinner
9. brush your hair
10. leave work
11. finish work
12. brush your teeth
13. go home
14. have dinner
15. go to school
16. get dressed
17. go to bed
18. take a shower
19. wake up
20. iron a shirt
21. dawn
22. day
23. dusk
24. night
25. do the dishes
26. have breakfast
27. walk the dog

13

13.1

1. Marion has a shower at 6:45am.
2. Marion has breakfast at 7am.
3. Marion brushes her teeth at 7:20am.

4. Marion goes to work at 7:30am.
5. Marion gets the bus at 7:45am.
6. Marion gets to work at 8:30am.
7. Marion leaves work at 5pm.

13.2

1. I **wake** up at 6:30am.
2. He **gets** up at 6am.
3. She **has** a shower at 7am.
4. They **have** cereal for breakfast.
5. He **has** a shower before breakfast.
6. She **leaves** home at 7:15am.
7. The bus **goes** every half hour.
8. I **get** to work at 8:30am.
9. He **starts** work at 9am.
10. She **takes** an hour for lunch.
11. I **go** to the sandwich shop for lunch.
12. They **eat** lunch in the canteen.
13. He **finishes** work at 5pm.
14. They **go** home on the bus.
15. He **washes** his car every weekend.
16. I **watch** TV after dinner.
17. They **go** to bed at 11pm.
18. He **sleeps** for eight hours.

13.3

1. He **has**
2. It **starts**
3. He **leaves**
4. She **gets up**
5. It **goes**
6. She **wakes up**
7. He **washes**
8. She **watches**
9. It **finishes**

13.4

1. He **gets** up at 6:30am.
2. He **has** breakfast at 7am.
3. She **leaves** home at 8am.
4. I **drive** to work.
5. I **have** lunch in the park.
6. I **work** eight hours every day.
7. He **goes** to bed at 10:30pm.

13.5

1. goes
2. washes
3. wakes
4. gets
5. watches
6. leaves
7. has
8. finishes

14

14.1

1. I go to the movies **on** the weekend.
2. Joe starts work at 6pm **on** Mondays.
3. You watch TV **in** the afternoon.
4. Harry plays tennis **on** Wednesdays.
5. Lin goes swimming **in** the evening.
6. Alex goes fishing **on** the weekend.
7. He eats lunch at 1pm **on** Fridays.
8. Sam goes to the gym **in** the morning.

14.2

1. I work from Monday to Thursday.
2. My sister goes swimming every day.
3. We go to the gym on Saturdays.
4. You read the newspaper on Sundays.
5. Peter goes to work on the weekend.
6. Jennifer goes to a café on Fridays.
7. Sam and Pete work from 9am to 5pm.

14.3

1. Pam works **from** Monday **to** Friday.
2. I work at home **on** Thursdays.
3. Tom goes to the cinema **on** Fridays.
4. I play soccer **on / at** the weekend.
5. They work **from** Monday **to** Thursday.
6. We go to bed at 9pm **on** Mondays.
7. Laura goes shopping **on** Tuesdays.
8. Peter gets up at 8am **on** Mondays.
9. We go the gym **on** Thursdays.
10. Gerald reads a book **on / at** the weekend.
11. Jane swims **from** Monday **to** Friday.
12. John takes a bath **on** Fridays.
13. Lizzy starts work at 9am **on** Fridays.

14.4

1. Dan goes to the gym three times a week.
2. Sam goes to the cinema twice a week.
3. We go to bed at 11:30pm every day.
4. Joe goes to college five times a week.
5. Clarice washes her clothes once a week.
6. Jennifer gets up at 10am twice a week.
7. We eat dinner at 7pm every day.

14.5

1. Bob **goes swimming** on Thursdays.
2. I play tennis **on the weekend / at the weekend**.
3. Jane and Tom go to the gym **three times** a week.
4. Angus works from **Monday to Thursday**.
5. I go to the movies **on the weekend / at the weekend**.
6. Sam goes to **college on Wednesdays**.
7. Jenny gets up **at 7am** every day.
8. Peter **works from** Monday to Friday.
9. Nina **goes to bed** at 11pm every day.

14.6

1. False 2. True 3. False 4. True
5. False 6. True

14.7

A. 3
B. 6
C. 4
D. 5
E. 1
F. 2

14.8

1. farmer
2. nurse
3. restaurant
4. 8am
5. Saturday
6. theater
7. three days
8. waitress
9. 6pm

15

15.1

1. Paula is not a teacher.
2. We are not from England.
3. This is not my phone.
4. Kirsty is not 18 years old.
5. Frank is not my father.
6. This is not my purse.
7. They are not engineers.
8. That is not a salon.
9. Kim is not a teacher.

15.2

1. That **is not** a castle.
2. They **are not** at school.
3. He **is not** a grandfather.
4. We **are not** engineers.
5. She **is not** 70 years old.
6. You **are not** French.
7. This **is not** my dog.

8 I **am not** a doctor.
9 It **is not** 11 o'clock.

15.3

A 3
B 1
C 2
D 4

15.4

1 Fredo is not a chef.
Fredo isn't a chef.
2 Susie's not my cat.
Susie isn't my cat.
3 My dad is not at work.
My dad's not at work.
4 They are not at the theater.
They aren't at the theater.

15.5

1 True
2 False
3 True
4 True
5 False

15.6

1 This **isn't** his umbrella.
2 Pedro **isn't** Spanish.
3 Pete and Terry **aren't** hairdressers.
4 It **isn't** a snake.
5 My cousins **aren't** 21 years old.
6 It **isn't** half past six.
7 **I'm not** your friend.

15.7

1 True
2 True
3 False
4 True
5 True
6 False

15.8

1 I'm a student. I'm not a teacher.
2 I'm 30 years old. I'm not 40.
3 I'm a farmer. I'm not a police officer.
4 I'm French. I'm not English.
5 I'm an uncle. I'm not a father.
6 I'm 18. I'm not 21.
7 I'm a waitress. I'm not a chef.
8 I'm Spanish. I'm not Italian.

15.9

1 You're 28. You're not 29.
2 You're a scientist. You're not a gardener.
3 You're Austrian. You're not English.
4 You're a contractor. You're not an actor.
5 You're 16. You're not 18.
6 You're an uncle. You're not a grandfather.
7 You're a mechanic. You're not an engineer.
8 You're a police officer. You're not a firefighter.

15.10

1. I'm not at work.
2. I'm not an actor.
3. I'm not American.
4. I'm not 40 years old.
5. You aren't at work.
6. You aren't an actor.
7. You aren't American.
8. You aren't 40 years old.
9. She isn't at work.
10. She isn't an actor.
11. She isn't American.
12. She isn't 40 years old.

16

16.1

1 Jane **does not** walk to work.
2 My brother **does not** watch TV.
3 I **do not** read a book in the evening.
4 Frank **does not** work at the museum.
5 They **do not** go dancing on the weekend.
6 We **do not** go to work on Fridays.
7 I **do not** get up at 7:30am.
8 You **do not** have a car.
9 My dad **does not** work in an office.
10 You **do not** have a dog.
11 My sister **does not** work with children.
12 They **do not** live in the country.
13 Freddie **does not** eat meat.

16.2

1 Tony doesn't live in New York.
2 Sebastian doesn't work on a farm.
3 My uncle doesn't work in a factory.
4 We don't play soccer on Thursdays.
5 I don't learn German at school.
6 Carlo doesn't work on Mondays.
7 You don't take a bath at night.

16.3

1 Tim does not play tennis.
Tim doesn't play tennis.
2 You do not have a black cat.
You don't have a black cat.
3 Jules does not read a book every day.
Jules doesn't read a book every day.
4 Sam does not work in a restaurant.
Sam doesn't work in a restaurant.
5 They do not play soccer.
They don't play soccer.
6 Emily does not work with animals.
Emily doesn't work with animals.
7 Mel and Greg do not have a car.
Mel and Greg don't have a car.
8 You do not work in a factory.
You don't work in a factory.

16.4

1 Chloe **doesn't** play tennis with her friends.
2 You **don't** work outside.
3 Sal and Doug **don't** have a car.
4 We **don't** watch TV at home.
5 Mrs. O'Brien **doesn't** work in an office.
6 You **don't** wake up at 6am.
7 They **don't** eat lunch at 1pm.
8 Virginia **doesn't** speak good English.
9 Trevor **doesn't** live near here.
10 My dad **doesn't** live in Los Angeles.
11 David **doesn't** play chess.

16.5

1 Jean doesn't cycle to work.
2 They don't live in the city.
3 Mr. James doesn't go to the theater.
4 He doesn't read a newspaper.
5 My cousins don't have tickets.
6 Sally doesn't go to the gym.
7 Our dog doesn't have a ball.
8 I don't have a laptop.
9 My mom doesn't get up at 7:30am.
10 You don't live in the country.
11 Claude doesn't have a dictionary.

16.6

1 False 2 False 3 True 4 False
5 True 6 False 7 True

16.7

1 Carla 2 Sam 3 Greg 4 Carla
5 Sam 6 Greg 7 Sam 8 Carla

16.8

1. I don't go swimming.
2. I don't have a car.
3. I don't speak Japanese.
4. Frank doesn't go swimming.
5. Frank doesn't have a car.
6. Frank doesn't speak Japanese.
7. We don't go swimming.
8. We don't have a car.
9. We don't speak Japanese.

17

17.1

1. Is this his passport?
2. Is it 6 o'clock?
3. Are Doug and Jim hairdressers?
4. Are these my glasses?
5. Is Sally his sister?
6. Are those your letters?
7. Is she a nurse?
8. Is this your snake?
9. Is it 3pm?
10. Is his wife a chef?
11. Are Katie and Jess my friends?

17.2

1. Are you an actor?
2. Are you a teacher?
3. Are you engineers?
4. Are they engineers?
5. Is she a teacher?
6. Is she an actor?

17.3

1. **Is** Dorota at school?
2. **Is** this your parrot?
3. **Is** there a bank near here?
4. **Are** you a gardener?
5. **Are** these Jean's keys?
6. **Is** there a castle in your town?
7. **Is** that your bag?
8. **Are** they your cousins?
9. **Are** they from France?
10. **Is** she Sam's sister?
11. **Is** this my burger?
12. **Is** there a church in this town?
13. **Are** those Brooke's shirts?

17.4

1. Is Paula from Italy?
2. Is it half past two?
3. Is Ronaldo your father?
4. Is there a bank on your street?
5. Are these your dad's glasses?
6. Is this your laptop?
7. Are those Katherine's books?

17.5

1. **Do** you work in a hospital?
2. **Does** your dog like children?
3. **Do** you get up at 10am on Sundays?
4. **Does** Simone work with children?
5. **Do** they live in the town?
6. **Do** we finish work at 3pm today?
7. **Does** Frank play tennis with Pete?

17.6

1. **Do** you read a newspaper every day?
2. **Does** he go to bed at 11pm?
3. **Do** they live in a castle?
4. **Does** Pedro come from Bolivia?
5. **Does** she work with children?
6. **Do** Claire and Sam eat lunch at 2pm?
7. **Does** your brother work with animals?
8. **Does** Tim play soccer on Mondays?
9. **Do** they work in a café?
10. **Do** you have a shower in the evening?
11. **Do** we start work at 10am on Thursdays?
12. **Does** Pamela work in a bank?

17.7

1. Do they work in a museum?
2. Do you work with children?
3. Does Shane live in Sydney?
4. Does John play tennis on Wednesdays?
5. Do Yves and Marie eat dinner at 6pm?
6. Does Seth work in a post office?

17.8

1 No 2 No 3 Yes 4 Yes
5 Yes 6 No 7 Yes

17.9

1. **Do** you go to a restaurant on Fridays?
2. **Does** Peter live near the museum?
3. **Do** Sam and Doug work with animals?
4. **Does** she get up at 7am on the weekend?
5. **Do** they play tennis in the evening?

18

18.1

1. Yes, I do.
2. No, they aren't.
3. Yes, it is.
4. Yes, she does.
5. Yes, it is.

18.2

1. No, **I don't.**
2. Yes, **she is.**
3. No, **he doesn't.**
4. No, **they don't.**
5. Yes, **he is.**

18.3

1. No, she isn't.
2. No, she doesn't.
3. No, it isn't.
4. Yes, she does.
5. No, she doesn't.

18.4

1 True 2 False 3 False 4 True
5 True 6 Not given 7 True

19

19.1

1. Franco. And yours?
2. I'm fine, thanks.
3. It's half past seven.
4. That's my wife, Vicky.
5. It's across from the bank.
6. It's his birthday.
7. He's the boy with red hair.
8. It's at 3 o'clock.
9. It's on Saturday.
10. I'm twenty-three.

19.2

1. **Why** does the dog keep barking?
2. **Where** are your parents now?
3. **Who** is your brother?
4. **What** is your name?
5. **When** is Carla's birthday?
6. **Where** is your sister's house?
7. **Which** car is yours?

8 **When** are your exams?
9 **Where** did you park the car?
10 **Why** are you sad?
11 **When** can I go home?
12 **Where** does your brother live?
13 **What** is your first memory?

19.3

1 84 years old
2 Near the supermarket
3 At a school
4 She's a receptionist
5 19

19.4

1 Which shirt do you prefer?
2 Where does your son go to college?
3 How do you get to work?
4 Where do you go swimming?
5 What time do you go to bed?
6 When does Jane start work?
7 What do you eat for breakfast?

19.5

1 **What** do you study?
2 **Which** do you want?
3 **Which** building is your college?
4 **Where** do you live?
5 **What** time do you wake up?
6 **How** many shirts do you own?
7 **What** do you want for lunch?
8 **When** does the course finish?
9 **What** do you do in the evening?

19.6

1 Which school does he go to?
2 Why does Kevin work there?
3 Where does your friend live?
4 Where is your car?
5 What does your brother do?

19.7

1 How is your uncle?
2 Which woman is your wife?
3 Where do you work?
4 What time is the meeting?
5 When do you finish work tonight?

19.8

1. Where does he play soccer?
2. Where does Jane play soccer?
3. Where do you play soccer?
4. Where does he live?
5. Where does Jane live?
6. Where do you live?
7. When does he play soccer?
8. When does he finish work?
9. When do you play soccer?
10. When do you finish work?
11. When does Jane play soccer?
12. When does Jane finish work?

19.9

1 Blois
2 Janet
3 Near the castle
4 French bread
5 In a café
6 Explore the old town
7 About 1,000 years old
8 Some beautiful paintings

20

20.1

1 school
2 police station
3 supermarket
4 bridge
5 hotel
6 here
7 post office
8 mosque
9 town
10 park
11 library
12 airport
13 there
14 hospital
15 pharmacy
16 bank
17 train station
18 factory
19 bar
20 near
21 castle
22 bus station
23 restaurant
24 office building
25 swimming pool
26 café
27 far

21

21.1

1 **There is** a station.
2 **There is** a swimming pool.
3 **There are** two theaters.
4 **There is** a factory.
5 **There are** two parks.
6 **There are** three cafés.

21.2

1 There **isn't** a restaurant.
2 There **aren't** any schools.
3 There **isn't** a post office.
4 There **aren't** any cafés.
5 There **aren't** any bars.
6 There **isn't** a train station.
7 There **isn't** a library.
8 There **aren't** any supermarkets.
9 There **aren't** any parks.
10 There **isn't** a town hall.

21.3

1. There is a hotel.
2. There is no hotel.
3. There are three parks.
4. There are no parks.
5. There aren't any parks.
6. There are three books.
7. There are no books.
8. There aren't any books.

21.4

A 3
B 2
C 1
D 4
E 5

21.5

1 There isn't a school.
2 There aren't two churches.
3 There isn't a café.
4 There isn't a library.
5 There aren't two airports.
6 There aren't three hotels.
7 There aren't two parks.
8 There isn't a town hall.

21.6

1 churches
2 primary school

3 café
4 hospital
5 police officer

21.7

1 There is a supermarket.
2 There aren't any restaurants.
3 There are no hotels.
4 There are three schools.
5 There is a bus station.

21.8

1 False
2 True
3 False
4 False
5 True
6 False
7 True

21.9

1 There are three stores.
2 There are two castles.
3 There isn't a church.
4 There is a hospital.
5 There isn't a post office.

22

22.1

1 **The** new doctor is called Hilary.
2 Sammy is **a** nurse.
3 There is **a** bank downtown.
4 Is there **a** hospital near here?
5 **The** gym is near Sam's house.
6 There is **a** new café in town.
7 **The** hotel on Elm Lane is nice.
8 **The** new teacher is good.
9 There's **an** old theater in town.

22.2

1 I have **a** sister and **a** brother.
2 There is **a** library on Queens Road.
3 I bought **an** apple and **an** orange.
4 Is there **a** bank near here?
5 There is **a** café at the bus station.
6 My dad is **an** engineer.
7 There is **a** cell phone on the table.

22.3

Dear Bob and Sally,
We are in Glenmuir, **a** quiet town in Scotland. There's **a** castle and **a** cathedral here. They're beautiful, and **the** castle is really old. There are **some** interesting stores, which we visit every day. We also have **a** new friend here. He's called Alfonso and he works as **a** waiter in **the** Italian restaurant next to **the** shopping mall. He's great!
Jane

22.4

1 Are there **any** factories in your town?
2 Is there **a** gym downtown?
3 Are there **any** pencils in your bag?
4 Is there **an** old church on Station Road?
5 Is there **a** hospital in the town?
6 Is there **a** salon near here?
7 Is there **an** apple in the basket?
8 Are there **any** restaurants in your town?
9 Is there **a** library downtown?
10 Are there **any** books on the table?
11 Is there **a** café nearby?
12 Is there **a** cathedral in that town?
13 Is there **a** bank near the supermarket?
14 Are there **any** kittens here?
15 Is there **a** school in this neighborhood?

22.5

1 Is there a supermarket near here?
2 There are some cafés on Beech Road.
3 There are some horses on Frank's farm.
4 There are some hotels near the airport.

22.6

1 Is **there a** museum?
2 Are **there any** cafés?
3 Are **there any** parks near here?
4 Is **there a** mosque in the town?
5 Is **there an** airport in Saltforth?
6 Are **there any** factories in Halford?
7 Is **there a** castle in your town?

22.7

1 Yes, **there are**.
2 No, **there isn't**.
3 Yes, **there are**.
4 No, **there isn't**.
5 Yes, **there is**.
6 No, **there aren't**.
7 Yes, **there are**.

22.8

1 Stonehill
2 Museum
3 Lots
4 French
5 None
6 Two
7 Some

23

23.1

1 put
2 read
3 work
4 start
5 eat
6 have
7 stop
8 wake up
9 run
10 come
11 be

23.2

1 present simple
2 imperativo
3 present simple
4 imperativo
5 imperativo
6 imperativo
7 present simple
8 present simple
9 imperativo

23.3

1 Go straight ahead. The swimming pool is opposite the station.
2 Take the second left. The school is opposite the factory.
3 Turn right and take the first left. The church is opposite the hotel.
4 Take the third left and go straight ahead. The theater is on the right.

23.4

1 Go past the house.
2 Take the second right.
3 Go straight ahead.
4 Turn left.
5 Take the third right.

23.5

1. on the left
2. opposite
3. on the right
4. behind
5. on the corner

23.6

1. Don't go straight ahead.
2. Don't come with me.
3. Don't take the first left.
4. Don't turn left at the intersection.
5. Don't read this daily planner.

23.7

A 5 B 2 C 6 D 4 E 9
F 8 G 3 H 7

23.8

1. The museum is **next to** the library.
2. The restaurant is **opposite** the store.
3. The hospital is **in front of** the theater.
4. The post office is **behind** the school.

24

24.1

1. My cousin lives and **works in Los Angeles.**
2. I play soccer and **basketball in the evening.**
3. There's a library and **a bookstore in my town.**
4. I eat two eggs and**a banana for breakfast.**
5. Pete's uncle and **aunt live in Arizona.**
6. I read a book and **watch TV on the weekend.**

24.2

1. restaurant
2. hospital
3. supermarket
4. movie theater
5. church

24.3

1. Three chefs and four waiters work in my hotel.
2. There's a park, a café, and a theater in Pella.
3. I have one aunt, two sisters, and a niece.
4. Ben eats breakfast, lunch, and dinner.
5. I play tennis and soccer.
6. We have a dog and a cat.
7. I read a book and take a bath on Sundays.
8. Jen speaks French, Spanish, and Japanese.
9. Pete has two dogs and a cat.

24.4

1. This is my brother and these are my sisters.
2. I speak English, but I don't speak French.
3. I play video games and I watch TV.
4. I have one uncle, but I don't have any aunts.
5. There are two stores and three hotels.
6. I eat lunch every day, but I don't eat breakfast.
7. There's a hotel, but there isn't a store.
8. I have a sandwich and an apple.
9. This is my house, but these aren't my keys.
10. Those are Sarah's magazines and that is her ID card.
11. This phone is Joe's, but this laptop isn't.

24.5

1. There's a library, a store, **and** a café.
2. There's a castle and a church **but** there isn't a museum.
3. Pete eats apples **but** doesn't eat bananas.
4. Greg reads magazines **and** a newspaper.
5. I have a calendar **and** a notebook.
6. He goes swimming **but** he doesn't play soccer.

24.6

1. Meg likes this restaurant **but** she doesn't like that café.
2. There are two schools **but** there isn't a library in my town.
3. I have a pen, a notebook, **and** a calendar in my bag.
4. My sister goes to the gym on Mondays **and** Thursdays.
5. Pedro works in a school **but** he isn't a teacher.

25

25.1

1. I am a busy man.
2. There is a new restaurant.
3. My friend is a beautiful woman.
4. We have a very old cat.
5. These are my new clothes.

25.2

1. good
2. beautiful
3. wonderful
4. busy
5. interesting
6. old
7. large

25.3

1. The children are small.
   They are small.
2. The waiter is good.
   He is good.
3. The dog is big.
   It is big.
4. The town is quiet.
   It is quiet.

25.4

1. new
2. large
3. bad
4. beautiful
5. old
6. slow
7. easy

25.5

1 False 2 True 3 False 4 True
5 False 6 True

25.6

1. **The** sea **is** blue **and the** sun **is** hot.
2. **The** beach **is** busy **and the** hotels **are** ugly.
3. **The** city **is** old **and the** buildings **are** beautiful.
4. **The** restaurant **is** good **and the** waiter **is** friendly.
5. **The** countryside **is** beautiful **and the** mountains **are** large.

6 **The** town **is** small **and the** shops **are** quiet.

25.7

1 **There are some** shops.
2 **There are some** trees.
3 **There are lots of** cars.
4 **There are a few** churches.
5 **There are a few** flowers.
6 **There are some** cafés.
7 **There are a few** parks.

26

26.1

1 Fred works outside because **he's a farmer.**
2 Mick travels to Switzerland because **he goes skiing there.**
3 Saul goes to bed late because **he works in a restaurant.**
4 I get up at 5am because **I'm a mailman.**
5 Marion goes to the library because **she's a student.**
6 Colin works with children because **he's a teacher.**

26.2

1 he's a farmer
2 she's a teacher
3 he's a student
4 she goes to the gym
5 he's an actor
6 he has the flu
7 she's a chef

26.3

1 Aziz lives in the countryside because **he thinks it's beautiful**.
2 We don't have breakfast because **we're very busy**.
3 Mr. Aspinall gets up early because **he takes his dog for a walk**.
4 Arnold wears a suit because **he works in a bank**.
5 Vicky works outside because **she is a gardener**.
6 I work in a hospital because **I'm a doctor**.

26.4

1. Clara works in a theater because she is an actor.
2. Clara lives on a farm because she is a farmer.
3. Clara works in a hotel because she is a receptionist.
4. Mike lives on a farm because he is a farmer.
5. Mike works in a theater because he is an actor.
6. Mike works in a hotel because he is a receptionist.

27

27.1

1 kitchen
2 toilet
3 television
4 house
5 closet (US) / wardrobe (UK)
6 bathtub
7 garage
8 bedroom
9 apartment block (US) / block of flats (UK)
10 couch (US) / sofa (UK)
11 shower
12 dining room
13 door
14 window
15 table
16 chair
17 lamp
18 refrigerator (US) / fridge (UK)
19 study
20 bed
21 bookcase
22 bathroom
23 armchair

28

28.1

1 My friend **has** new glasses.
2 John **has** two dogs.
3 We **have** an old castle in our city.
4 They **have** a lot of parks in their town.
5 I **have** a beautiful necklace.
6 Alex **has** a new camera.
7 Our house **has** a lovely yard.
8 Phil and Sue **have** four daughters.
9 Pete **has** a new cell phone.
10 Your town **has** a big hotel.
11 I **have** a lot of friends.

28.2

1 Bob and Shirley **have** a big dog.
2 She **has** some new friends.
3 We **have** two sons at home.
4 James **has** two cars.
5 His house **has** three bedrooms.
6 Pam **has** lots of books at home.
7 He **has** two cats.
8 Sally's house **has** a new kitchen.
9 You **have** a beautiful house.
10 I **have** three sisters.
11 Kelly and Mark **have** a microwave.
12 We **have** a castle in our town.
13 Sanjay **has** a cat and a dog.
14 You **have** three brothers.
15 Ross **has** a new cell phone.
16 Our house **has** two bathrooms.
17 I **have** a couch in my room.
18 Washington **has** some lovely parks.

28.3

1 I have two sisters.
2 You have a beautiful house.
3 We have a garden.
4 Sam and Greg have a dog.
5 Marlon has a brother.
6 Fardale has an old castle.
7 They have a new car.

28.4

1 False
2 False
3 False
4 True
5 False
6 False
7 True

28.5

1 We don't have a computer at home.
2 My city doesn't have a castle.
3 Rob's house doesn't have a garage.
4 You don't have any sisters.
5 The village doesn't have any stores.

28.6

1. You have got a beautiful necklace.
2. She has not got any sisters.
3. We have not got a microwave.
4. Greg has not got a bike.
5. My town has got two theaters.
6. Chloe has not got a cat.
7. They have got a new house.

28.7

1. Our town
2. Adam and I
3. Sally and Jonathan
4. My friend Sam
5. Our house

28.8

1. I have a computer.
2. I have a sofa.
3. I have some tables.
4. We have a computer.
5. We have a sofa.
6. We have some tables.
7. He has a sofa.
8. He has a computer.
9. He has some tables.
10. He doesn't have a computer.
11. He doesn't have a sofa.

28.9

1. She has two bedrooms.
   She's got two bedrooms.
2. They have not got a dog.
   They haven't got a dog.
3. We have some chairs.
   We have got some chairs.
4. He has a brother.
   He's got a brother.
5. Carla has not got a sister.
   Carla hasn't got a sister.
6. You have a car.
   You've got a car.
7. Phil has a dog.
   Phil has got a dog.
8. You have got a yard.
   You've got a yard.
9. Jamal doesn't have a sofa.
   Jamal has not got a sofa.
10. They have a shower.
    They've got a shower.
11. May has a couch.
    May has got a couch.
12. He has not got a cat.
    He hasn't got a cat.

29

29.1

1. fork
2. washing machine
3. kettle
4. toaster
5. refrigerator
6. sink
7. plate

29.2

1. Does the house have a yard?
2. Does their kitchen have a refrigerator?
3. Does Bill's house have a big garage?
4. Do you have a sofa?
5. Does Barry have a kettle?
6. Does she have a barbecue at her house?
7. Does Marge have a new washing machine?
8. Do Jack and Marienne have a TV?
9. Does Leela's brother have a knife and fork?

29.3

1. Claudia
2. Paul
3. Jenny
4. Colin
5. Roberto

29.4

1. Yes, I do.
2. No, I don't.
3. Yes, I do.
4. Yes, I do.
5. No, I don't.

29.5

1. Do you have any chairs?
2. Do you have any knives?
3. Do you have a refrigerator?
4. Does he have any chairs?
5. Does he have any knives?
6. Does he have a refrigerator?
7. Do they have any chairs?
8. Do they have any knives?
9. Do they have a refrigerator?

29.6

1. Yes, **she does**.
2. Yes, **he does**.
3. No, **he doesn't**.
4. Yes, **it does**.
5. No, **they don't**.
6. No, **she doesn't**.
7. Yes, **he does**.

29.7

1. Have they got a microwave?
2. Have Shaun and Shania got a pet snake?
3. Has Charles got a camera?
4. Has Clarissa got a new laptop?
5. Has Carol's house got a big yard?
6. Have your friends got my book?
7. Has Brian got a new TV?

29.8

1. Has the kitchen got a microwave?
2. Has your house got a yard?
3. Have the Hendersons got a car?
4. Has Claire got my glasses?
5. Have your parents got a computer?
6. Has Paul got my book?
7. Has Brian got a magazine?
8. Have your neighbors got a basement?
9. Has your cell phone got a camera?
10. Has Sam got any money?
11. Has your town got a supermarket?
12. Has Brian got a sister?
13. Have your children got a cat?
14. Has your husband got a camera?
15. Has your school got a library?
16. Has Jane got a cell phone?
17. Have the kids got their bikes?

29.9

1. Have you got a refrigerator?
2. Have you got a car?
3. Have you got any brothers or sisters?
4. Has John got a refrigerator?
5. Has John got a car?
6. Has John got any brothers or sisters?
7. Has your kitchen got a refrigerator?

30

30.1

1. burger
2. spaghetti
3. juice
4. bread
5. fish

6 apple
7 eggs
8 drinks
9 banana
10 seafood
11 milk
12 strawberry
13 chocolate
14 cheese
15 orange
16 cereal
17 potatoes
18 sugar
19 butter
20 salad
21 meat
22 coffee
23 pasta
24 vegetables
25 cake
26 water
27 fruit
28 rice
29 breakfast
30 lunch
31 dinner

31

31.1

CONTABLES: **apple**, **burger**, **egg**
INCONTABLES: **coffee**, **rice**, **juice**

31.2

1 There **is** some orange juice.
2 Sam has **some** milk.
3 We have **some** salt.
4 There **are** some apples.
5 Rita has **a** banana.
6 I've got **some** eggs.

31.3

1 four bananas
2 two eggs
3 some cheese
4 two burgers
5 one bar of chocolate

31.4

1 There is some salt.
There isn't any salt.
2 Is there any wine?
There isn't any wine.
3 There are some burgers.
There aren't any burgers.
4 Are there any cookies?
There aren't any cookies.
5 Are there any pastries?
There are some pastries.
6 There is some bread.
There isn't any bread.
7 Is there any rice?
There isn't any rice
8 Is there any butter?
There is some butter.
9 There are some pizzas.
There aren't any pizzas.
10 Is there any cheese?
There isn't any cheese.

31.5

1 False
2 True
3 False
4 True
5 False
6 True
7 True
8 False
9 False

31.6

1 There's a **glass** of milk.
2 There are two **bags** of rice.
3 There's a **bar** of chocolate.
4 There's a **carton** of juice.
5 There are three **bottles** of water.
6 There's a **bowl** of pasta.
7 There are two **cups** of tea.

31.7

1 There **is** a jar of coffee.
2 There **isn't** any rice.
3 There **are** two cartons of juice.
4 There **is** some meat.
5 There **are** two bottles of wine.
6 There **isn't** any bread.
7 There **is** a bag of flour.
8 There **is** some pasta.
9 There **are** two bars of chocolate.
10 There **isn't** any sugar.
11 There **is** some butter.

31.8

1 bowl
2 jar
3 bar
4 glass
5 carton
6 bag
7 cup
8 bottle
9 tube

31.9

1 How **much** meat is there?
2 How **many** cartons of milk are there?
3 How **many** bowls of rice are there?
4 How **much** juice is there?
5 How **much** bread is there?
6 How **many** cups of tea are there?
7 How **many** bars of chocolate are there?
8 How **much** coffee is there?
9 How **many** jars of jam are there?
10 How **much** milk is there?
11 How **many** bags of flour are there?
12 How **much** pizza is there?
13 How **many** eggs are there?

31.10

1. How many burgers are there?
2. How many eggs are there?
3. How many people are there?
4. How much rice is there?
5. How much water is there?
6. How much coffee is there?

32

32.1

1 There are **too many** pears.
2 There is **too much** milk.
3 She has **too much** pasta.
4 We have **too many** bananas.
5 There is **too much** butter.
6 There are **too many** apples.
7 There are **too many** tomatoes.
8 I have **too much** juice.
9 There are **too many** mushrooms.
10 They have **too many** burgers.
11 Sue owns **too many** shoes.

32.2

1. There **are enough** pineapples.
2. There **are enough** mangoes.
3. There **is enough** sugar.
4. There **is enough** bread.
5. There **is enough** milk.
6. There **is enough** pasta.
7. There **are enough** apples.
8. There **are enough** oranges.
9. There **are enough** bananas.
10. There **is enough** chocolate.
11. There **are enough** eggs.
12. There **is enough** cheese.
13. There **are enough** tomatoes.
14. There **is enough** butter.
15. There **is enough** juice.

32.3

1. You have enough oranges.
   You have too many oranges.
2. There isn't enough sugar.
   There's too much sugar.
3. We don't have enough butter.
   We have enough butter.
4. There aren't enough eggs.
   There are too many eggs.
5. There is enough flour.
   There is too much flour.
6. There aren't enough potatoes.
   There are enough potatoes.
7. You don't have enough melons.
   You have too many melons.
8. He has enough bread.
   He has too much bread.
9. There isn't enough tea.
   There is enough tea.
10. We don't have enough milk.
    We have too much milk.
11. You have enough rice.
    You have too much rice.
12. There aren't enough mangoes.
    There are enough mangoes.
13. Martha doesn't have enough onions.
    Martha has too many onions.
14. You have enough carrots.
    You have too many carrots.

32.4

1. True
2. True
3. False
4. False
5. False

32.5

1. There are **not enough** carrots.
2. There are **enough** potatoes.
3. There are **not enough** tomatoes.
4. There is **not enough** pasta.
5. There is **too much** oil.
6. There is **enough** bread.
7. There is **enough** butter.
8. There is **too much** flour.
9. There is **not enough** sugar.
10. There are **enough** oranges.
11. There are **not enough** bananas.
12. There are **too many** eggs.
13. There is **enough** milk.

32.6

1. There **isn't** enough butter.
2. There **aren't** enough tomatoes.
3. There **aren't** enough mangoes.
4. You have too **many** bananas.
5. They don't have **enough** butter.
6. There **are** enough onions.
7. There **isn't** enough sugar.
8. You have **too** many pineapples.
9. They have too **much** bread.
10. You **don't** have enough apples.
11. They have **enough** flour.
12. There **are** too many potatoes.
13. There **is** too much salt.
14. There **is** too much chocolate.
15. There **are** too many mangoes.
16. You have **enough** eggs.
17. There **are** enough oranges.

32.7

1. There is enough butter.
2. There is not enough butter.
3. There is too much butter.
4. There are enough eggs.
5. There are not enough eggs.
6. There are too many eggs.
7. There is enough rice.
8. There is not enough rice.
9. There is too much rice.

33

33.1

1. gloves
2. hat
3. blue
4. boots
5. jeans
6. pink
7. red
8. suit
9. dress
10. belt
11. coat
12. green
13. skirt
14. shirt
15. black
16. scarf
17. yellow
18. sandals
19. socks
20. purple
21. extra small
22. small
23. medium
24. large
25. extra large
26. orange
27. shoes

34

34.1

1. That sweater **fits** you. It's the right size.
2. My mom always **chooses** my dad's clothes.
3. These jeans don't **fit**. They're too small.
4. I **own** 30 pairs of shoes.
5. I always **try on** clothes before I buy them.
6. Those shops **sell** very fashionable clothes.
7. We **buy** fruit at the market.
8. I **want** some shoes for my birthday.
9. I sometimes **pay** by credit card.

34.2

1. Ruth **does** a lot of her shopping on the internet.
2. The shop **doesn't** sell my size of clothes.
3. She **wears** short skirts.
4. Greg's jeans **don't** fit him.
5. Amy **owns** a lot of fashionable clothes.
6. We **pay** for our shopping with cash.
7. Duncan never **tries** on clothes before he buys them.

8. My parents usually **pay** for my clothes.
9. Peter **doesn't** own many clothes.

34.3

1. That blouse **doesn't** fit you.
2. Sue always **tries** on her new clothes.
3. Rob **wants** a new tie for Christmas.
4. Peter **buys** his meat at the butcher's shop.
5. Jose **owns** a beautiful house in France.
6. My jeans **don't** fit me. They're too big.
7. Samantha **chooses** high-quality clothes.
8. They **sell** vegetables in the market.
9. Do you **want** a new shirt for your birthday?

34.4

1. This is a **new** T-shirt.
2. These are **short** jeans.
3. This is an **expensive** tie.
4. This is a **large** sweater.
5. This is a **blue** dress.
6. This is an **old** T-shirt.
7. These are **cheap** shoes.
8. This is a **short** skirt.
9. This is a **red** shirt.
10. These are **big** shoes.
11. This is a **small** sweater.

34.5

1. a red skirt
2. a red scarf
3. brown shoes
4. blue jeans
5. green coat.

34.6

1. cheap
2. short
3. long
4. hard
5. soft

34.7

1. too hard
2. too old
3. too expensive
4. too long
5. too soft
6. too short

34.8

1. Claire's hat is **too small**.
2. These shoes are **too expensive**.
3. Sophie's pullover is **too small**.
4. Corrine's coat is **big enough**.
5. Emma's sweater is **too big**.
6. Chloe's scarf is **too long**.
7. Phoebe's shoes are **too big**.
8. Joshua's jacket is **too small**.

35

35.1

1 False 2 True 3 True 4 True 5 False
6 True 7 False 8 True 9 False

35.2

1. Our house has a pretty little yard.
2. James has an ugly leather jacket.
3. Pete has an old wooden table.
4. This is a brilliant new book.
5. Shelley's got a beautiful glass bottle.
6. That was such a boring old film.
7. That's an ugly woolen sweater.
8. Those are boring black shoes.
9. I've got a horrible old car.
10. Simone has a beautiful gray parrot.
11. That's a horrible old house!
12. You've got a nice red shirt.

35.3

1. Jill's got a beautiful black dog.
2. Simon has a nice new house.
3. They have an ugly old car.
4. Those are pretty red shoes.
5. That's an ugly pink hat.
6. Greg has a horrible brown snake.
7. You've got a beautiful black bag.
8. This is a great new book.

35.4

1. metal
2. paper
3. wool
4. glass
5. leather
6. wood

35.5

1 plastic 2 wooden 3 glass
4 leather 5 plastic 6 wool
7 wooden 8 paper 9 wool
10 plastic 11 leather 12 metal 13 metal

35.6

1. Four **plastic** cups.
2. An ugly **wooden** table.
3. An old **leather** jacket.
4. Three **metal** chairs.
5. A green **wool** sweater.
6. A brown **paper** bag.
7. Beautiful **fabric**.

36

36.1

1. roller-skating
2. rugby
3. golf
4. snowboarding
5. cycling
6. badminton
7. ice hockey
8. baseball
9. skateboarding
10. swimming
11. running
12. basketball
13. tennis
14. skiing
15. horse riding

36.2

1. baseball bat
2. golf course
3. snowboard
4. swimming pool
5. golf club
6. running track
7. skateboard
8. stadium
9. surfboard
10. tennis court
11. skis

37

37.1

1. Douglas **goes cycling** with his brother on Sundays.
2. Phil and John **go skating** in the winter.

3 Mr. Henderson **goes sailing** in the Mediterranean in the summer.
4 Veronica **goes dancing** with her friends on the weekend.
5 They **go hiking** in the mountains in Scotland.
6 Lawrence **goes swimming** on Tuesdays.
7 Ted **goes skateboarding** on Saturday morning.
8 I **go horseback riding** in France each year.
9 She **goes shopping** in Milan at Christmas.
10 We **go fishing** after work on Mondays.
11 Anne **goes surfing** in California.

37.2

1 Jane goes **dancing** on Friday nights.
2 Our dad goes **sailing** in the summer.
3 I go **fishing** in the evening.
4 Do you go **running** in the morning?
5 They go **cycling** in the summer.
6 Sam goes **swimming** on Sundays.
7 I go **horseback riding** daily.
8 Claire goes **shopping** in London.
9 Omar goes **skateboarding** daily.
10 Do you go **dancing** with her?
11 Rachel goes **hiking** in Peru.
12 I go **snowboarding** in the winter.
13 Bob and Steve go **surfing** in Tahiti.

37.3

1 snowboarding
2 running
3 fishing
4 swimming
5 skateboarding
6 dancing
7 surfing
8 shopping
9 cycling
10 sailing
11 riding

37.4

1 I **go** shopping in the evening.
2 Jan **goes** skateboarding on Fridays.
3 Pete **goes** sailing on the weekend.
4 Sam **goes** skating every December.
5 I **go** running on Wednesday.
6 They **go** fishing with their friends.
7 Sarah **goes** dancing on Saturdays.

37.5

1 Do you **play** chess?
2 Paolo **plays** badminton at the weekend.
3 My father **plays** golf with his friends.
4 We **don't play** baseball anymore.
5 I **play** tennis with my brother.
6 Greg **doesn't play** basketball.
7 Liz **plays** racquet ball on the weekend.
8 Your dad **doesn't play** soccer.
9 Our dog **plays** with its ball.
10 Mike **plays** soccer on Saturdays.
11 We **don't play** golf in the winter.
12 Pammy **doesn't play** tennis.

37.6

1 Does he play badminton on Fridays?
2 Does Noah play golf with his grandpa?
3 Do they play basketball with their friends?
4 Does Georgia play baseball at school?
5 Do we play tennis in the summer?
6 Do Tim's parents play chess in the evening?

37.7

1 False 2 True 3 False 4 True
5 False 6 True 7 True

37.8

1 John **plays** badminton on Wednesday.
2 You **go** fishing with your brother.
3 My uncle **plays** chess with my aunt.
4 We **go** dancing in the evening.
5 Sally's dad **plays** rugby.
6 Bartou **goes** cycling in the mountains.
7 Ramona **plays** racquet ball with her dad.
8 Our kids **play** baseball after school.
9 Simon and Pam **go** surfing in the summer.
10 They **play** basketball every Saturday.
11 We **go** snowboarding in Austria.

37.9

1 I **play baseball** with my friends at school.
2 Anna **goes skateboarding** in the afternoon on Sundays.
3 Mrs. Amir **plays chess** with her husband in the evening.
4 Max **plays badminton** on Tuesdays and Fridays.
5 Peter **goes fishing** with his brother on Mondays and Wednesdays.

38

38.1

1 play a musical instrument
2 write
3 do yoga
4 play video games
5 watch television
6 walk / hike
7 go the gym
8 sew
9 go shopping
10 do the gardening
11 draw
12 go camping
13 bake
14 listen to music
15 do puzzles
16 watch a movie
17 visit a museum
18 play cards
19 see a play
20 meet friends
21 knit
22 paint
23 read
24 go bird watching
25 go out for a meal
26 play chess
27 take photos

39

39.1

1 True 2 False 3 False 4 False
5 True 6 False 7 True

39.2

1 They sometimes go to the theater.
2 Mike never goes running after work.
3 You always go to bed early.
4 Jane often goes shopping on Saturday.
5 We usually eat dinner at 6pm.

39.3

1 never 2 sometimes 3 often
4 usually 5 always 6 often

39.4

1 Clara **never** plays chess with her grandfather.
2 Enzo **always** eats chocolate ice cream.
3 Paul **sometimes** goes fishing in the morning.
4 My parents **usually** drive to work.
5 Gill **never** goes shopping with her mom.

6 You **sometimes** go to the gym in the town.
7 Shelley **usually** watches TV in the evening.
8 My dog **always** sleeps under the table.
9 We **sometimes** play baseball in the summer.
10 Tim **usually** rides his horse on the weekend.

39.5

1 How often does Steph watch TV?
2 How often do you visit your dad?
3 When do they play soccer?
4 When do you usually go to bed?
5 How often does May go running?
6 How often do you play tennis?
7 How often does Jo read a book?

39.6

1 **She goes to the gym** on Wednesdays.
2 **He plays soccer** in the evening.
3 She never **goes to the theater**.
4 He sometimes **reads a newspaper**.
5 **She visits her family** four times a year.
6 **He plays baseball** every afternoon.
7 **She goes shopping** twice a week.
8 **I read** a book every evening.
9 She sometimes **makes a cake**.

39.7

1 How often does Jimmy play soccer?
2 How often do you phone your grandma?
3 How often does Sheila get up at 7am?
4 How often do you read a book?
5 How often does Sally go to work?
6 How often do you play badminton?
7 How often does your daughter go running?
8 How often does Megan go fishing?
9 How often do you watch TV?

39.8

1 She always **goes** dancing on the weekend.
2 I often **go** fishing.
3 My mom never **gets up** early.
4 Seb usually **plays** soccer on weekends.
5 Tracy never **watches** TV in the evening.
6 We sometimes **take** the bus to work.
7 Doug often **plays** tennis on Fridays.

40

40.1

1 We like cake.
2 I hate tennis.
3 We love basketball.
4 Shelley loves pizza.
5 They hate board games.
6 I don't like pasta.
7 Samantha likes chocolate.

40.2

1 salad 2 sports 3 playing tennis 4 golf
5 listening to music 6 classical music
7 going shopping 8 going to the cinema
9 scary films 10 taking photos

40.3

1 Chris doesn't like spiders.
2 They hate Paris.
3 Mrs. McGregor doesn't like cats.
4 We hate soccer.
5 We don't like wine.
6 Simone hates her horse.
7 He doesn't like your necklace.
8 Jean-Marie hates sports.
9 Colin doesn't like pizza.
10 Douglas doesn't like Anne.
11 Cynthia loves dogs.
12 We hate chocolate.
13 You don't like cheese.
14 Susan doesn't like pizza.

40.4

1. They love cats.
2. They love running.
3. They love pizza.
4. They love snakes.
5. Arnold hates cats.
6. Arnold hates running.
7. Arnold hates pizza.
8. Arnold hates snakes.
9. My mother hates cats.
10. My mother hates running.
11. My mother hates pizza.
12. My mother hates snakes.

40.5

1 She likes cooking.
2 Her favorite is Italian food.
3 She doesn't like cooking meat.
4 She cooks for her friends and family.
5 She doesn't like fast food.
6 She hates candy.

40.6

1 I **hate** cities, but I **love** the country.
2 Archie **likes** ice cream, and he **loves** pizza.
3 He **loves** meat, but he **hates** fish.
4 Francis **doesn't like** coffee, but he **likes** tea.
5 We **hate** Mondays, but we **love** Fridays.
6 My dad **dislikes** classical music, but he **loves** rock.

40.7

1 Sam likes watching soccer **because it's exciting.**
2 Marie loves pizza. **She thinks it's delicious.**
3 I love reading history books **because they're really interesting.**
4 Sally doesn't like running **because it is tiring.**
5 Peggy does not like eating meat **because she is a vegetarian.**
6 Paolo does not eat chocolate **because he doesn't have a sweet tooth.**
7 Jemma hates snakes. **She thinks they are scary.**

40.8

1 hot
2 interesting
3 delicious
4 boring
5 tiring

41

41.1

1 sing a song
2 dance
3 electric guitar
4 headphones
5 opera
6 keyboard
7 piano
8 rap
9 country
10 album
11 rock

12. guitar
13. Latin
14. orchestra
15. jazz
16. flute
17. conductor
18. saxophone
19. audience
20. guitar player
21. play the trumpet
22. trumpet
23. concert
24. violin
25. drum
26. microphone
27. harmonica

42

42.1

1. Nick's favorite uncle is an actor.
2. Jo's favorite book is *Puzzling People*.
3. Jay's favorite instrument is the piano.
4. Paul's favorite drink is orange juice.
5. Blake's favorite animal is the tiger.
6. Dan's favorite place is his garden.
7. Sanjay's favorite season is winter.
8. Max's favorite hobby is painting.
9. Greg's favorite food is rice.
10. Levi's favorite sport is baseball.
11. Martha's favorite country is France.
12. Simone's favorite lesson is science.
13. Maya's favorite dessert is cake.
14. Karina's favorite fruit is pineapple.
15. Their favorite city is London.
16. Kate's favorite pet is her parrot.
17. Zoe's favorite pastime is dancing.

42.2

1. math
2. Friday
3. red
4. chocolate cake
5. baseball
6. fall

42.3

1. Barbara likes listening to music in the evening.
2. Arnold's favorite food is ice cream and pizza.
3. Craig doesn't like getting up in the morning.
4. Seb's favorite type of music is hip-hop.
5. Ruth likes orange juice.
6. Daniel's favorite animal is the lion.
7. I like bacon and eggs for breakfast.
8. Aziz doesn't like lasagna or spaghetti.
9. Miguel loves going to the movie theater.

42.4

1 True 2 False 3 False 4 False
5 True 6 False 7 False 8 True 9 True
10 True

42.5

1. Arnie's favorite sport is **tennis**.
2. Joan's favorite animal is a **dolphin**.
3. Hassan's favorite actor is **Chris Minota**.
4. Pam's favorite number is **21**.
5. Jane's favorite sport is **badminton**.
6. Dora's favorite ice cream is **strawberry**.
7. Jim's favorite food is **spaghetti**.

42.6

1. She loves salsa dancing.
2. She loves sailing.
3. She loves chocolate ice cream.
4. Simon loves salsa dancing.
5. Simon loves sailing.
6. Simon loves chocolate ice cream.
7. She likes salsa dancing.
8. She likes sailing.
9. She likes chocolate ice cream.
10. Simon likes salsa dancing.
11. Simon likes sailing.
12. Simon likes chocolate ice cream.
13. Her favorite food is chocolate ice cream.
14. Her favorite sport is sailing.

43

43.1

1. talk
2. shout
3. throw
4. listen
5. lift
6. hit
7. walk
8. add
9. kick
10. make (a snowman)
11. carry
12. fly
13. sit
14. act
15. see
16. do (homework)
17. ride
18. catch
19. spell
20. move
21. stand up
22. understand
23. jump
24. climb
25. subtract
26. drive
27. work

44

44.1

1. I can ride a horse.
   I can't ride a horse.
2. I cannot climb a tree.
   I can't climb a tree.
3. I can speak French.
   I cannot speak French.
4. I can sing.
   I can't sing.
5. I can lift a box.
   I cannot lift a box.
6. I can fly a kite.
   I can't fly a kite.
7. I cannot catch a fish.
   I can't catch a fish.
8. I can swim.
   I can't swim.

44.2

1. Kate **can hit** the ball.
2. Paul **can't do** math.
3. Helen **can spell** very well.
4. Ivan **can't run** very fast.
5. Sara **can move** the chair.
6. Alex **can't play** badminton.
7. Lynn **can ride** a bicycle.

44.3

1. Eliza cannot drive a car.
2. Jonathan can play the piano.

3. Cathy can't jump very high.
4. Mick can throw a stick.
5. Laura can't do math.
6. Alan can lift the box.
7. Julia can't swim very far.

44.4

1. Can 2. Can't 3. Can't 4. Can 5. Can

44.5

1. Can Maria and Juan spell English words?
2. Can the children do their math homework?
3. Can you sing difficult jazz songs?
4. Can Mark ride a horse?
5. Can Jack climb a tree?
6. Can he carry that box?
7. Can Carlos kick a football?
8. Can Adam and Ella dance the tango?
9. Can Peter and John swim?

44.6

1. Jack is a diving teacher. He can **swim very well**.
2. Carla lives on a farm. She can **ride a horse** and look after animals.
3. Bobby is good at languages. He can **speak Russian**.
4. Nuna likes going on winter vacations. She can **ski well**.
5. Jim is a great children's teacher. He can **tell stories** well.

44.7

1. Yes, **I can**. 2. No, **I can't**. 3. Yes, **I can**. 4. No, **I can't**. 5. No, **I can't**. 6. Yes, **I can**. 7. No, **I can't**. 8. No, **I can't**. 9. No, **I can't**. 10. Yes, **I can**. 11. Yes, **I can**.

44.8

1. I can ride a bicycle.
2. I can't ride a bicycle.
3. She can ride a bicycle.
4. She can't ride a bicycle.
5. They can ride a bicycle.
6. They can't ride a bicycle.
7. I can swim a mile
8. I can't swim a mile.
9. She can swim a mile
10. She can't swim a mile.
11. They can swim a mile
12. They can't swim a mile.
13. I can play tennis.
14. I can't play tennis.
15. She can play tennis.
16. She can't play tennis.
17. They can play tennis.
18. They can't play tennis.

45

45.1

1. My friend speaks too **quietly**.
2. A turtle walks very **slowly**.
3. Alan can speak German **well**.
4. My dog can run very **fast**.
5. I get up very **early**.

45.2

1. Patrick is good at dancing.
2. Caitlin bakes well.
3. My mother is good at writing.
4. Ethan plays the guitar well.
5. Aimee is good at skiing.
6. They swim well.
7. We are good at speaking English.
8. Lara climbs trees well.

45.3

1. Haruda sometimes arrives **late** for school.
2. My cousin Paul runs **quickly**.
3. Shelley sings **beautifully**.
4. Our neighbors talk so **noisily** at night.
5. Rosa reads very **slowly**.
6. I can pass this exam **easily**.
7. My aunt drives very **carefully**.
8. Anita works very **hard**.
9. We **usually** go to bed at 11pm.
10. Angela speaks English **badly**.
11. A cheetah runs very **fast**.
12. Sarah eats her food very **quickly**.
13. Andrew does his homework **well**.

45.4

1. I am good at drawing.
2. I am good at playing the drums.
3. I am good at English.
4. I am bad at drawing.
5. I am bad at playing the drums.
6. I am bad at English.
7. Jennifer is good at drawing.
8. Jennifer is good at playing the drums.
9. Jennifer is good at English.
10. Jennifer is bad at drawing.
11. Jennifer is bad at playing the drums.
12. Jennifer is bad at English.
13. We are good at drawing.
14. We are good at playing the drums.
15. We are good at English.
16. We are bad at drawing.
17. We are bad at playing the drums.
18. We are bad at English.

46

46.1

1. Pedro is really good at history.
2. You speak French really well.
3. Sandra is very good at singing.
4. Sal is quite good at skiing.
5. Your uncle can swim very well.
6. They can run quite fast.
7. Mr. Henderson is really good at golf.

46.2

1. Arnold isn't very good at art and design.
2. My cousin is really good at speaking English.
3. Jean is quite good at climbing mountains.

46.3

1. My aunt is quite good at speaking Polish.
2. Your brother surfs really well.
3. Katie paints very well.
4. Silvia is really good at singing.
5. Martina is very good at dancing.
6. Serge cooks quite well.
7. Sonia is really good at playing chess.
8. Ricky runs very well.
9. Peter is quite good at drawing.
10. My mom speaks Greek really well.
11. David is very good at playing the drums.

46.4

1. Charlotte can ski quite well.
2. Harry sings really quietly.
3. My aunt walks very slowly.
4. Elizabeth speaks Russian very well.
5. My dog can jump quite high.
6. William speaks Japanese really badly.
7. Philip eats quite noisily.

47

47.1

1. She wants to have a cat.
   She'd like to have a cat.
2. They would like to visit Tokyo.
   They'd like to visit Tokyo.
3. I want to eat an orange.
   I would like to eat an orange.
4. You want to learn Spanish.
   You'd like to learn Spanish.
5. We want to go to a café.
   We would like to go to a café.
6. He would like to live in Germany.
   He'd like to live in Germany.
7. We want to swim in a lake.
   We'd like to swim in a lake.

47.2

1. They'd like to go sailing on a sailboat.
2. Dan would like to travel to New York.
3. Sharon wants to read her book.
4. Doug would like to climb a mountain.
5. We want to go on vacation to Tahiti.

47.3

1. Douglas wants to have pasta.
2. They'd like to go home tomorrow.
3. Does Chris want to go swimming later?
4. Sheila doesn't want to see Paul.
5. Would you like to visit us tomorrow?
6. Our children want to go to college.
7. She'd like to buy a new cell phone.
8. Jenny wants to go shopping on Friday.
9. Simon would like to be a doctor.
10. I would like to have a hamburger.
11. Would you like to be a vet?
12. Chloe doesn't want to eat that pizza.
13. Do you want to read this book?
14. They would like to watch TV.
15. She wants to go to the party.

47.4

1. I'd like to drive around America.
2. I'd like to travel around America.
3. We want to drive around America.
4. We want to travel around America.
5. Greg wants to drive around America.
6. Greg wants to travel around America.
7. I'd like to drive to Miami.
8. I'd like to travel to Miami.
9. We want to drive to Miami.
10. We want to travel to Miami.
11. Greg wants to drive to Miami.
12. Greg wants to travel to Miami.

47.5

1. Yes, he would.
2. No, he doesn't.
3. Yes, he would.
4. Yes, she does.
5. No, she doesn't.
6. No, he doesn't.
7. Yes, she does.

47.6

1. Marie wants to go snowboarding in Austria.
2. Mario doesn't want to go to school today.
3. She wants to climb that mountain.
4. Tony would like to play golf in Scotland.

47.7

1. Do you want **to** go home now?
2. Claude would **like** to learn French.
3. He would **like** to go swimming.
4. Paolo wants **to** get a new cat.
5. Would you like **to** visit China?
6. **He'd** like to go to work later today.
7. Peter **wants** to go to college next year.
8. They **don't** want to go to school today.
9. My sister **wants** to go to Greece this summer.

47.8

1. Would Peter like to go fishing?
2. Does Marion want to play tennis on Saturday?
3. Would he like to visit India?
4. Would Mr. Evans like to play chess tonight?
5. Would you like to play squash this evening?
6. Does Sam want to go to the park again?
7. Would they like to travel around China?

48

48.1

1. My mother would really like to travel to Spain.
2. Doug would quite like to learn French.
3. Sally would quite like to do an art degree.
4. Don's brother would like to practice the piano.
5. I'd really like to go to a rock concert tonight.
6. Martha would like to study chemistry in college.
7. My kids would quite like to study German at school.

48.2

1. Edith would really like to read her new book.
2. They'd really like to go to a concert.
3. I'd really like to go to France on vacation.
4. Jean-Paul would quite like to speak to you.
5. We'd quite like to eat pizza tonight.
6. Jeremy would really like to play his piano.
7. They'd really like to pass their chemistry exam.
8. Sophie would quite like to speak Mandarin.
9. David would really like to visit his son.

48.3

1. I'd really like to improve my English.
2. I'd really like to learn Japanese.
3. I'd really like to do a history degree.
4. I'd quite like to improve my English.
5. I'd quite like to learn Japanese.
6. I'd quite like to do a history degree.
7. Sam would really like to learn Japanese.
8. Sam would really like to do a history degree.
9. Sam would quite like to learn Japanese.
10. Sam would quite like to do a history degree.
11. We'd really like to learn Japanese.
12. We'd really like to do a history degree.
13. We'd quite like to learn Japanese.
14. We'd quite like to do a history degree.

48.4

1. history
2. review
3. music
4. study
5. drama
6. math
7. degree
8. exams

48.5

1. Phillipa goes to **college**.
2. Rome is **a beautiful city**.
3. We are at **home** at the moment.

4. Sharon goes to **school** at 9am.
5. **The college** is far away.
6. Peter goes **to bed** at 10pm.
7. My uncle is at **the mosque** today.
8. Jim goes to **church** on Sundays.
9. Sean leaves **home** at 7:30am.
10. Seb lives next to **the hospital**.

48.6

1. Carol leaves work at 6pm every day.
2. Jane can drive you to school tomorrow.
3. Chris lives across from the hospital.
4. Carl is at home at the moment.
5. Julia has a beautiful horse.
6. The hospital isn't very far.
7. We go to bed at 11pm usually.
8. Ottersley is a beautiful town.
9. Your shoes are under the bed.

48.7

1. Sally is **in hospital**. She is ill.
2. York is **a** pretty town.
3. She is **at home** now.
4. Lizzie goes **to church** on Sundays.
5. Bob is **at work** at the moment.
6. Christopher has **a** new car.
7. Jim goes **to bed** early on Sundays.
8. Carlos is **a** very talented boy.
9. Sarah and John are **a** great team.
10. Mary **bought three** new pens.
11. He jumped into **the** water and started swimming.
12. New York is **a** beautiful city.
13. **The** children were playing in the sun.
14. I can't **play soccer** on Monday.
15. Can you play **the** classical guitar?

48.8

1. Sarah
2. Eddie
3. Robert
4. Oliver

Agradecimientos

Los editores expresan su agradecimiento a: Jo Kent, Trish Burrow y Emma Watkins por la redacción de textos adicionales; Thomas Booth, Helen Fanthorpe, Helen Leech, Carrie Lewis y Vicky Richards por su asistencia editorial; Stephen Bere, Sarah Hilder, Amy Child, Fiona Macdonald y Simon Murrell por sus tareas de diseño; Simon Mumford por los mapas y banderas nacionales; Peter Chrisp por la comprobación de datos; Penny Hands, Amanda Learmonth y Carrie Lewis por la corrección de pruebas; Elizabeth Wise por el índice; Tatiana Boyko, Rory Farrell, Clare Joyce y Viola Wang por sus ilustraciones; Liz Hammond por la edición de los guiones de audio y la gestión de las grabaciones; Hannah Bowen y Scarlett O'Hara por compilar los guiones de audio; Jordan Killiard por hacer las mezclas y el master de las grabaciones de audio; Heather Hughes, Tommy Callan, Tom Morse, Gillian Reid y Sonia Charbonnier por su apoyo técnico creativo; Priyanka Kharbanda, Suefa Lee, Shramana Purkayastha, Isha Sharma y Sheryl Sadana por su apoyo editorial; Yashashvi Choudhary, Jaileen Kaur, Bhavika Mathur, Richa Verma, Anita Yadav y Apurva Agarwal por su apoyo en diseño; Deepak Negi y Nishwan Rasool por la documentación gráfica; y Rohan Sinha por sus tareas de gestión y su apoyo moral.